Publisher: Travis Rigby
Authors: Arthur Williams + Stacey Bal
Editor: Robin Avni
Art Director: Kathleen Dillinger
Copy Editor: David Coake

Cover design by Arthur Williams + Stacey Bal
Cover photography by Stacey Bal

Impermanent was produced by WildFlower Media, Inc.

Ft. Lauderdale, Florida
floristsreview.com

Printed in China

ISBN: 978-1-7337826-8-5

ARTHUR WILLIAMS + STACEY BAL

IMPERMANENT

Wildflower.Media

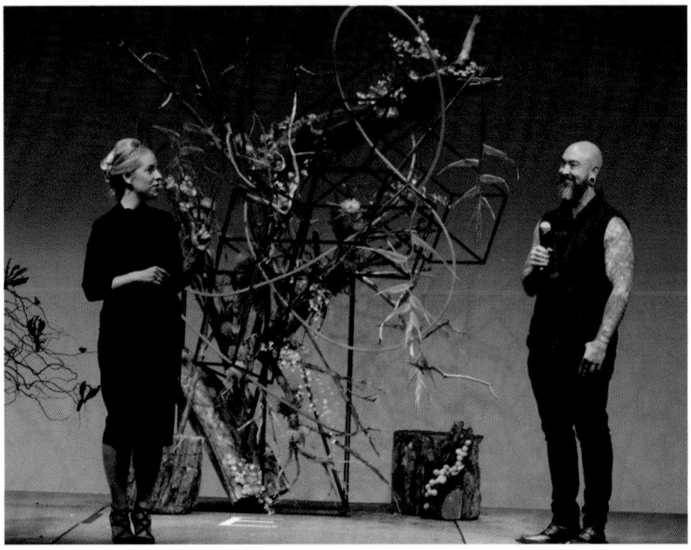

"What would I do without the absurd and the ephemeral?"

FRIDA KAHLO

DEDICATION

Arthur Williams and I initially embarked on this project expecting answers but found during this process that the more valuable outcome, the solutions, arrive in the form of questions. Growth and wealth, if you will, have deeproots in curiosity and true presence. Suffering significantly decreases when you (we) embrace impermanence, imperfection, and transience. But what is imperfection anyway?

In this concept-driven journey, Arthur and I explore the visual interpretations of twenty-one words we hold close to our hearts and souls, with impermanent materials as the medium. How do personal experiences influence one's definitions of words and concepts? Do they have the power to sway from positive to negative or vice versa? What makes anything negative in the first place? Does anything really last, or does everything evolve?

We did not travel this journey alone. It is here we give thanks to:
- Jet Fresh Flower Distributors
- Alexandra Farms
- Robin Avni
- Travis Rigby
- Kathleen Dillinger
- Hitomi Gilliam AIFD, CFD
- Tomas De Bruyne
- Rosie Carlton
- Joshua Landis
- Leon Gallery
- Calabrese Greenhouse
- Dan De Los Monteros
- Jonas De Vestel
- Mariya Byelikova
- Colin Gilliam
- Nicole Perez
- Peter Keltz
- Maxwell Frantz
- Kari Smith AIFD, CFD
- Amie Oakley
- Skyler Heck
- Chuck Hutson
- Dan Devlin
- Mary Pappas
- Sarah Melching, Director of Conservation, Denver Art Museum

We welcome you to step into our minds, our processes, our madness.
Learn with us, grow with us, evolve with us.

All the best,
Stacey

FOREWORD

This is exactly what has happened in the case of two floral peers Arthur Williams and Stacey Bal. They found each other through the common ground of exploring and sharing their emotional expression using impermanent materials to reflect their artistic skills.

The curiosity of acting with a conscious mind and feeling the ecstasy of a growing process is a liaison between these two artists. As both are true explorers, it is not about the outcome but all about the journey. Indeed, it was an educational journey that brought us together. I had the good fortune to meet them through the European Masters Certification (EMC) program.

When I got to see the first photographs of their work for this book, styles such as "Freakebana" and "eclectic" popped up—but all done in a concept with a harmonious flair. This, and the signature style of these two infinitely creative designers, is how they bring an essential statement to the surface: With art, they create an idealism with their interplay.

I do appreciate the inquisitiveness of these artists. Their ambition and drive to explore new possibilities, sometimes by revealing a botanical's soul or through the combination between all the elements, is refreshing.

This inspirational book is an invitation to action for anyone who is on a quest of how elements can be combined and interact one another overall. Arthur and Stacey challenge themselves to guide the materials into a story of synergy. Their message is an invitation to embrace the imperfection and the transience that make this medium so perfect.

Design should be an infinite process, a journey of growing and expressing recent emotions. Art will always be a barometer of time.

Congratulations! I am so proud of you both as you were able to artistically catch the spirit of time. I wish you both the best luck!

Tomas De Bruyne
Floral Experiences Worldwide

FOREWORD

There are riveting visual stories to be told,
There are experiential ways to give meaning to words,
Art is the creative expression—the means to this end.

In this inspirational book, Arthur Williams and Stacey Bal collaborated to create the visual narrative to skillfully define twenty-one thought-provoking words and to open a dialogue on their enigmatic aspects. The primary medium used for this collection of botanical art works are the IMPERMANENTS.

The mainstream art medium, be it paint, clay, metal, or glass, does not breathe REAL life into a composition as only flowers can. In a playful interplay with its contrasting and/or complementary elements, Arthur's and Stacey's art conveys the extraordinary temporal nature of our LIVING WORLD.

I have had the pleasure of working with these two talented artists over many years. I respect their curiosity-driven, avante-garde approach to capture the pure essence of artistry, in search of what intrigues them.

Collaboration brings depth to their collective experience.

The two voices forge compelling dialogues that you can hear and see. It manifests in different perspectives, contrasts ranging from similarities to opposition, from austerity to exuberance, positives and negatives. I especially feel an affinity to their vision for the four very special Japanese words.

Through the pages of this volume, be prepared to approach each word with your own vision.

And then be surprised by their profound interpretations to glean your triadic analysis of this compelling study and approach to FLORAL ART.

Hitomi Gilliam AIFD, CFD
Design358
Bowen Island, B.C. Canada

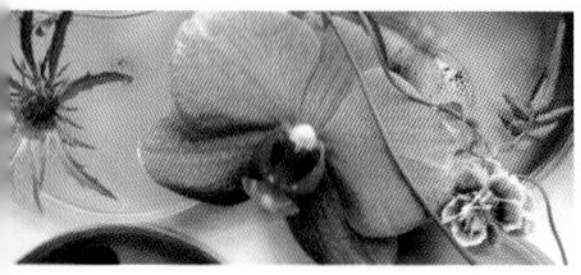

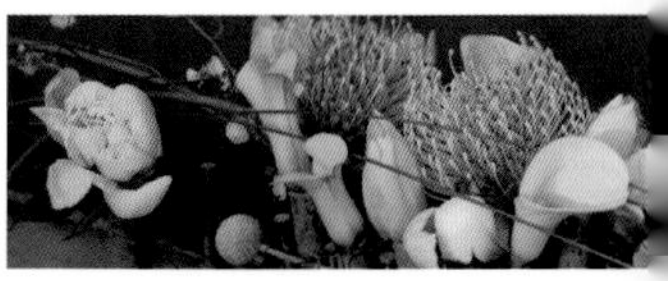

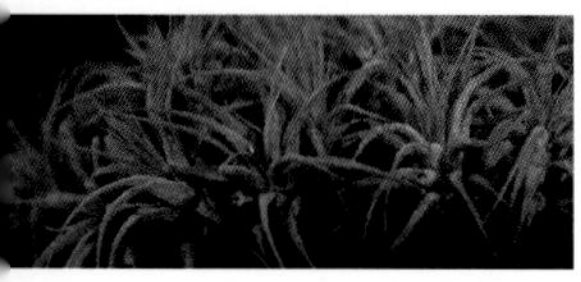

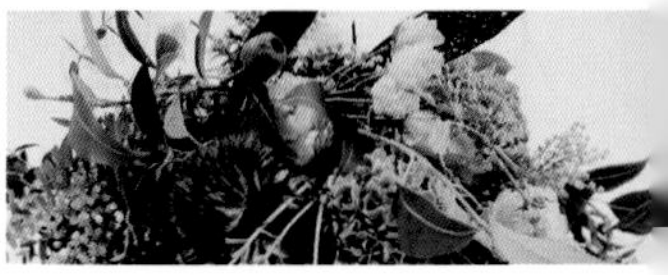

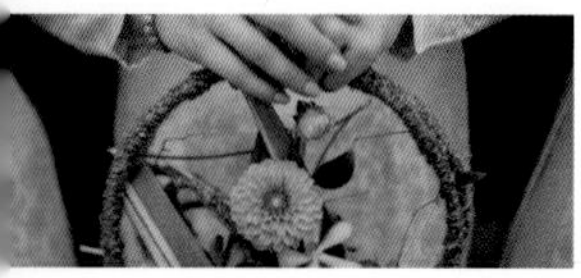

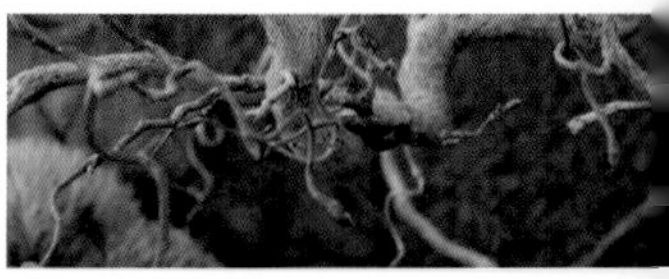

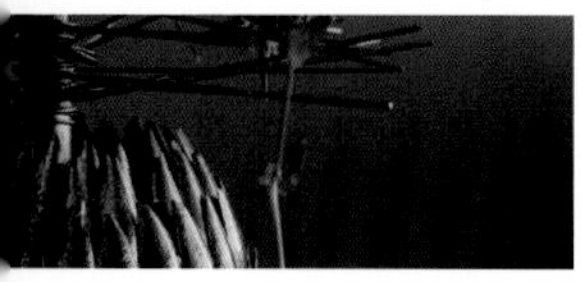

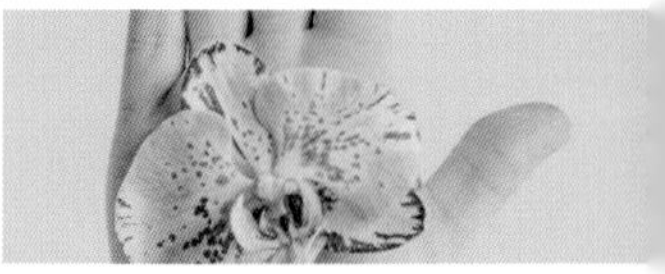

CONTENTS

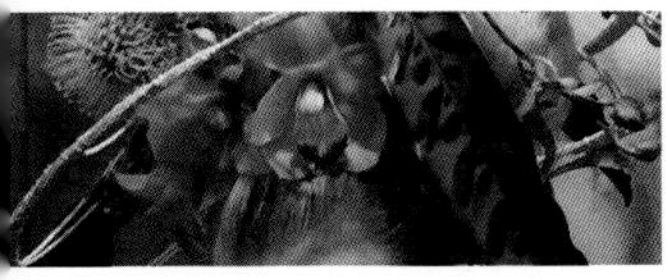
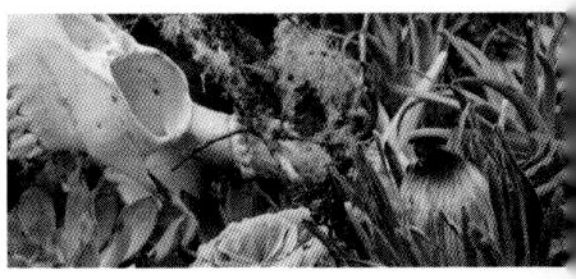

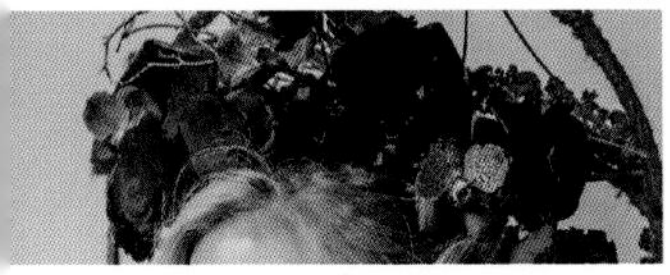
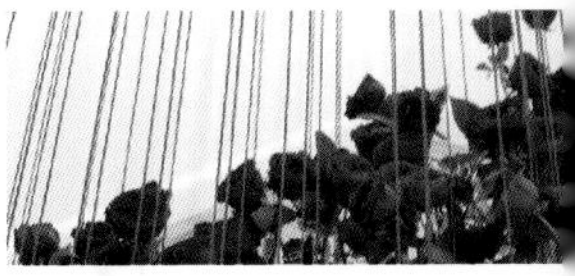

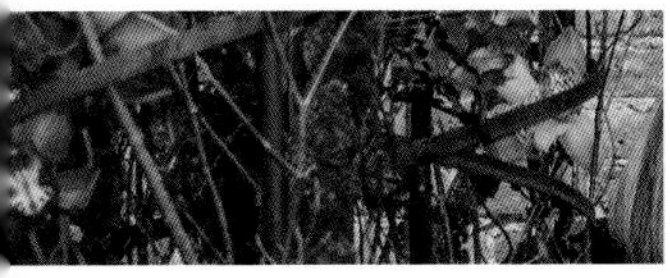
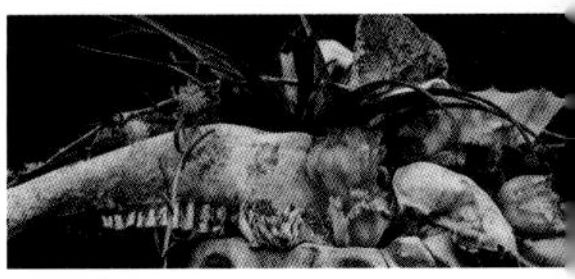

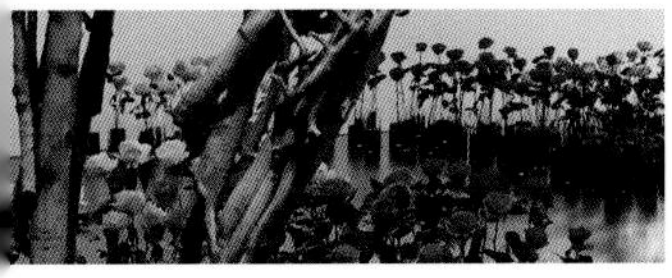
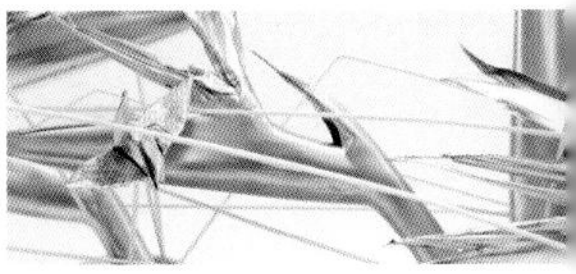

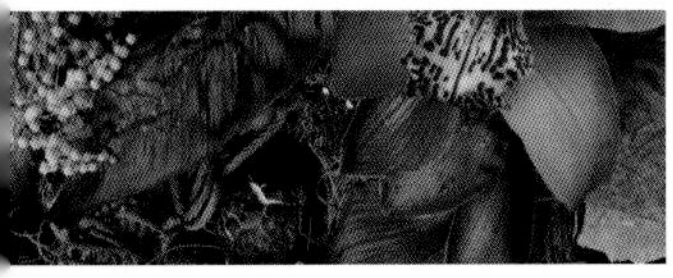
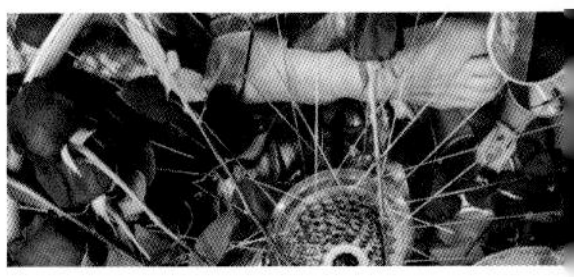

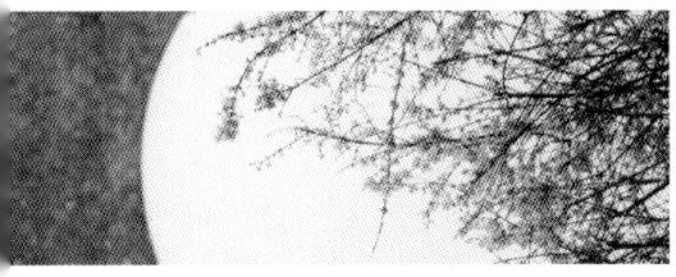
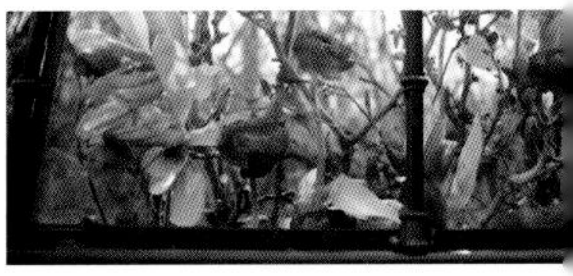

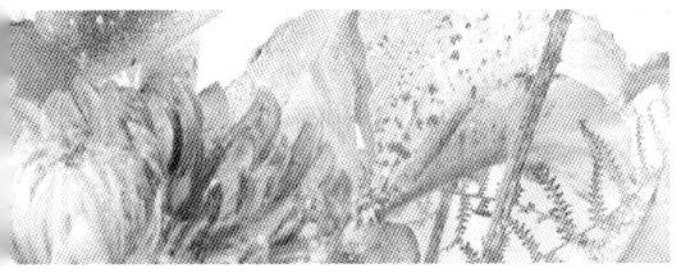

ARTHUR WILLIAMS ARTIST STATEMENT

My work is all about the tension of opposites: man versus nature, soft opposing harsh, new life sprouting from the remnants of last year's harvest.

My medium is botanical: fresh floral materials and dried branches.

I often use people in my work to give voice and movement to the flowers to create still-life performances where I selfishly incorporate models into floral moments.

I draw inspiration from tribal cultures and European myth, weaving stories into my work, giving people reference points from which to continue the stories for themselves. The ephemeral nature of my work forces me to push the boundaries of both my materials and the traditional conceptions of what floral art/design can be.

Nothing that comes from nature can be untrue.

STACEY BAL ARTIST STATEMENT

I work with nature for its improvisation and impermanence, for its delicacy and strength, for its innate realness and rawness, and its undeniable universal nostalgia. Curiously, I blur lines between the outside and inside worlds, boldly challenging the definition of what belongs where while intuitively exploring complex color stories. A rebel with a cause driven by the mutually beneficial nurturing partnership of nature and humanity.

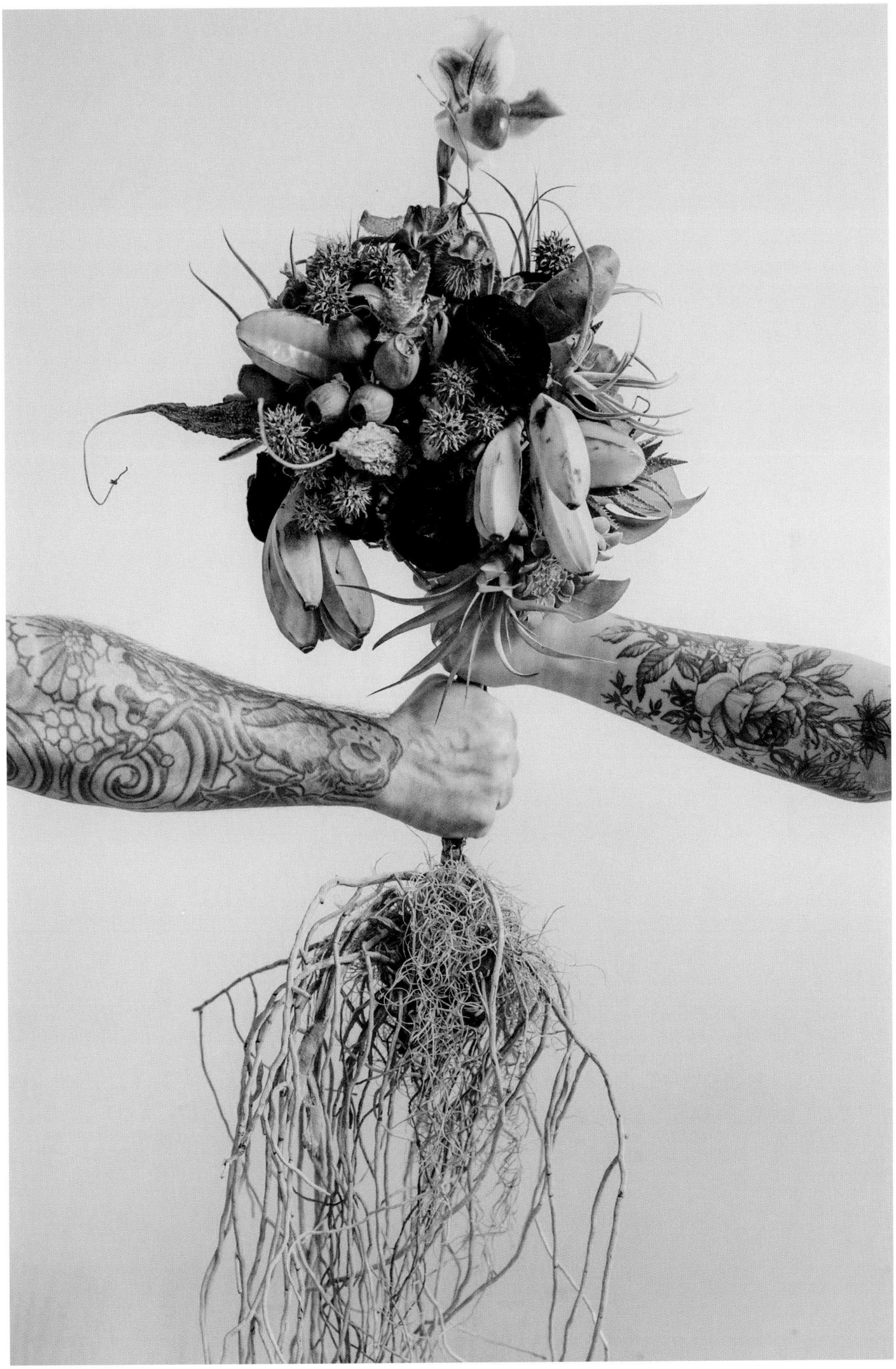

CULTURE

An integrated pattern
of thoughts, actions,
values, customs,
and beliefs that
connect us.

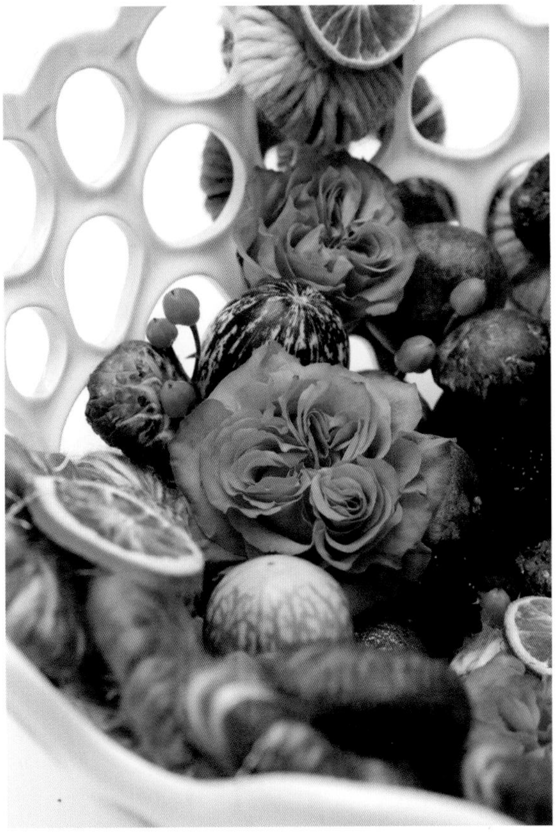

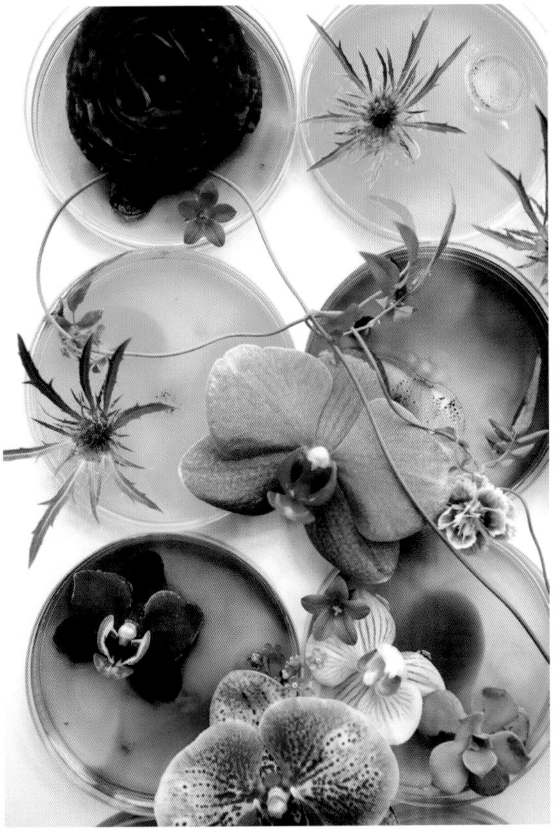

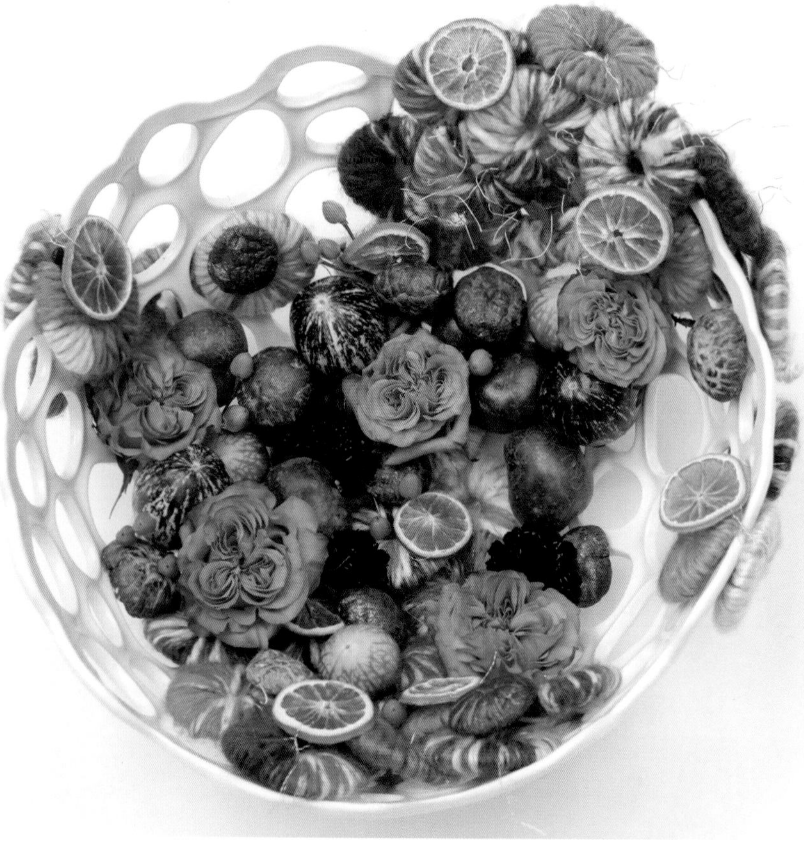

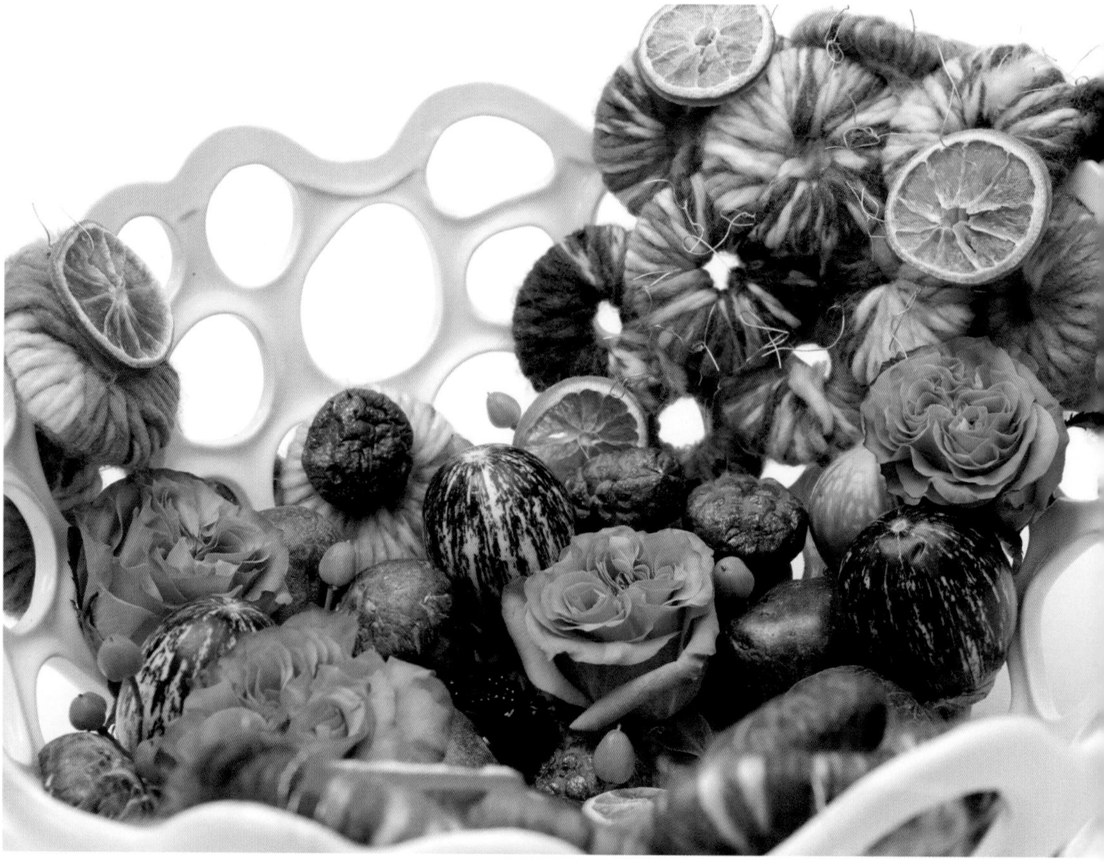

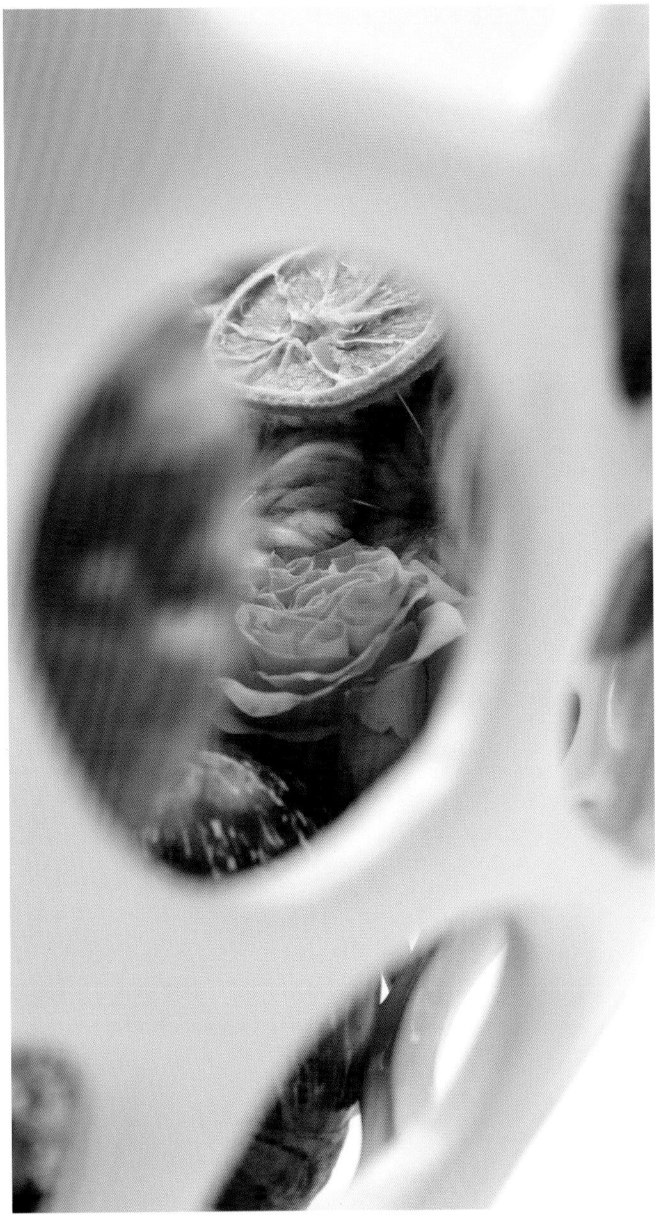

DESIGN BY ARTHUR WILLIAMS | PHOTOGRAPHY BY STACEY BAL
Denver, Colorado | January 2020

BIOLOGY VS CULTURE

"Culture is just a way to diffuse our primal needs so we can continue to pretend we are civilized."

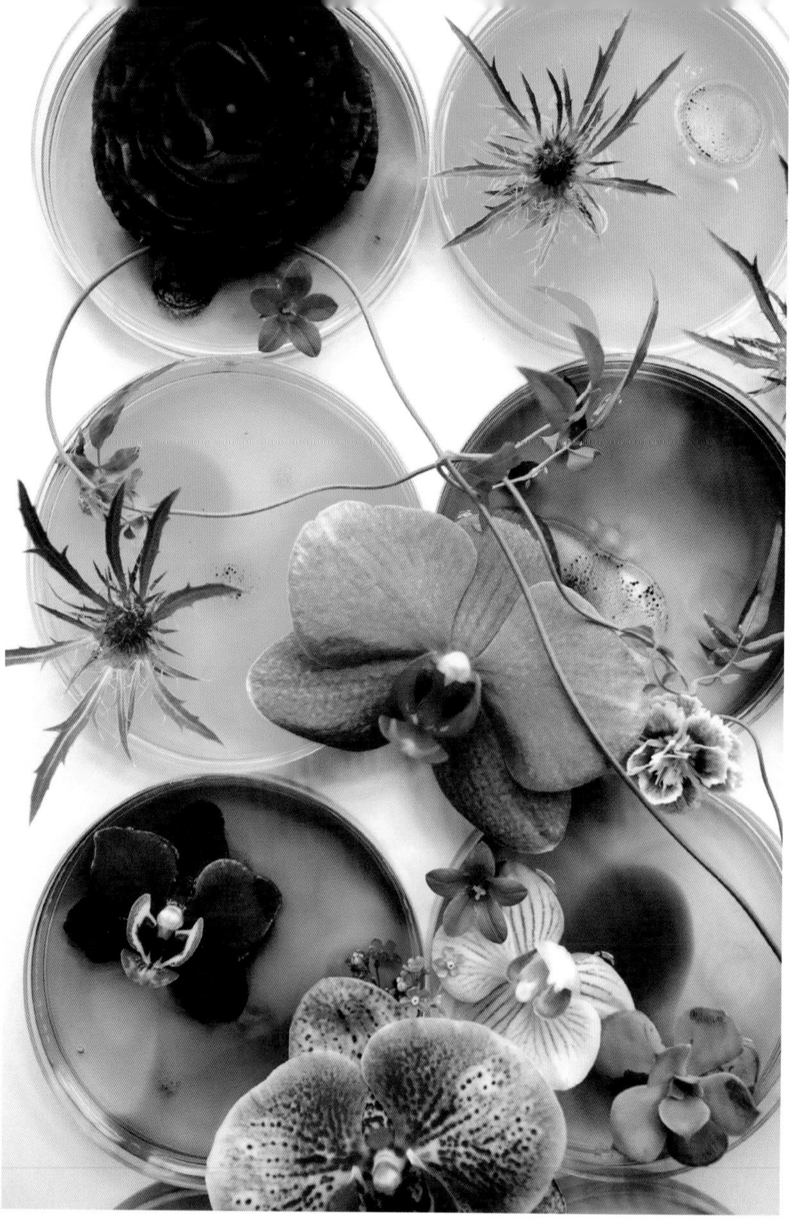

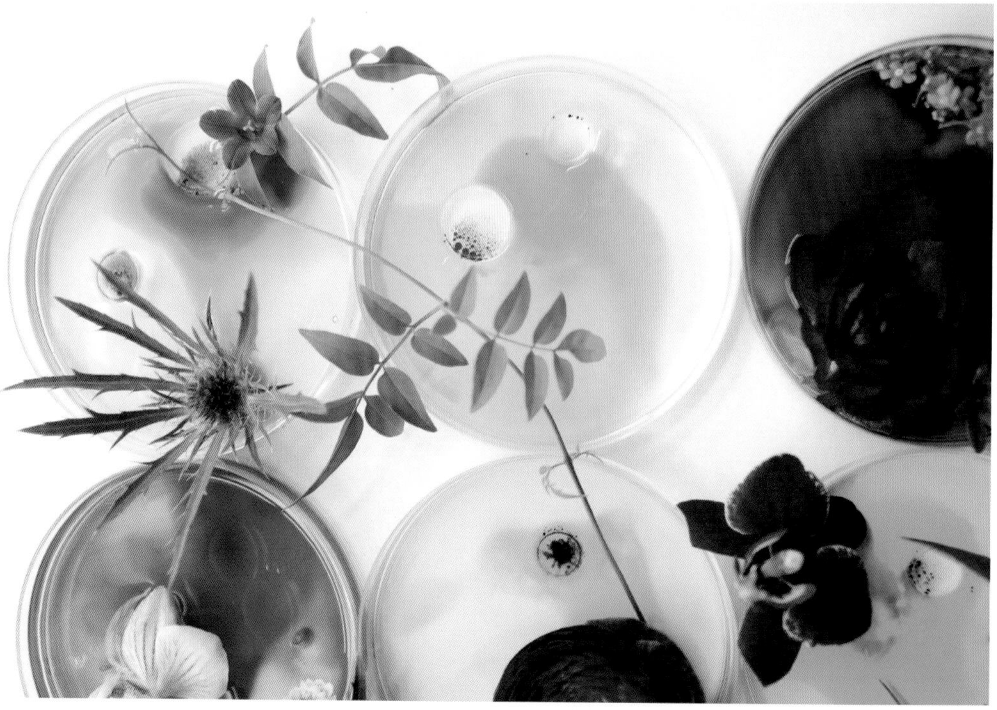

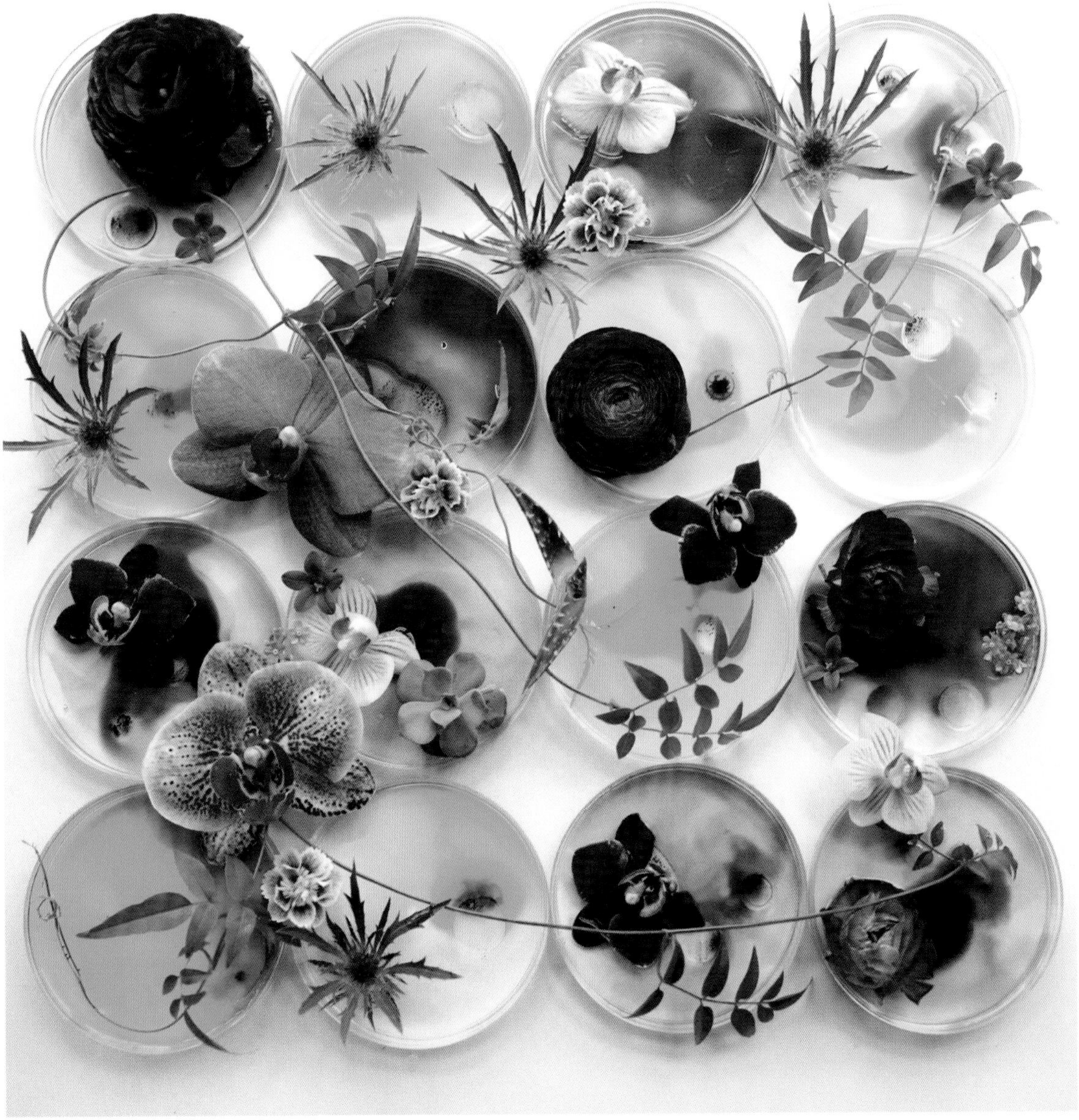

DESIGN BY STACEY BAL | PHOTOGRAPHY BY STACEY BAL
Riverside, Illinois | April 2020

PROBIOTIC

"Integrated pattern of thoughts, actions, values, customs, and beliefs that connect us. A strong showing of gestalt, an organized whole that is perceived as more than the sum of its parts."

KINTSUKUROI

KIN-TSU-KU-ROI

Golden repair: The Japanese art of repairing broken pottery by mending the fractured areas with lacquer dust mixed with powdered gold, silver or platinum. This ancient philosophy states that breakage and repair are part of the rich history of any object.

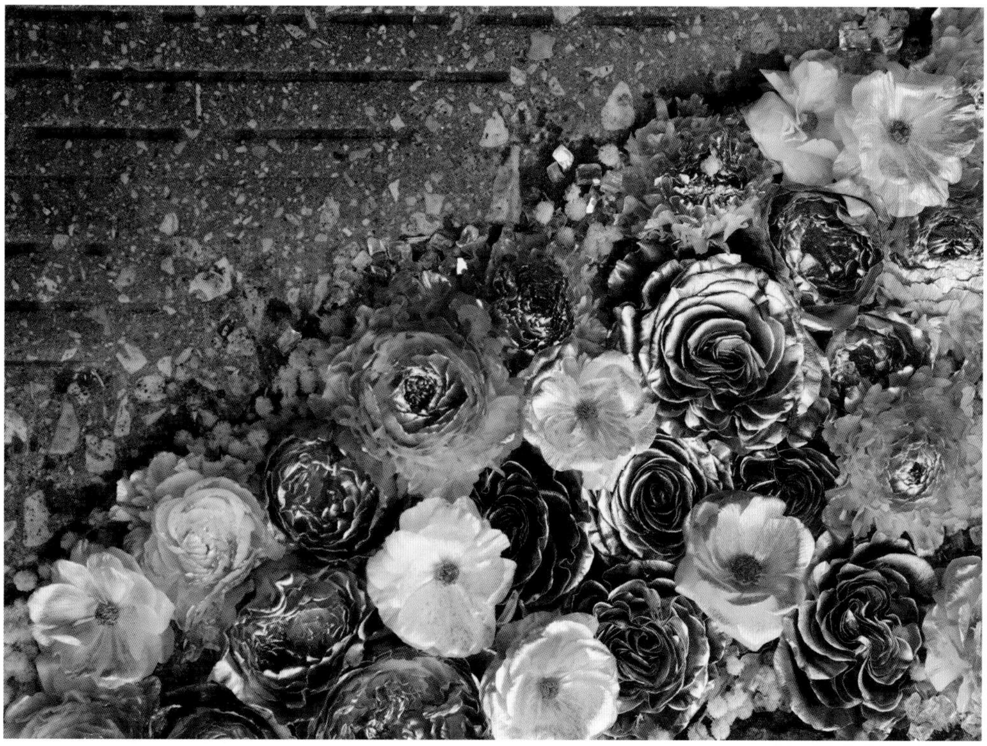

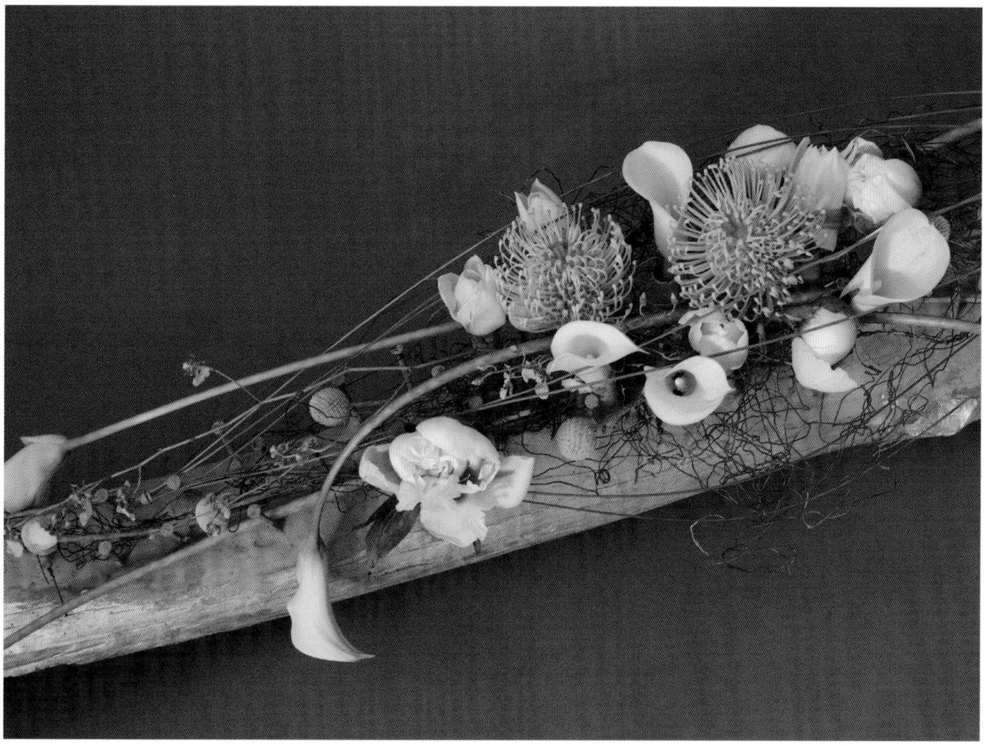

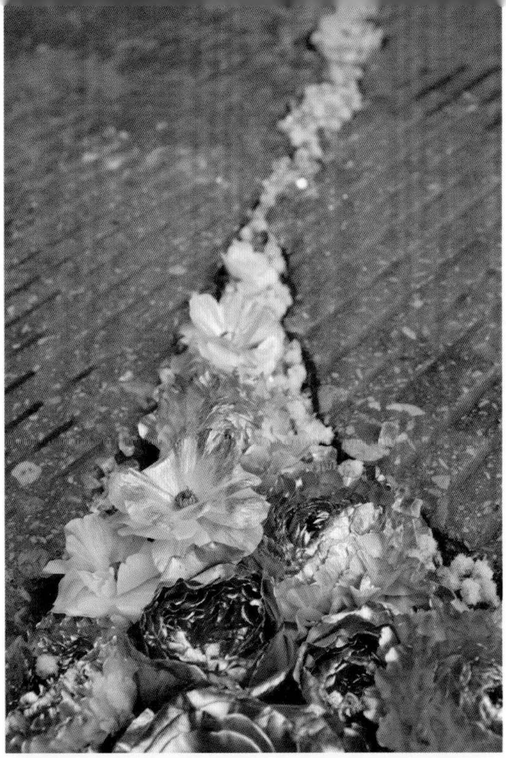

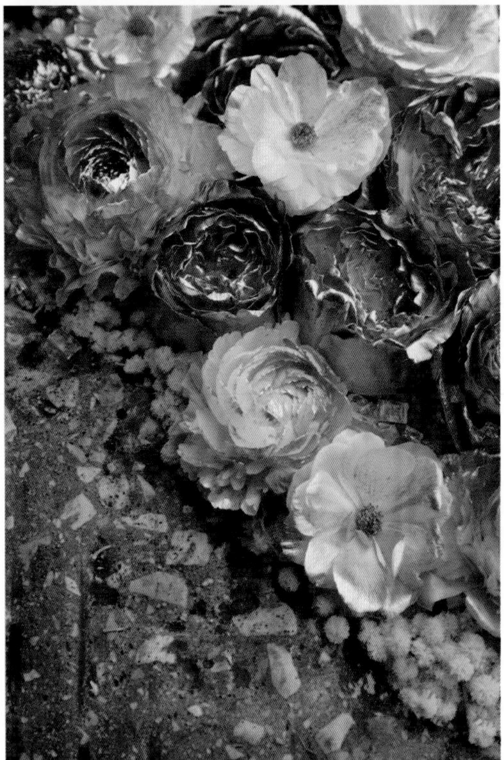

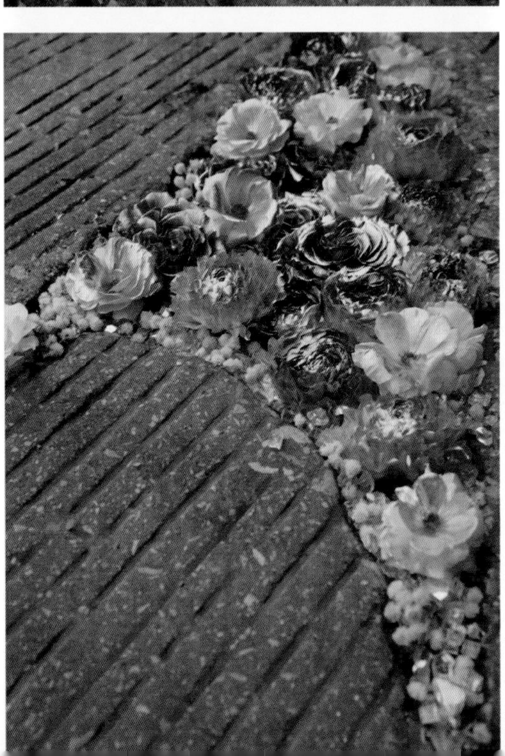

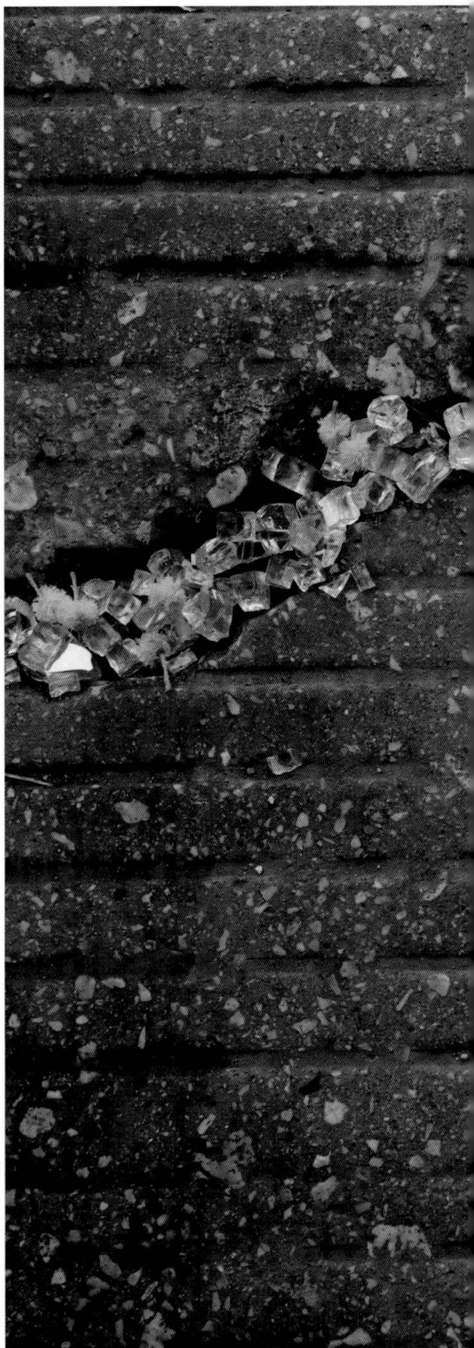

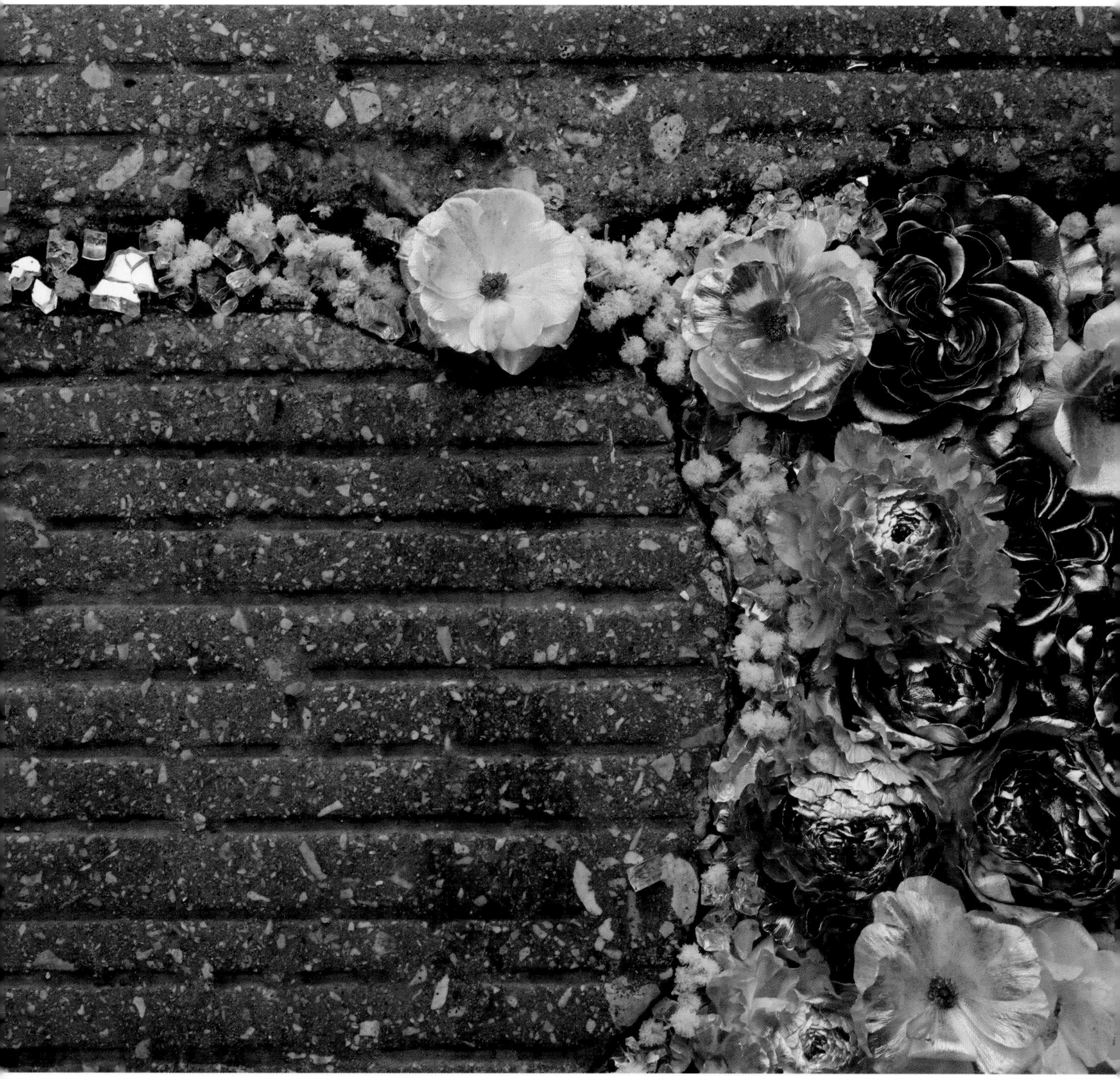

DESIGN BY STACEY BAL | PHOTOGRAPHY BY STACEY BAL
Chicago, Illinois | March 2020

URBAN SCARS

"Fill the cracks with gold!
There's beauty in the breakdown."

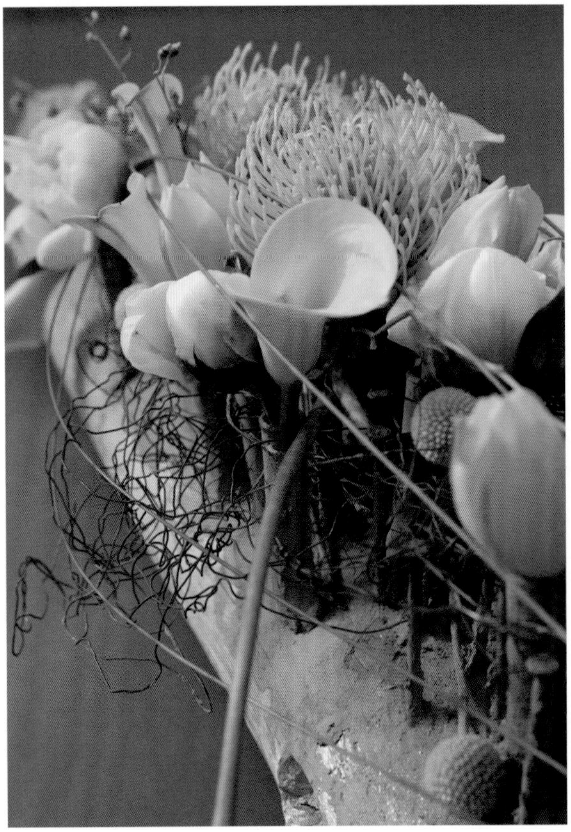

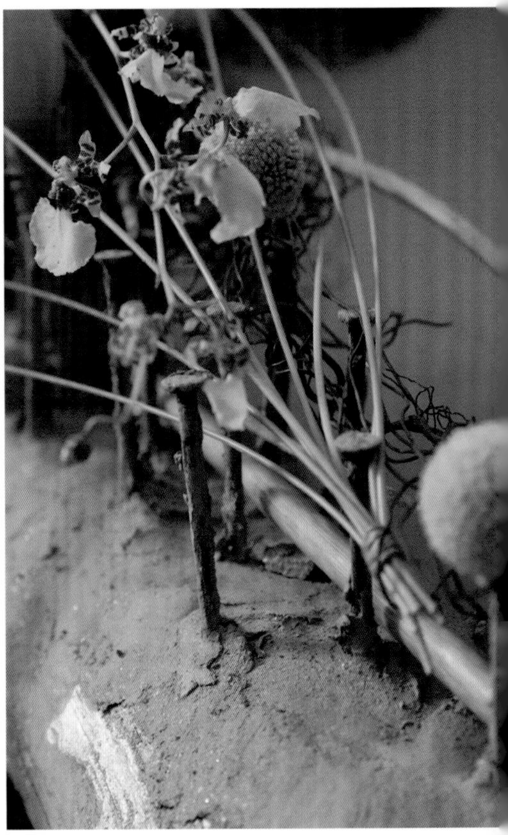

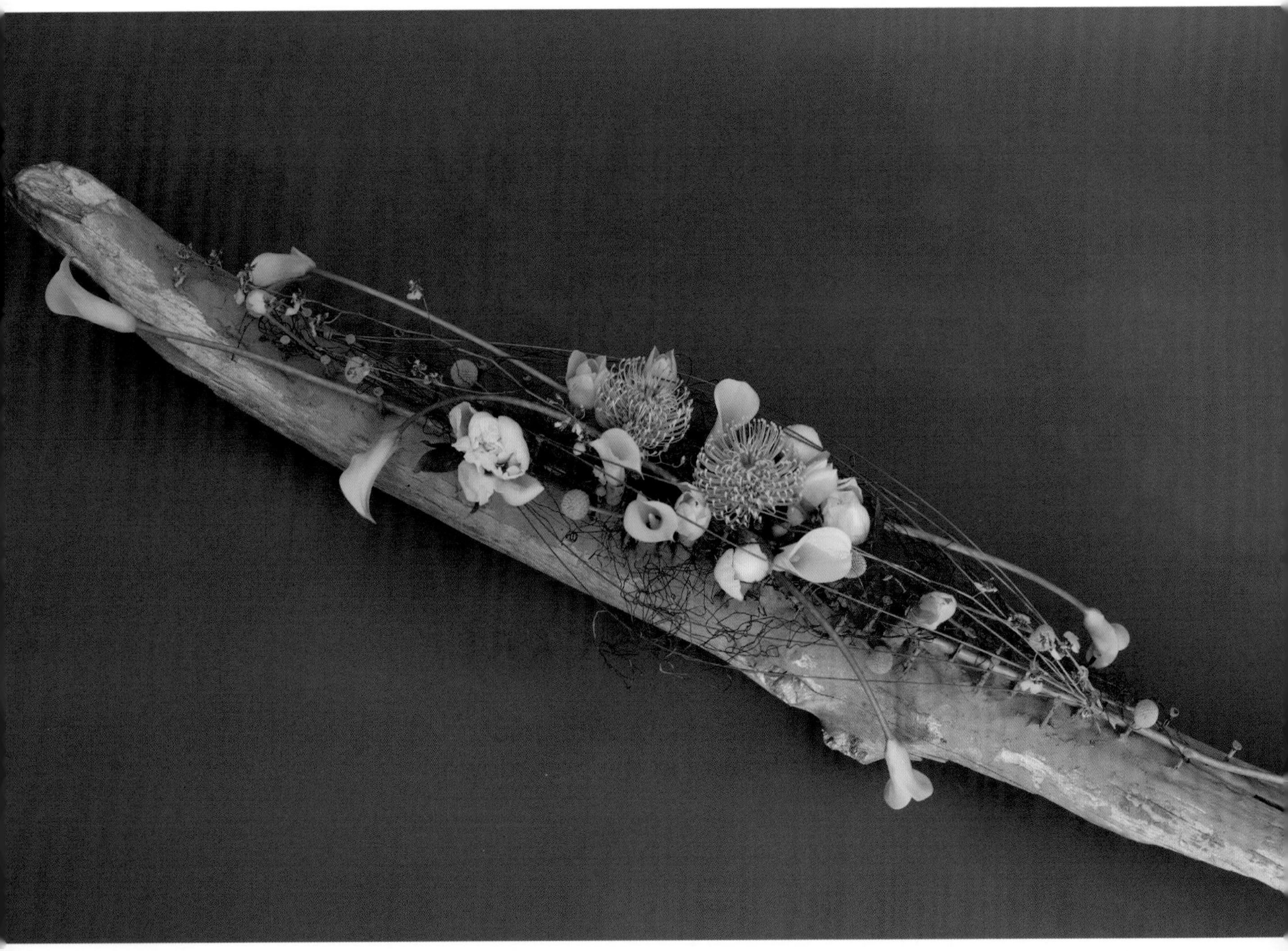

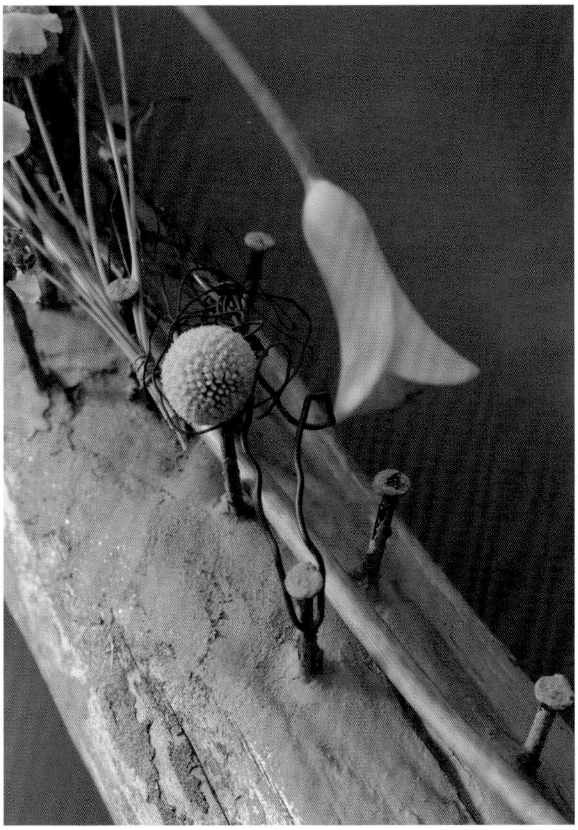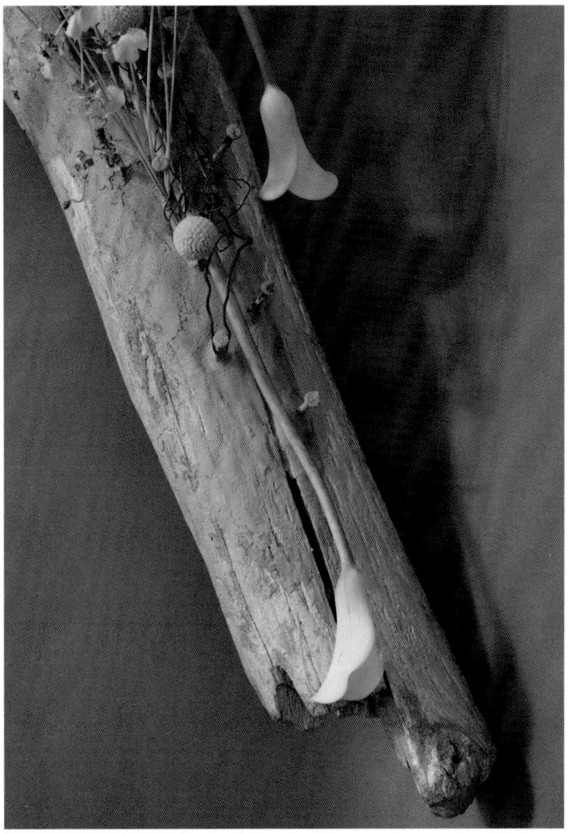

DESIGN BY ARTHUR WILLIAMS | PHOTOGRAPHY BY STACEY BAL

Denver, Colorado | January 2020

INTENTION

"Thought transmuting objects
cast away, reborn in golden light,
as art."

MA

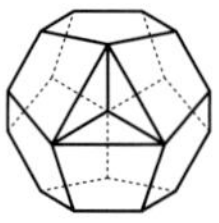

The Japanese word for "the space between two structural parts." To use negative space in a composition that creates dialogue between the elements. Also references what happens within a space, as in architecture and the silent pauses within a conversation.

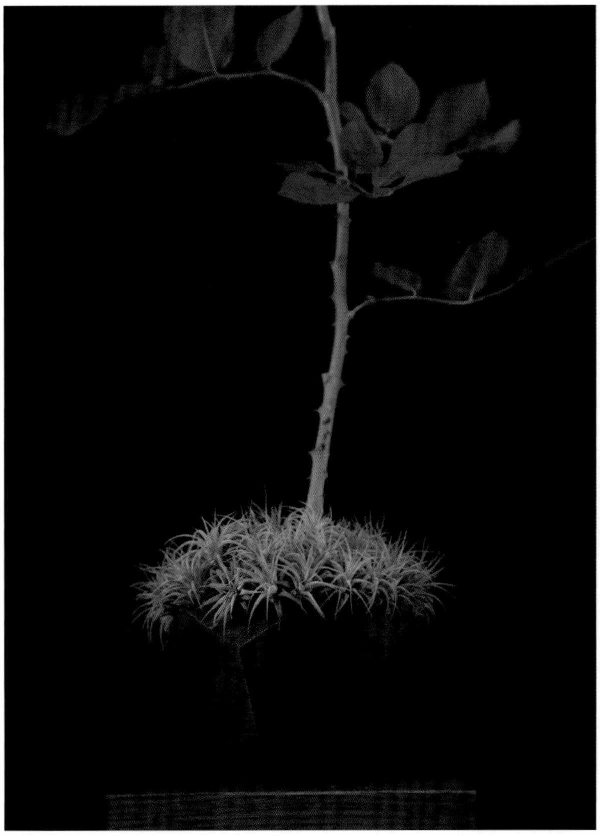

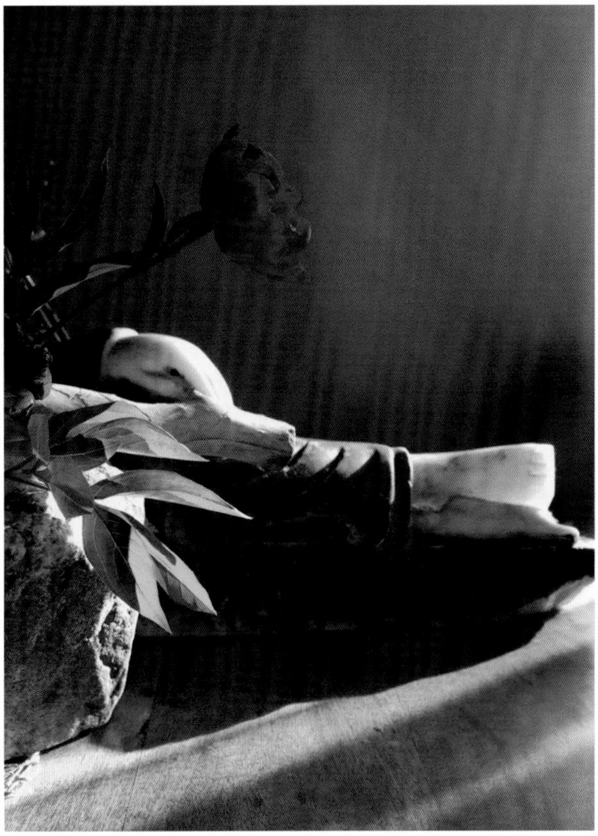

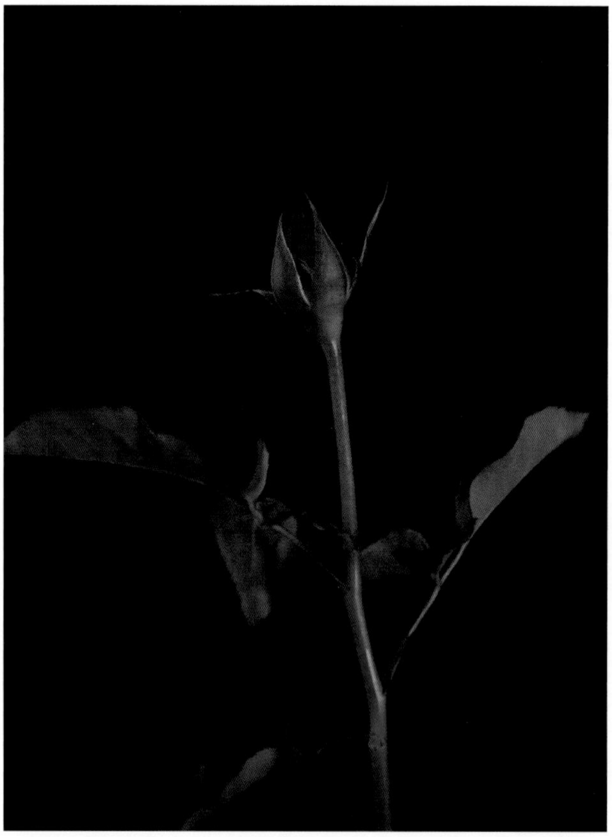

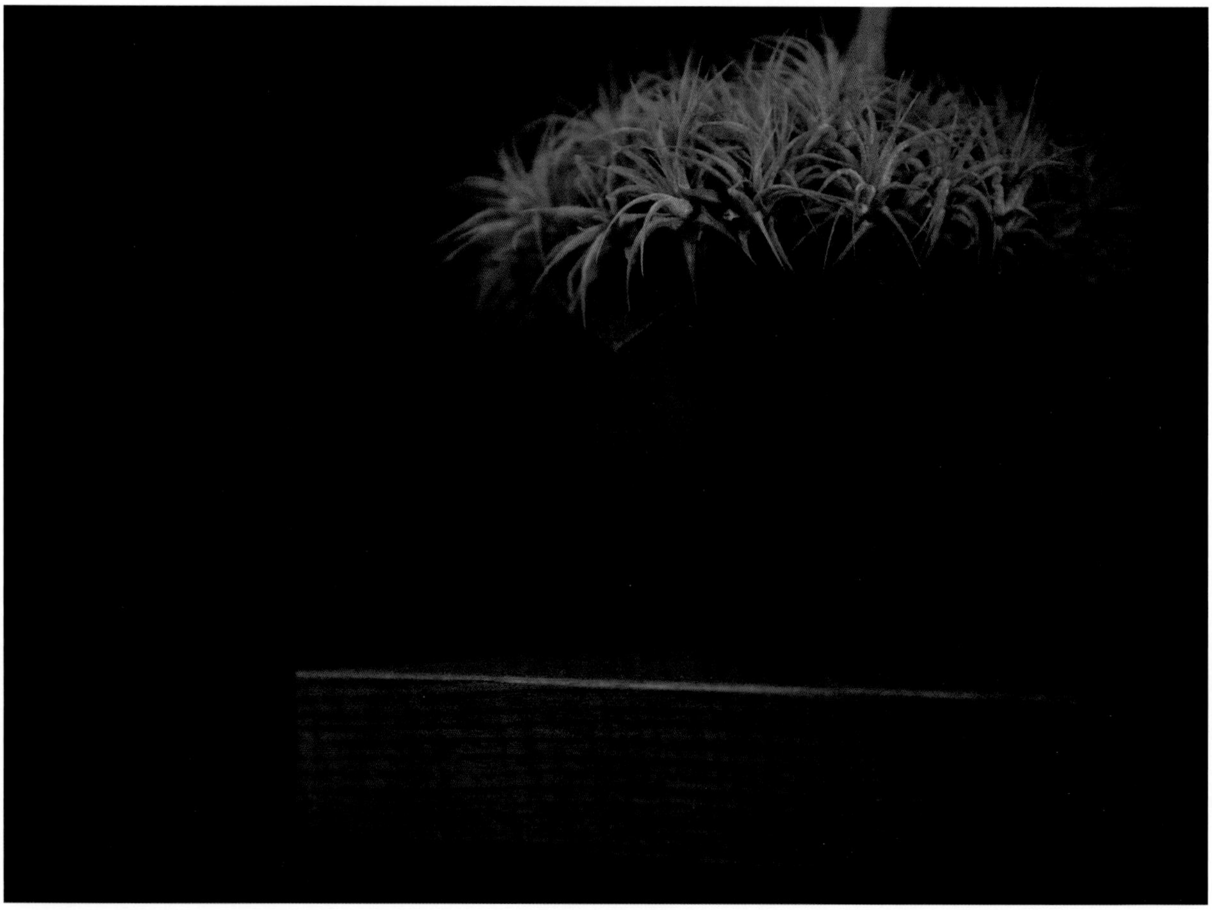

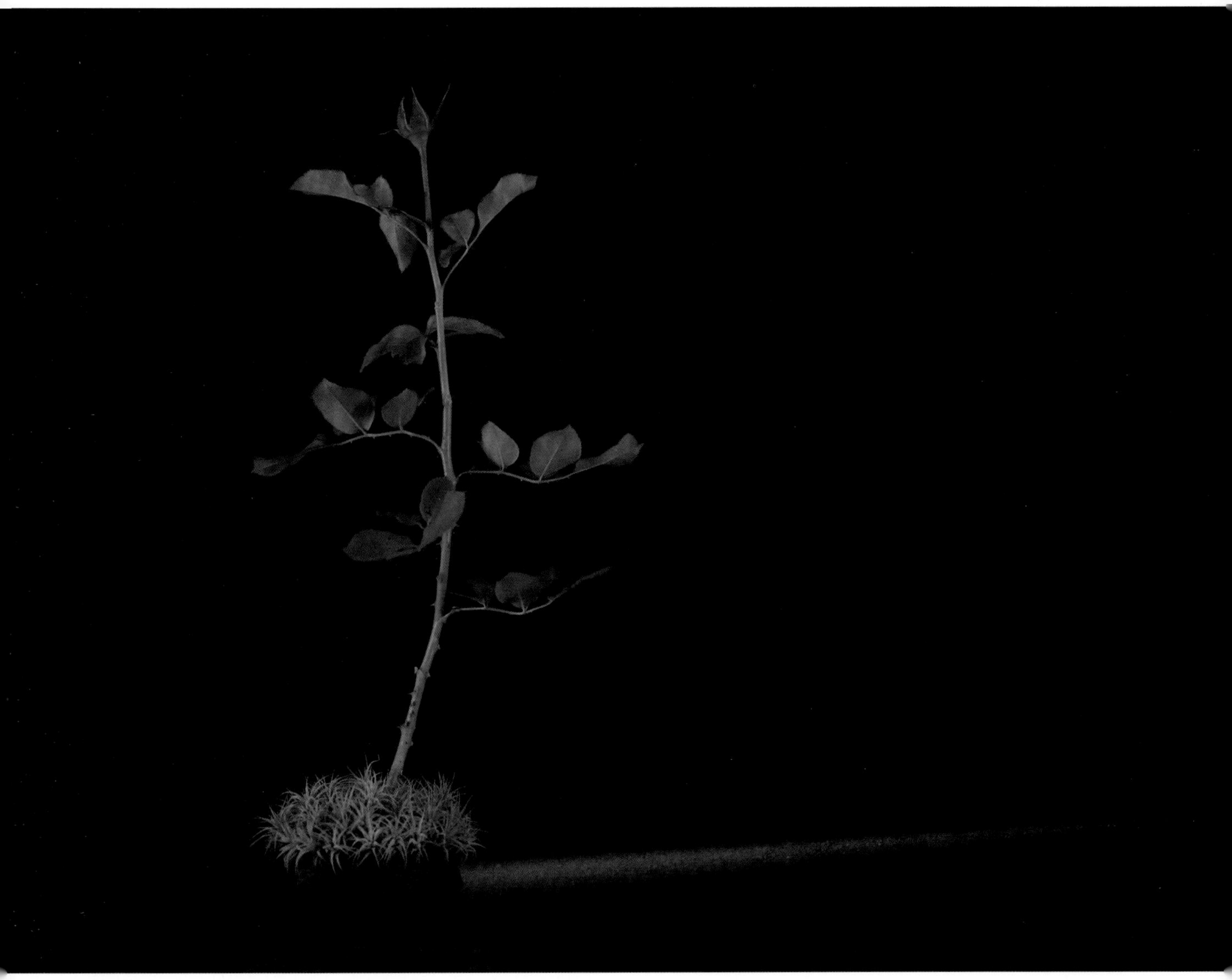

DESIGN BY STACEY BAL | PHOTOGRAPHY BY STACEY BAL
Chicago, Illinois | April 2020

AERODYNAMIC

"Challenging aesthetic assumptions, antigravity provides a sense of weightless relief. A visual silence where thoughts can rest, strengthen, and evolve."

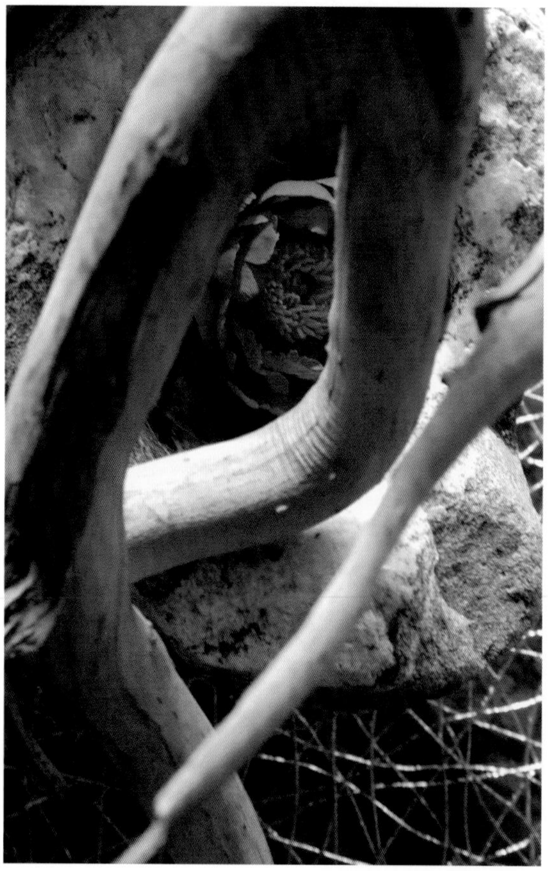

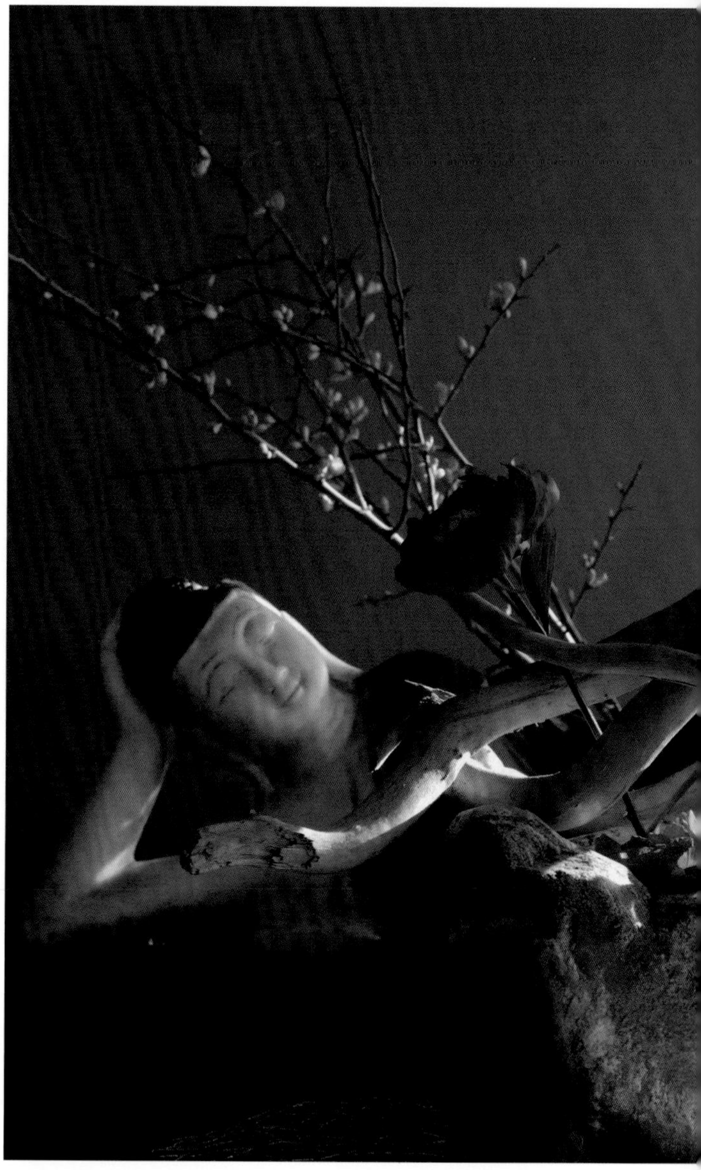

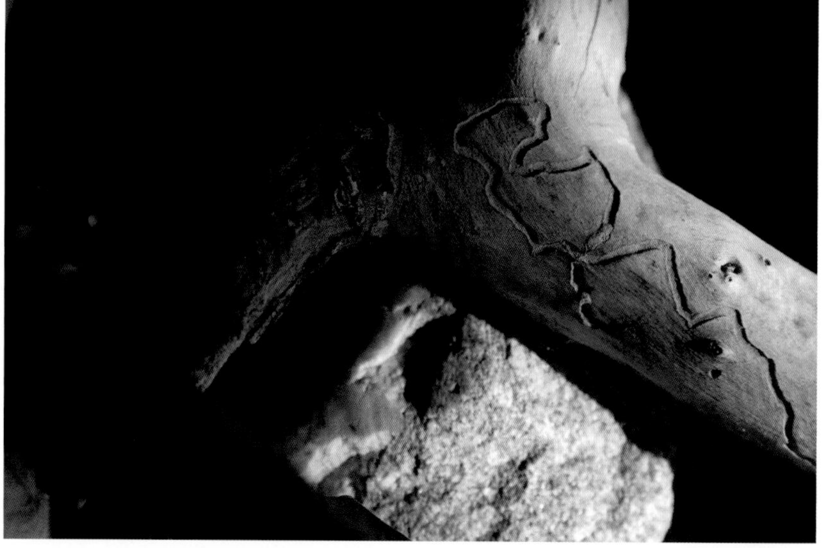

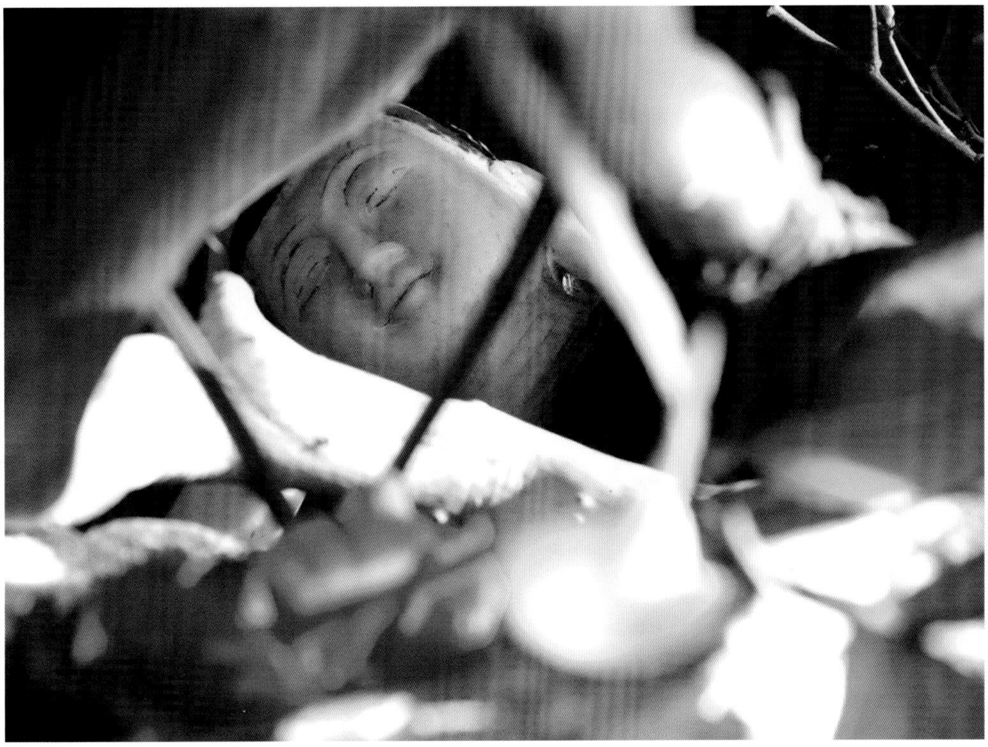

DESIGN BY ARTHUR WILLIAMS | PHOTOGRAPHY BY STACEY BAL
Denver, Colorado | January 2020

MOVEMENT BETWEEN TIME

"The silent conversation between stones
shaped by human hands."

TAKIWATANGA

TOCKI-WAA-TAN-GA

The Maori's (indigenous people of New Zealand) word for autism. It translates as "In his/her/my own space and time."

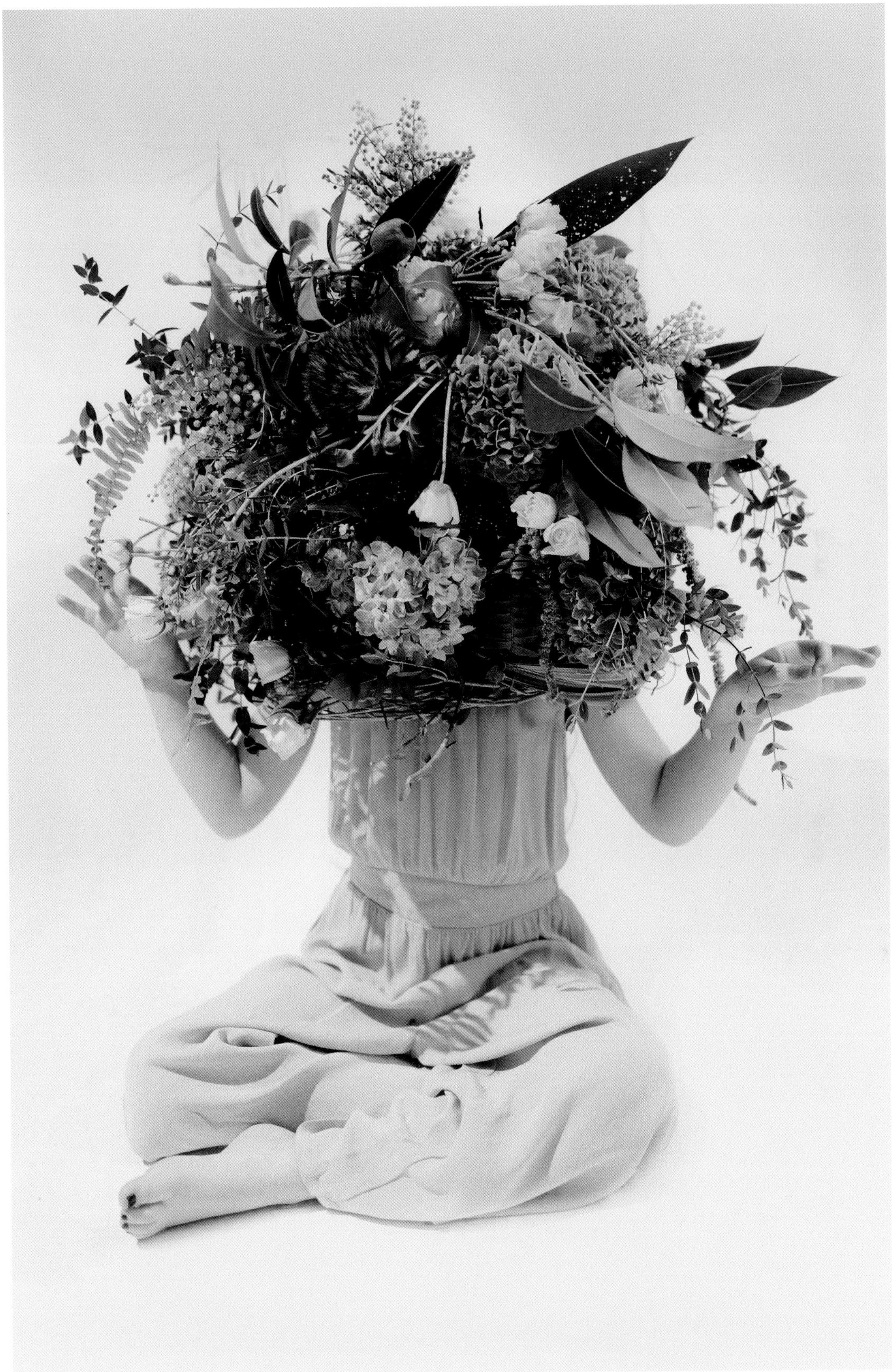

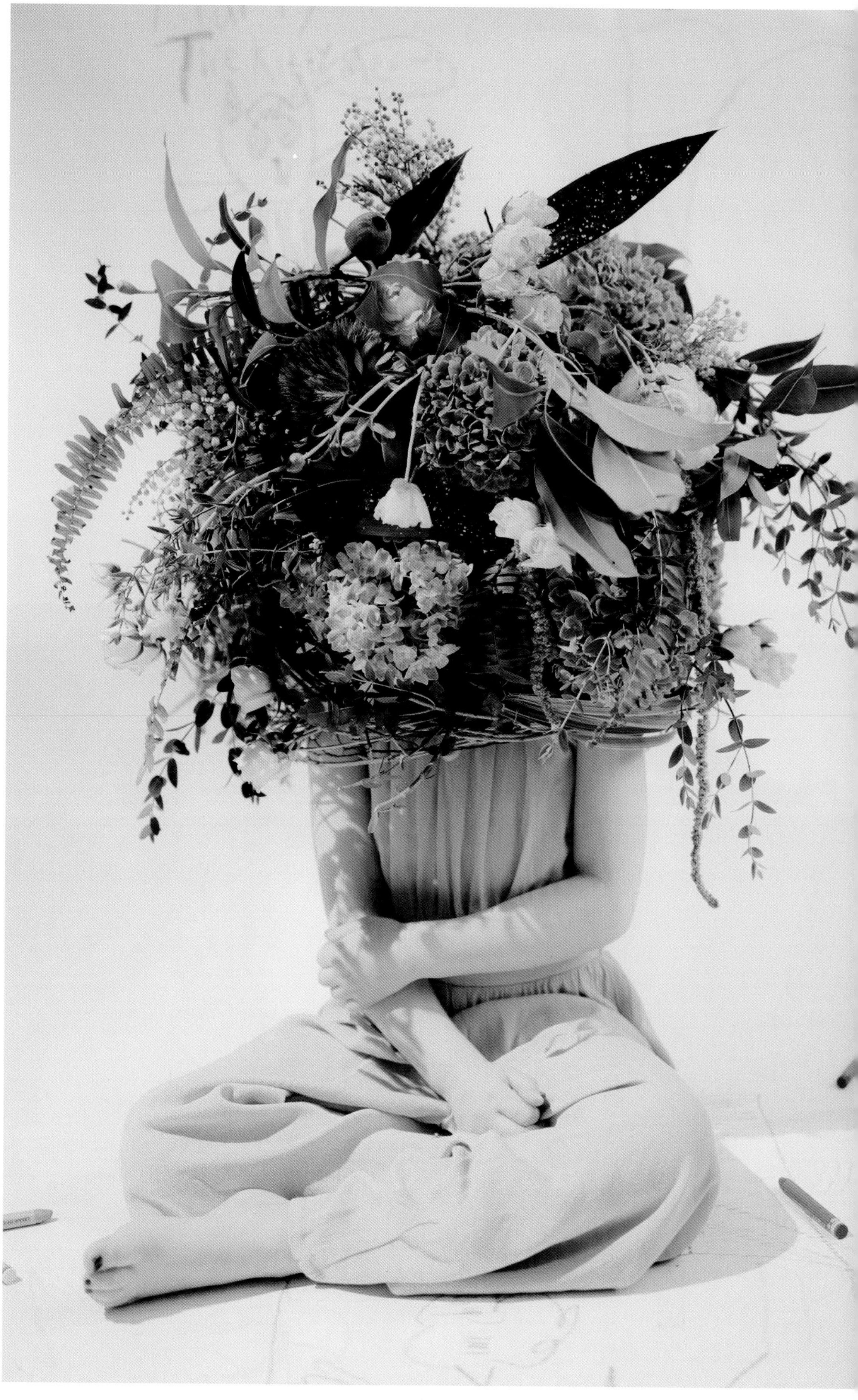

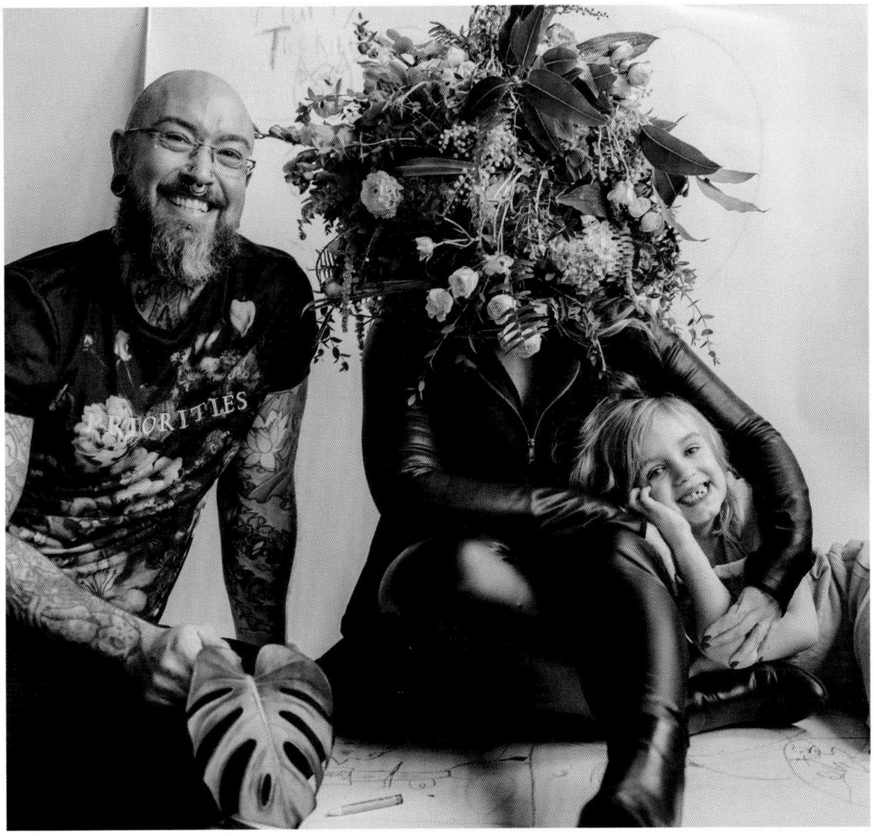

DESIGN BY ARTHUR WILLIAMS + STACEY BAL | PHOTOGRAPHY BY MARIYA BYELIKOVA

Muse: Rosie Carlton

Chicago, Illinois | March 2020

MONOTROPIC MIND

"It seems that for success in science or art, a dash of autism is essential."

Dr. Hans Asperger (1906-1980)

TRUST

A firm belief in the reliability,
truth, ability, or strength
of someone or something.

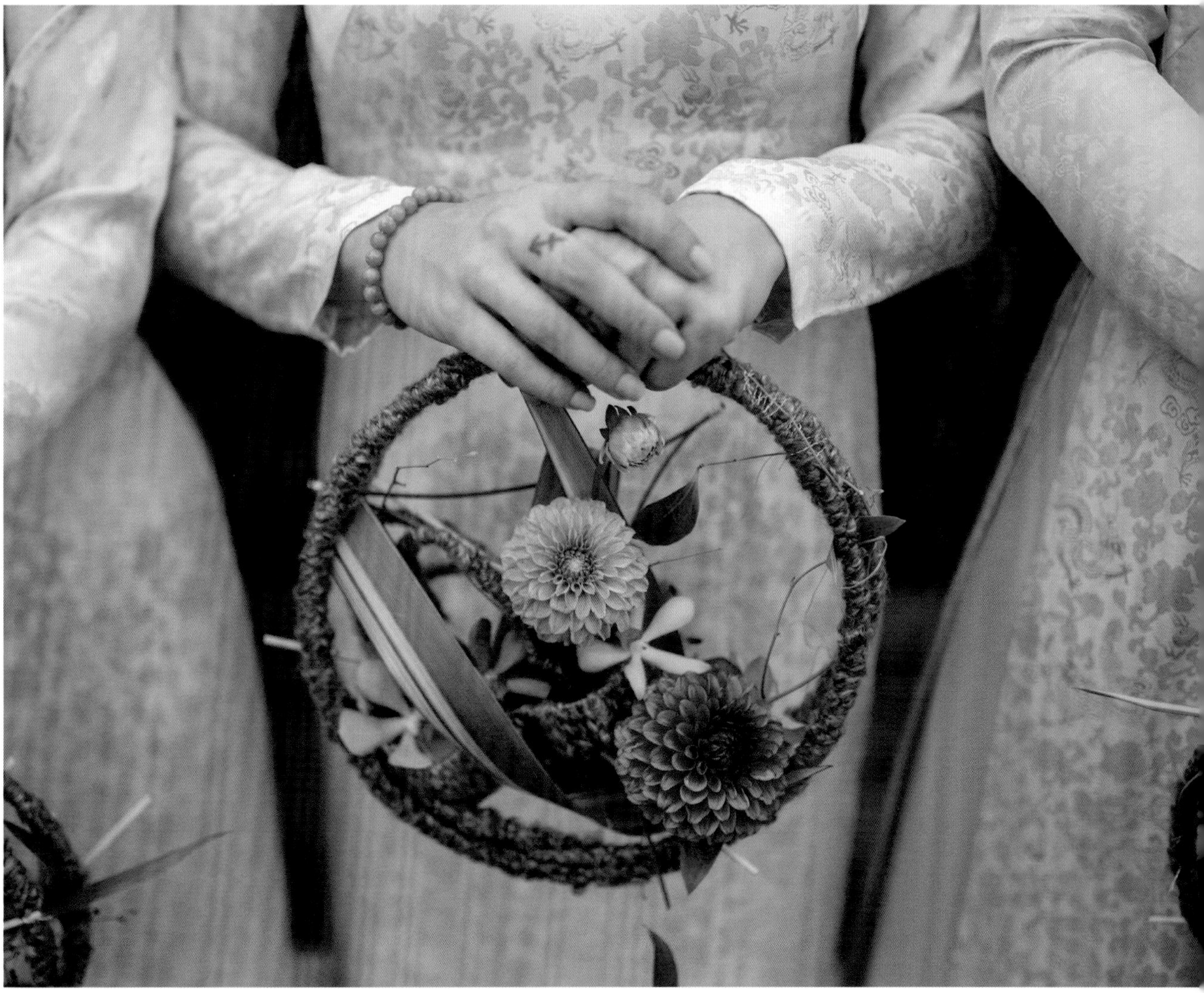

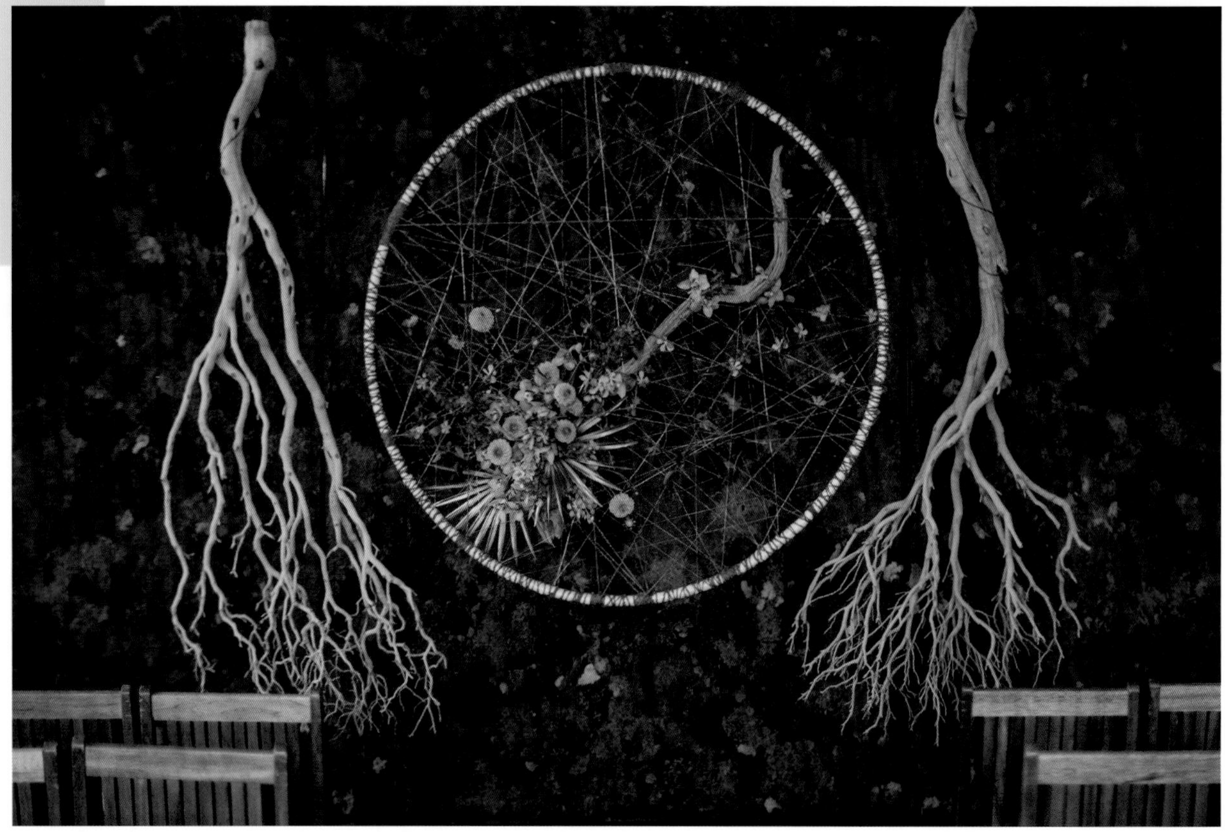

DESIGN BY ARTHUR WILLIAMS + STACEY BAL | PHOTOGRAPHY BY THE SCOBEYS
Denver, Colorado | August 2019

MATRIMONY: HUYEN + JOSH

From the very first meeting with this couple, the theme became apparent: Trust. Needless to say, we hit it off. Then, as it often happens in world of weddings, another client's wedding fell on the same date.

After a brief panic, I knew what I had to do. I turned to the only person who I knew had the knowledge and experience to pull off my favorite wedding of all time: Stacey. We had begun working together more and more on events, but this one was by baby; my most precious dream project.

I gave Stacey all the elements, the little bits of my soul to be included, and then stepped away, trusting that our shared education and the laws of nature would fall into place. That they did.

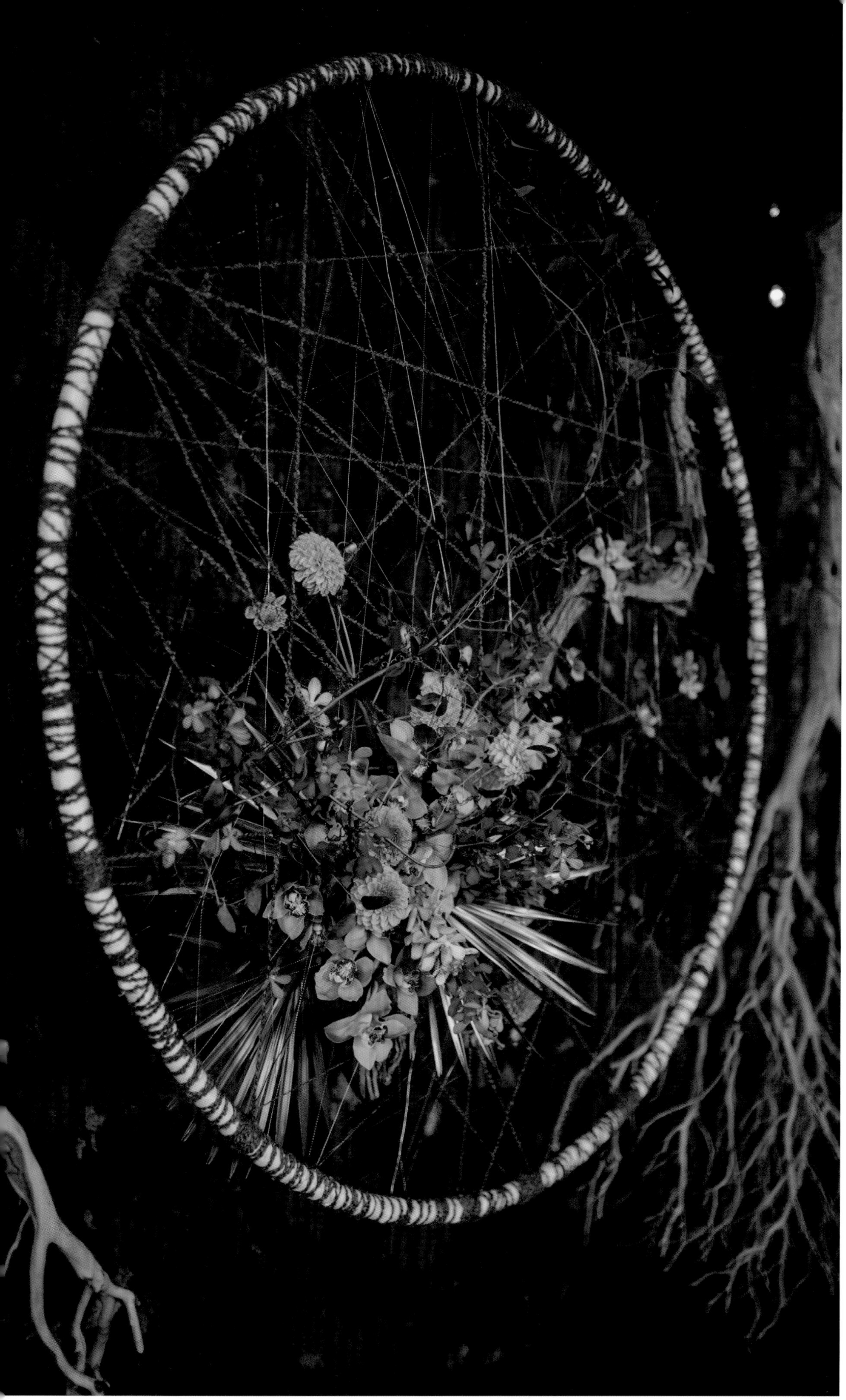

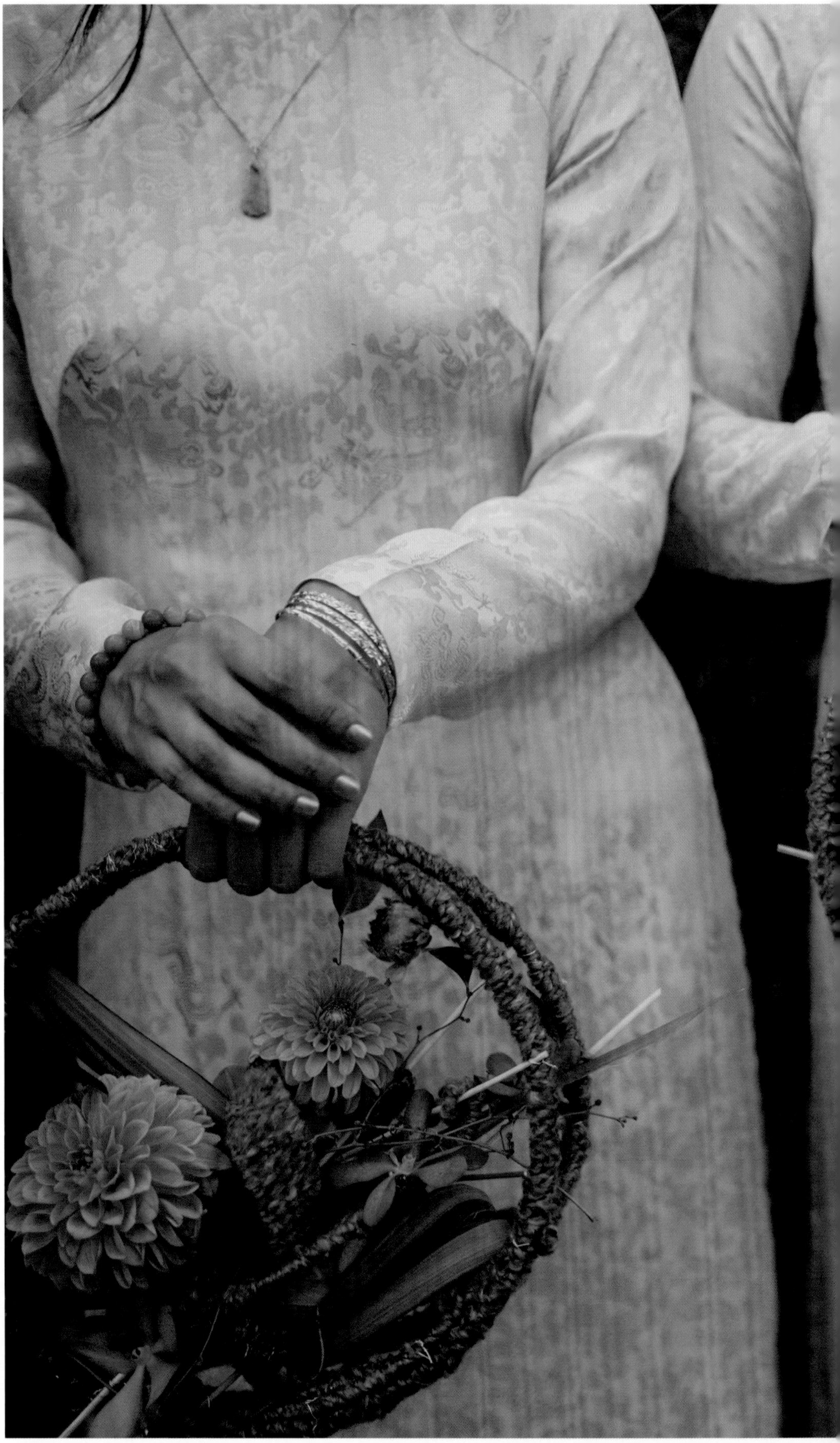

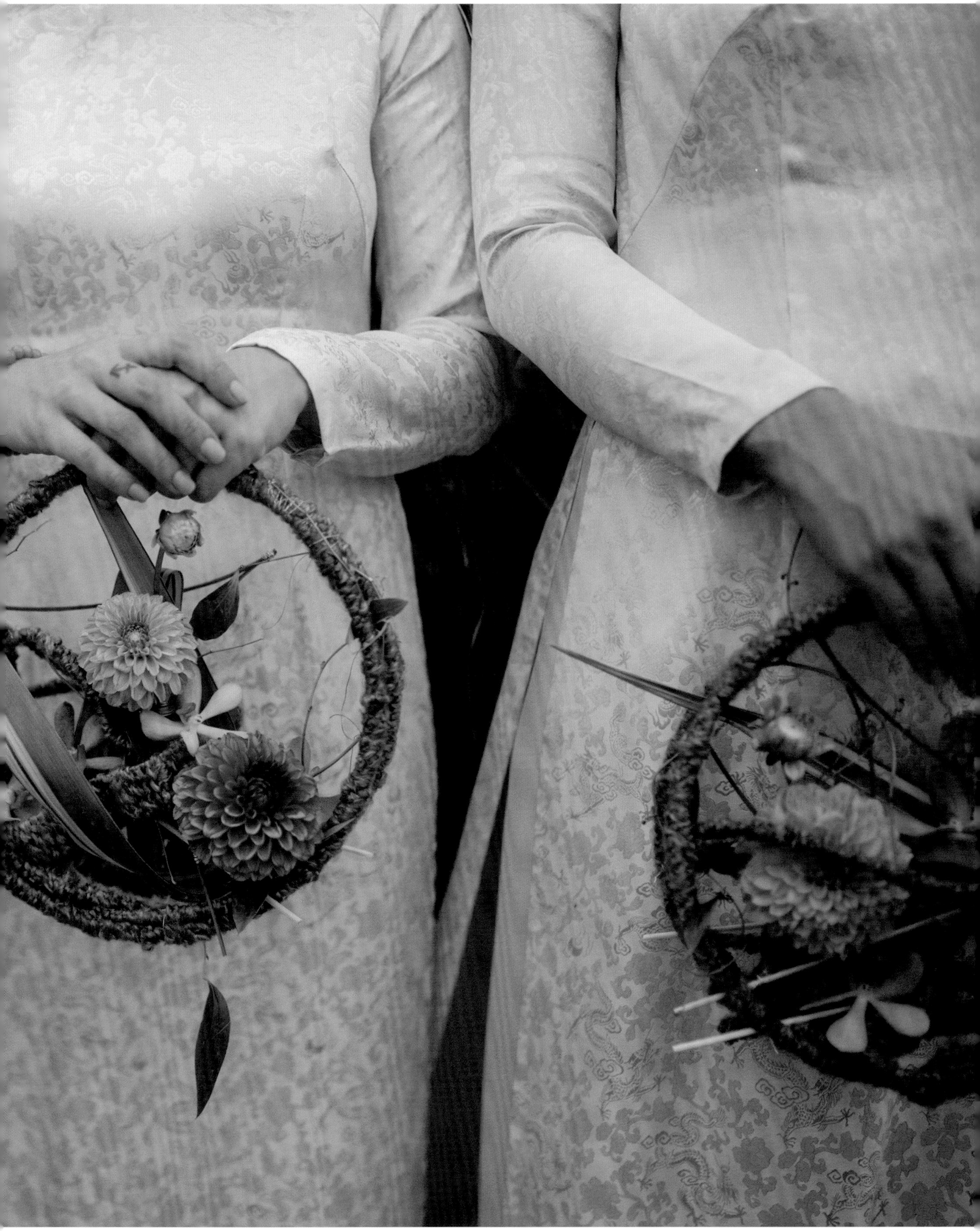

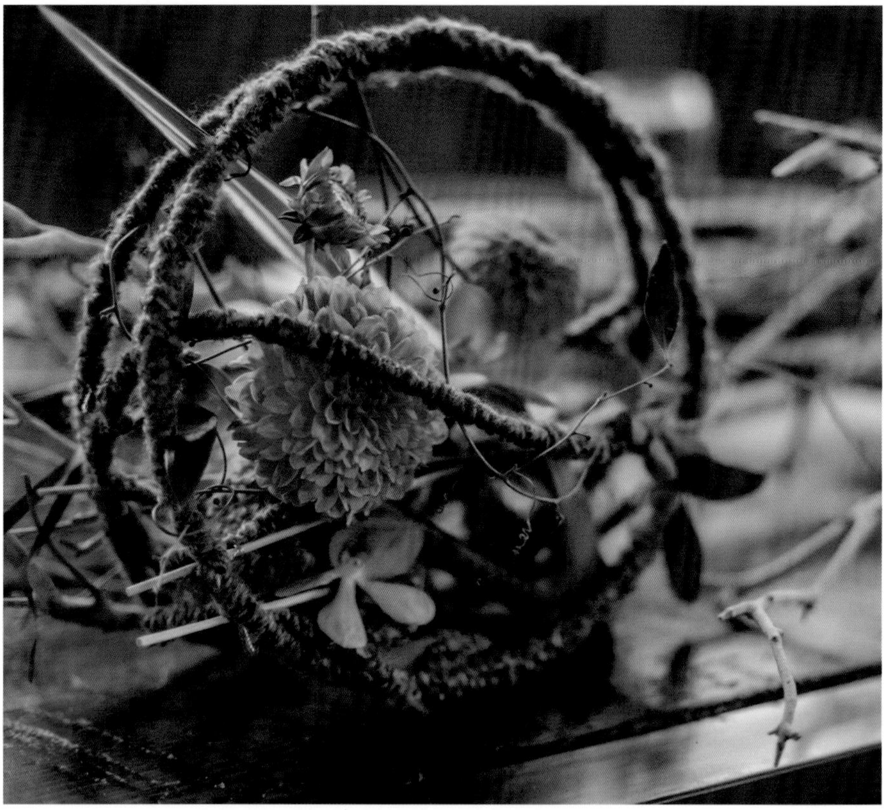

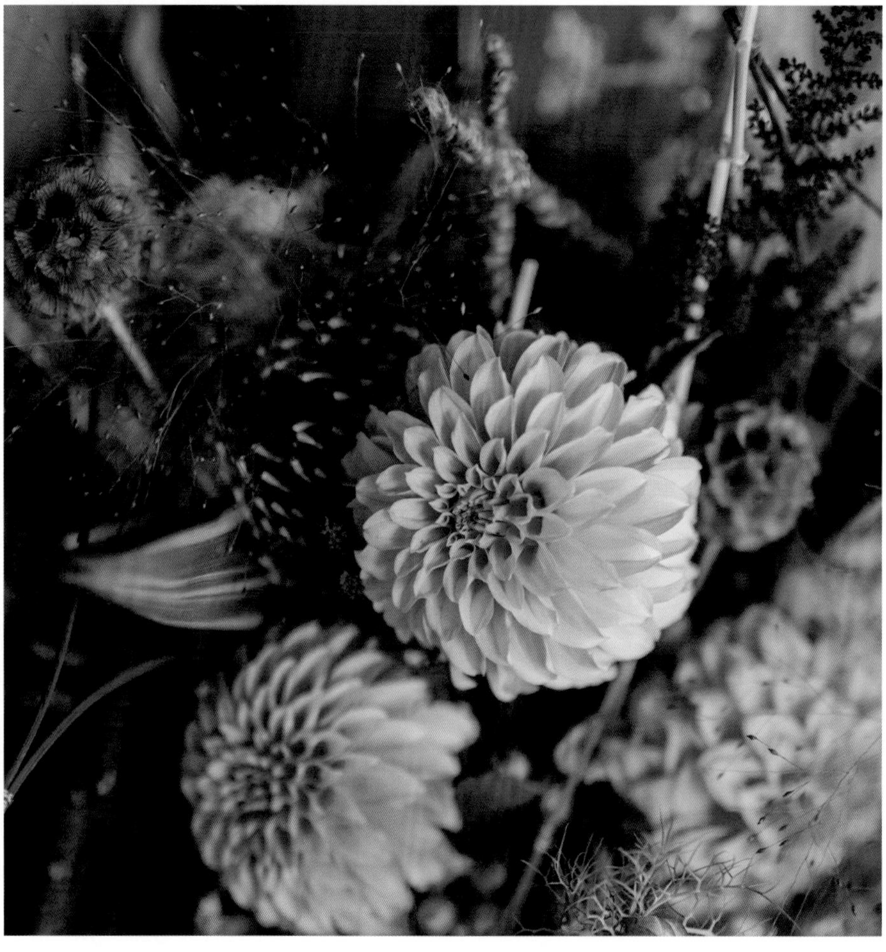

IMPERMANENT

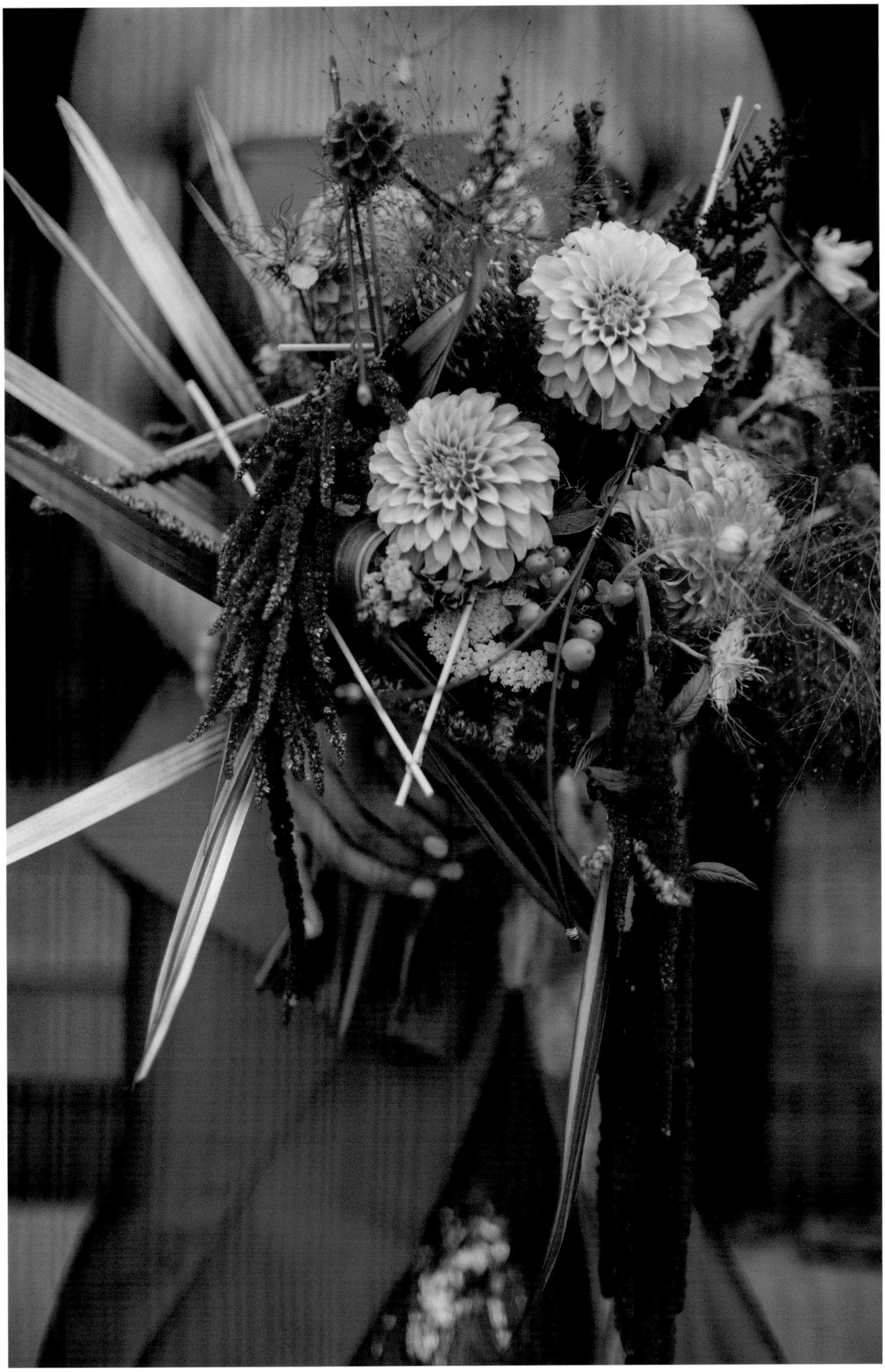

"Trust is a very powerful thing."

WAVE

A sudden occurrence
or increase in a specified
phenomenon or emotion.

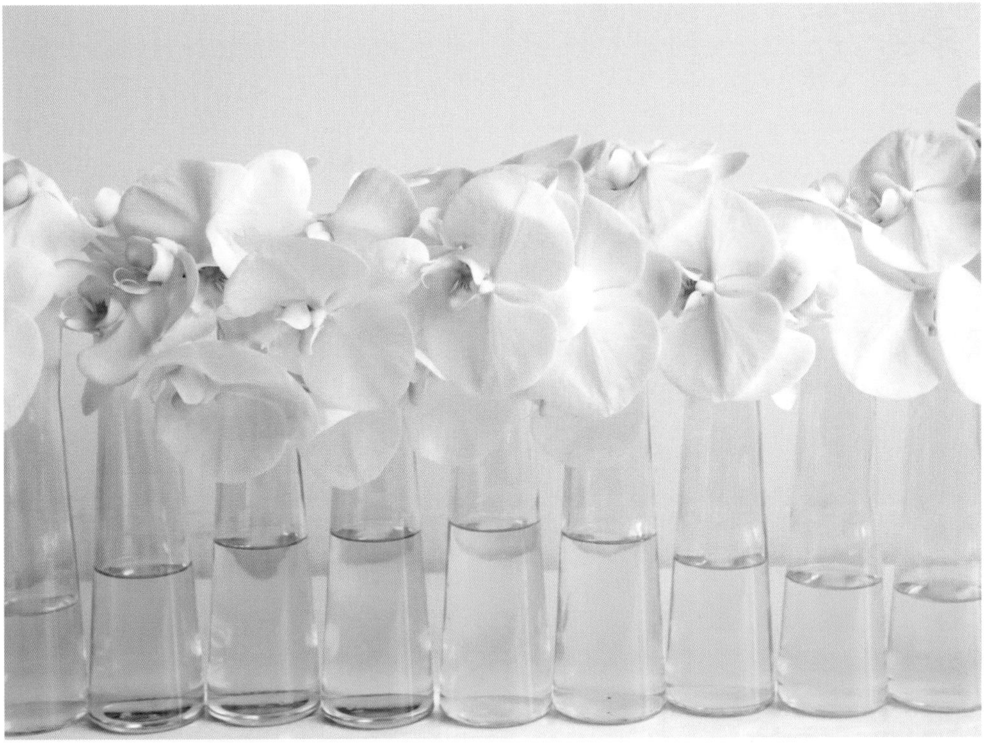

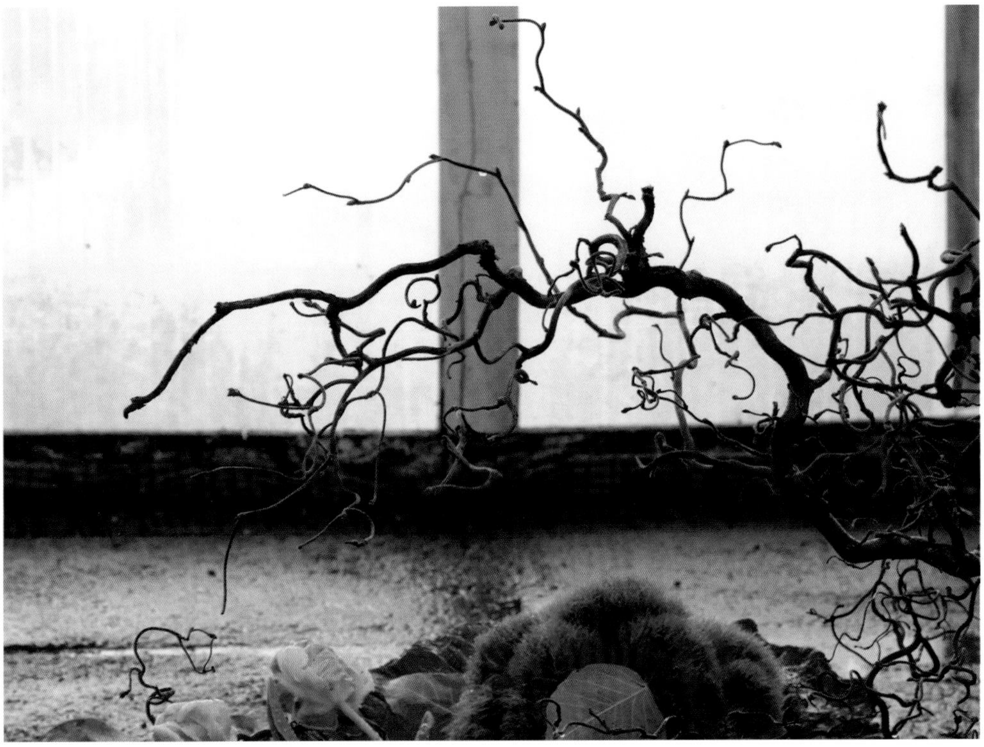

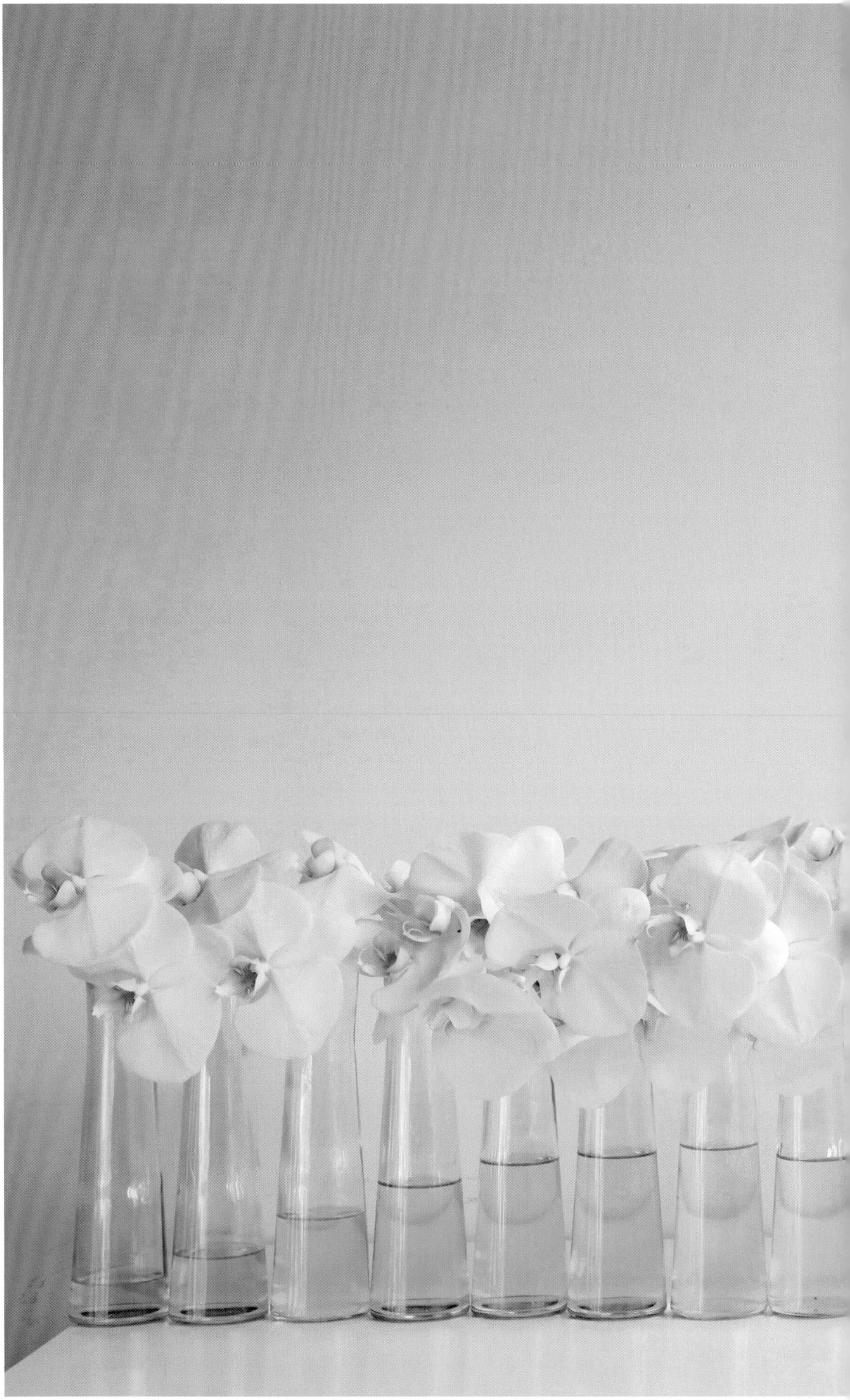

DESIGN BY STACEY BAL | PHOTOGRAPHY BY STACEY BAL

Chicago, Illinois | March 2020

MIND LIKE WATER

"Capable of stillness and strength.
Adaptable, evolving, and ready to
react to ever-changing circumstances."

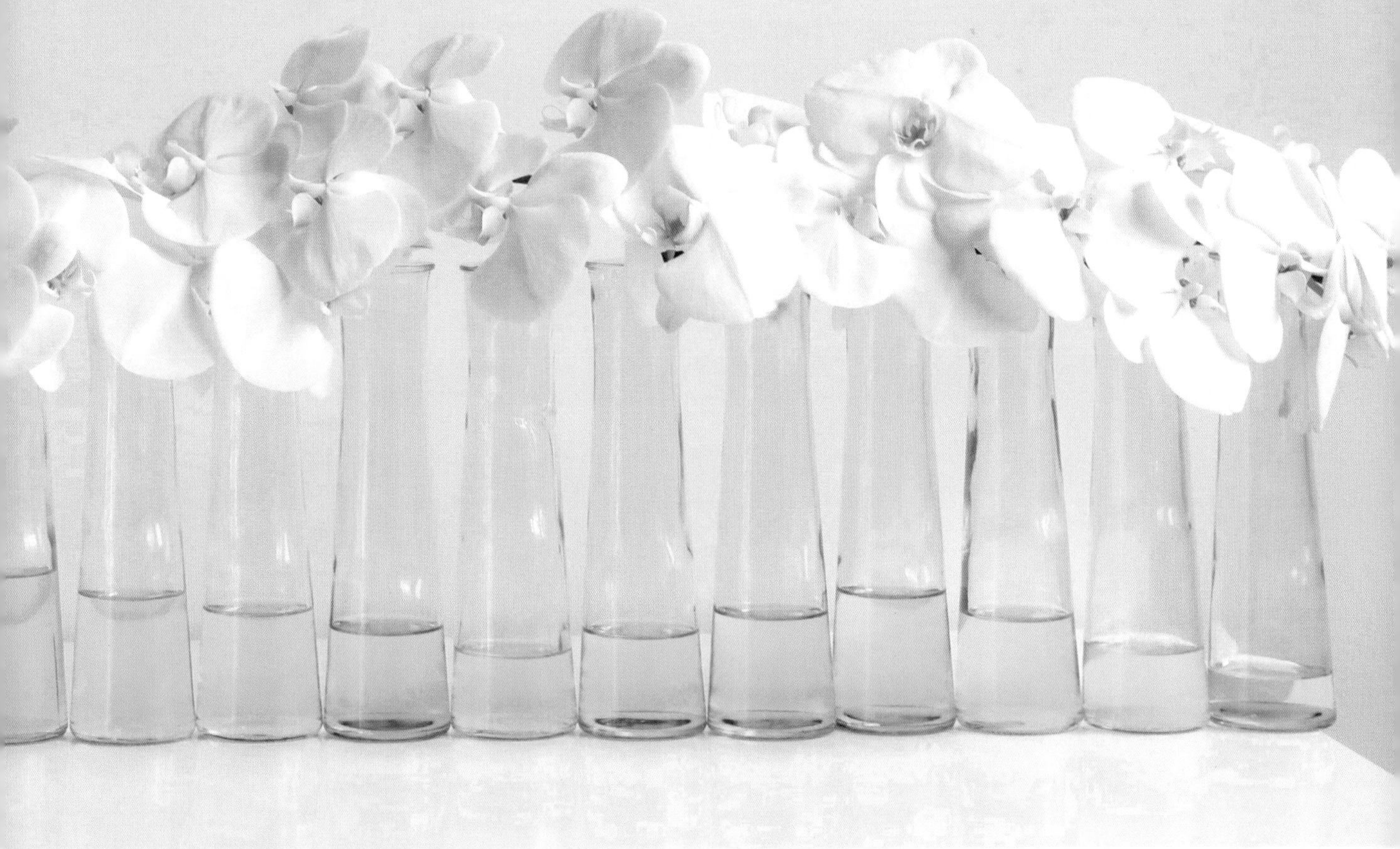

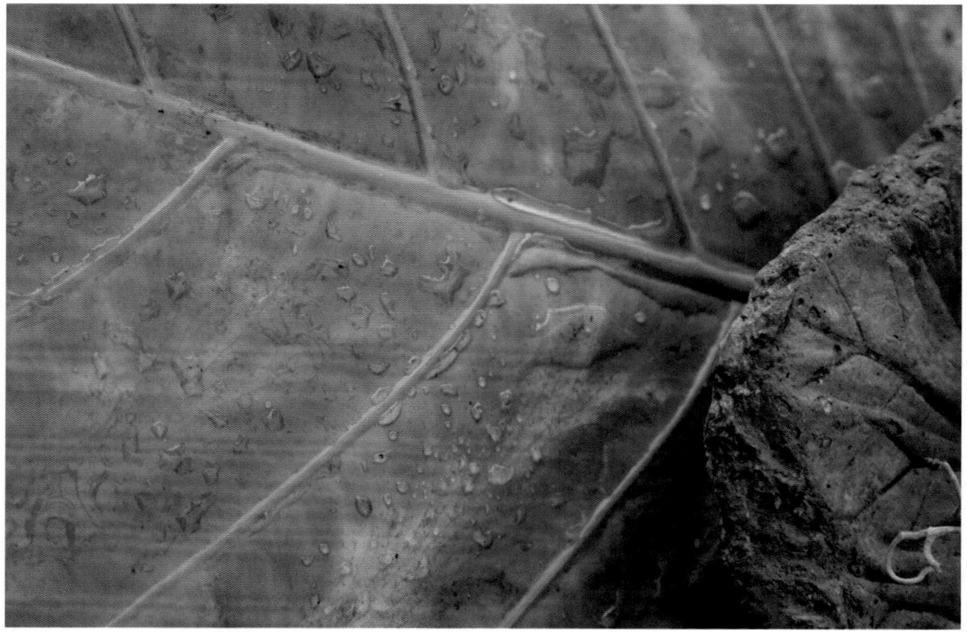

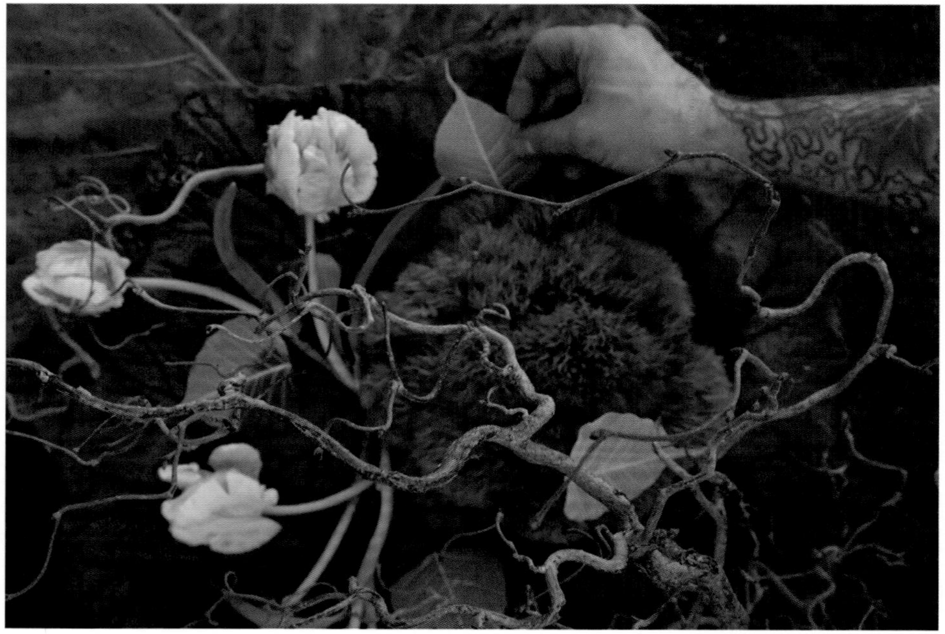

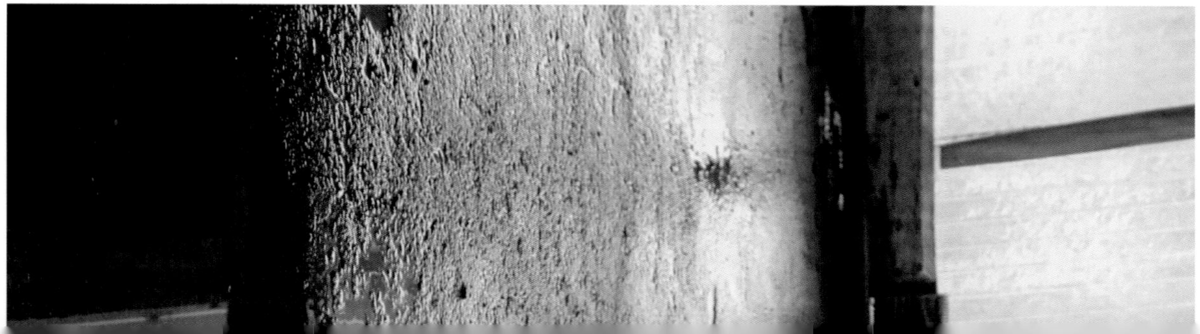

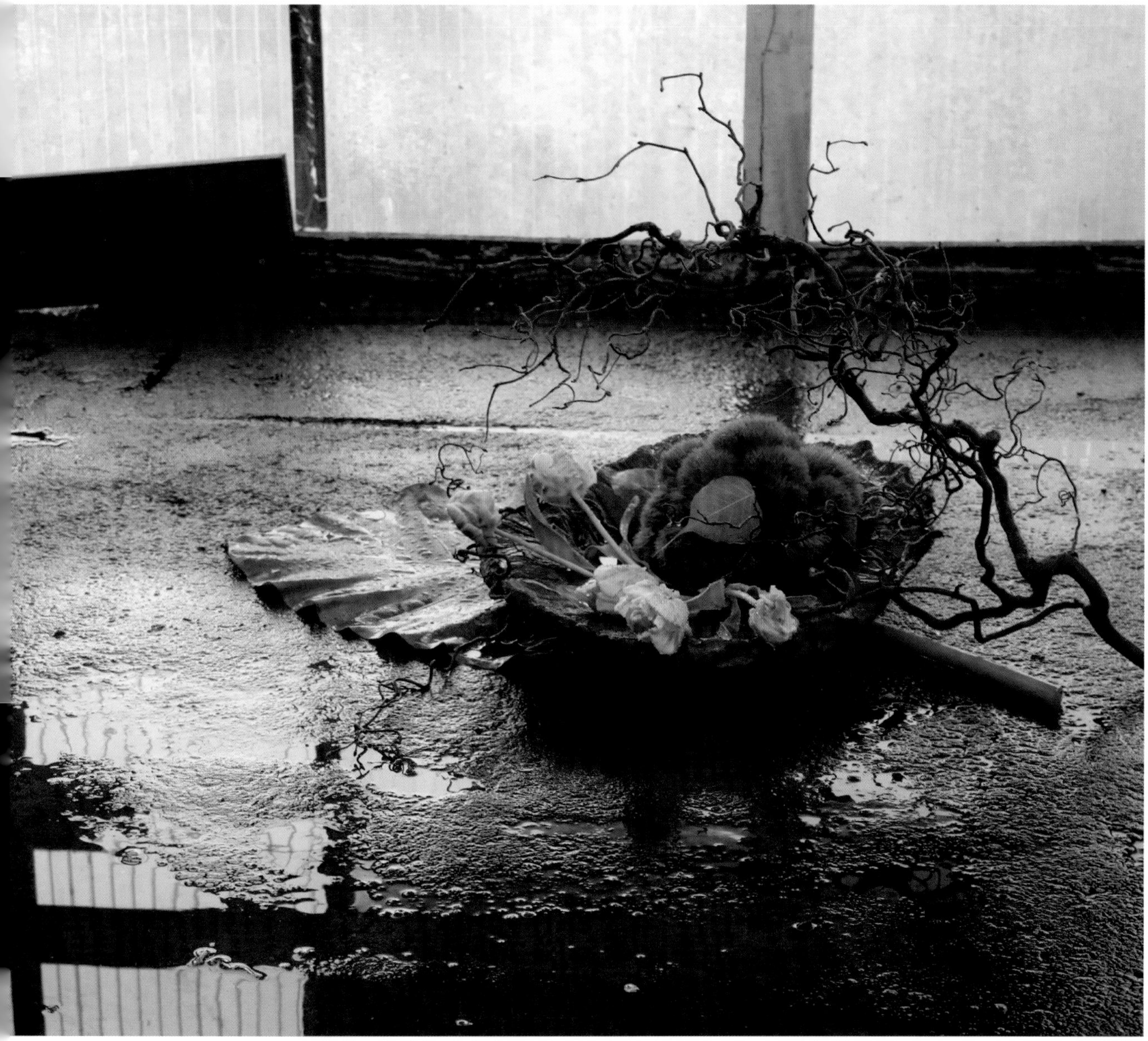

DESIGN BY ARTHUR WILLIAMS | PHOTOGRAPHY BY STACEY BAL

Denver, Colorado | January 2020

KOMOREBI

"My dreams, falling leaves, adrift on
a wave of unconscious lives lived.
The cycles continue, of death and birth,
like sunlight flickering through the
forest canopy."

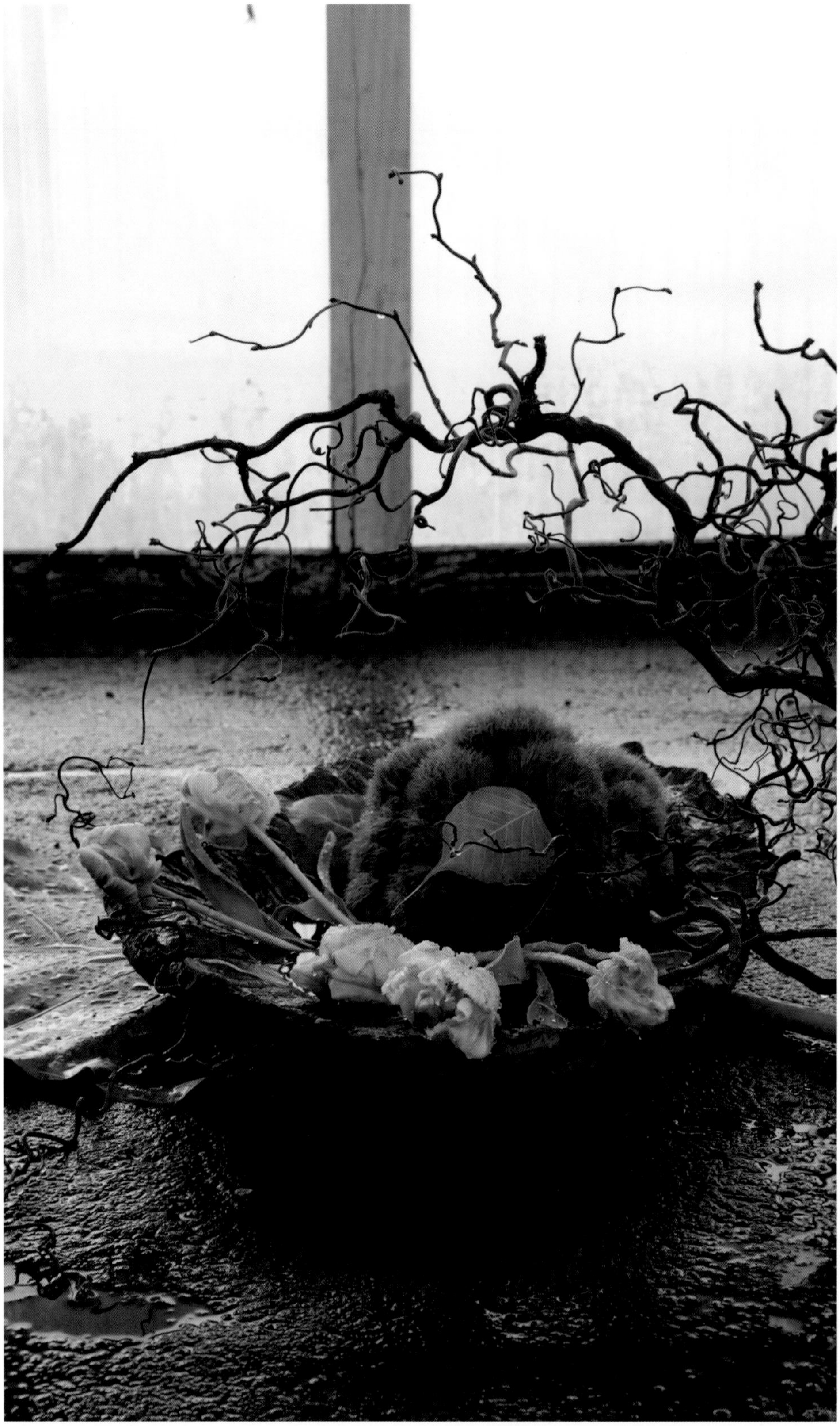

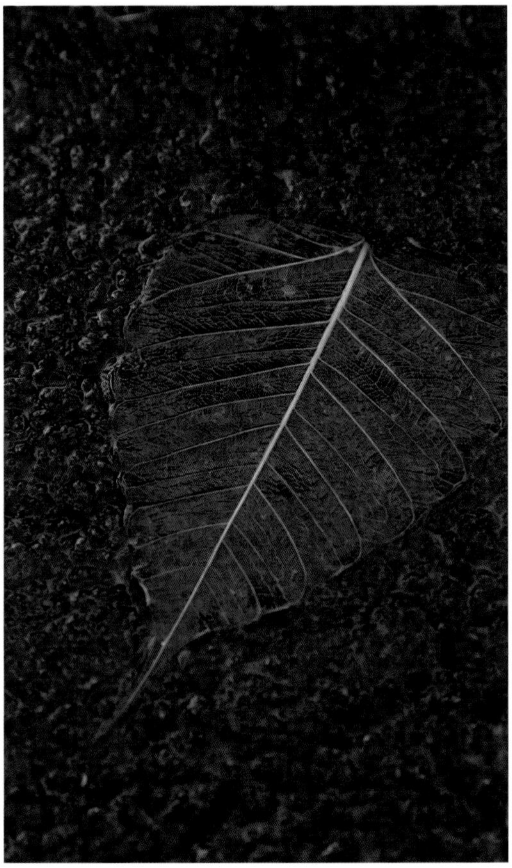
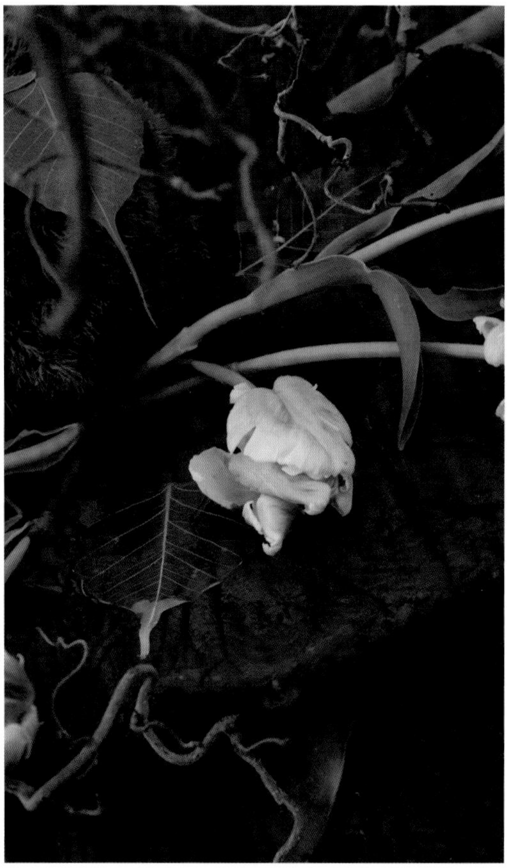
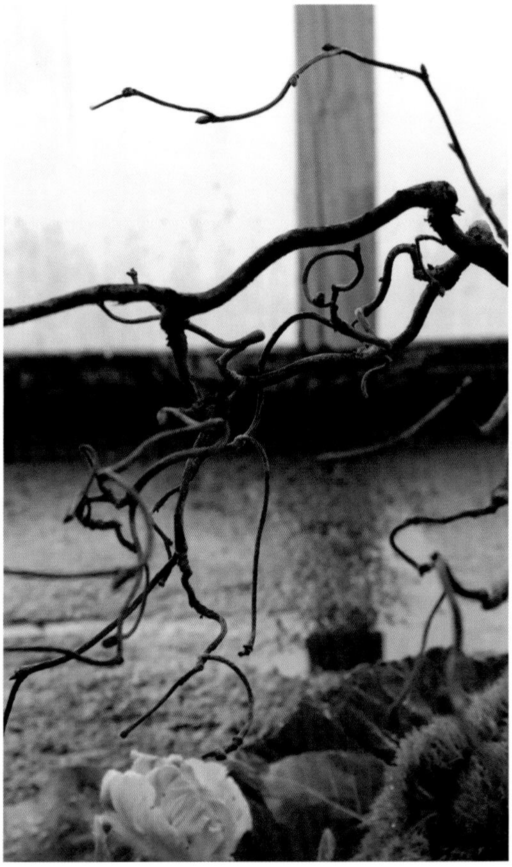
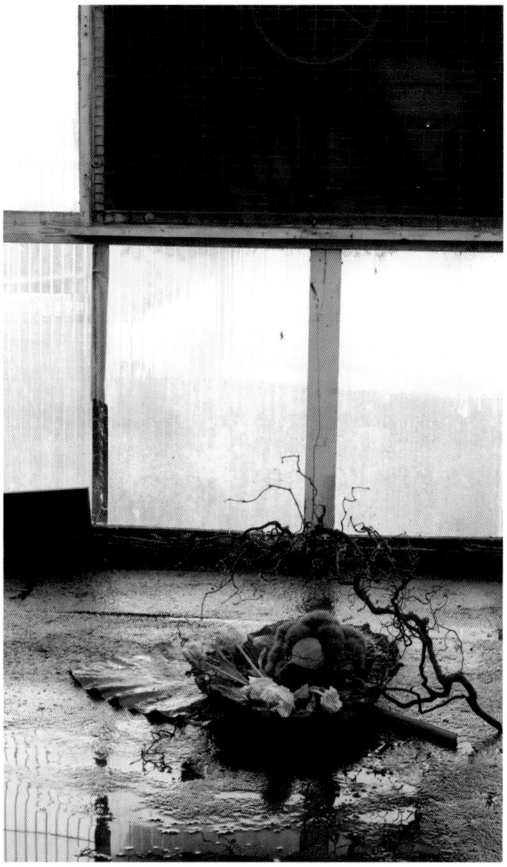

BIOMIMETIC

BI-O-MI-MET-IC

The imitation of the models, systems and structures of nature to solve complex problems with the intention to improve humanity.

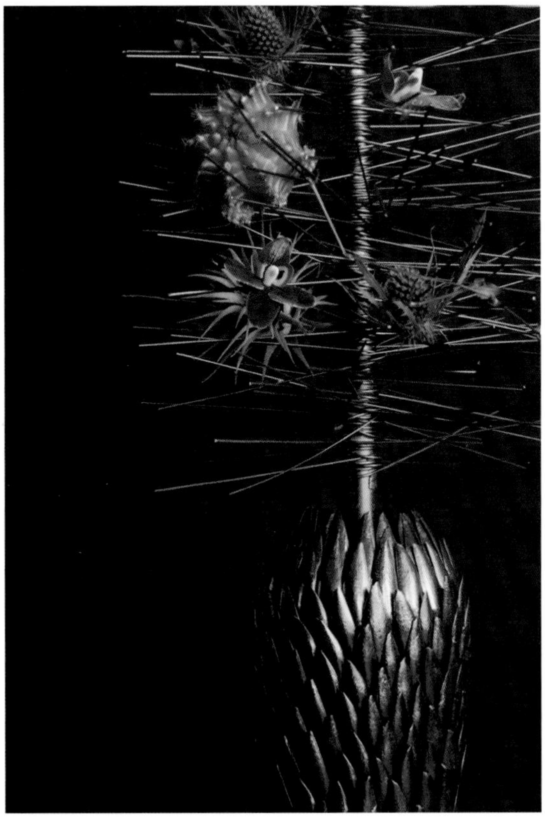

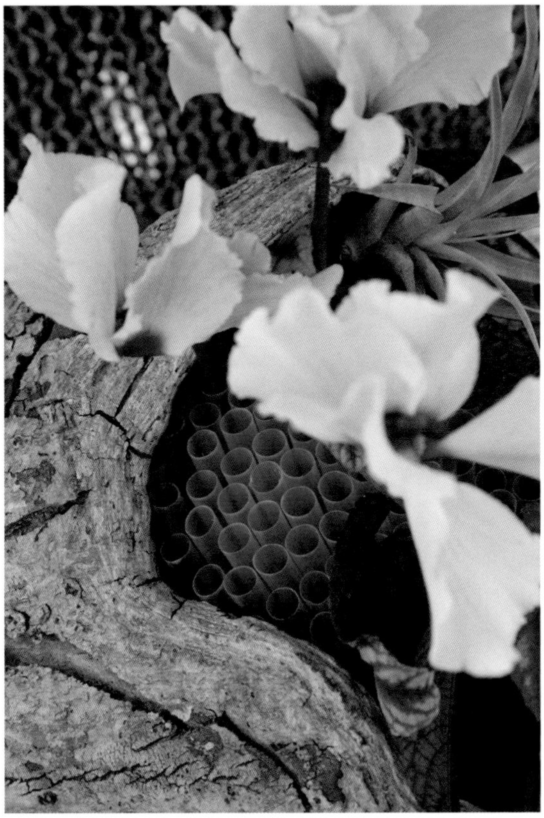

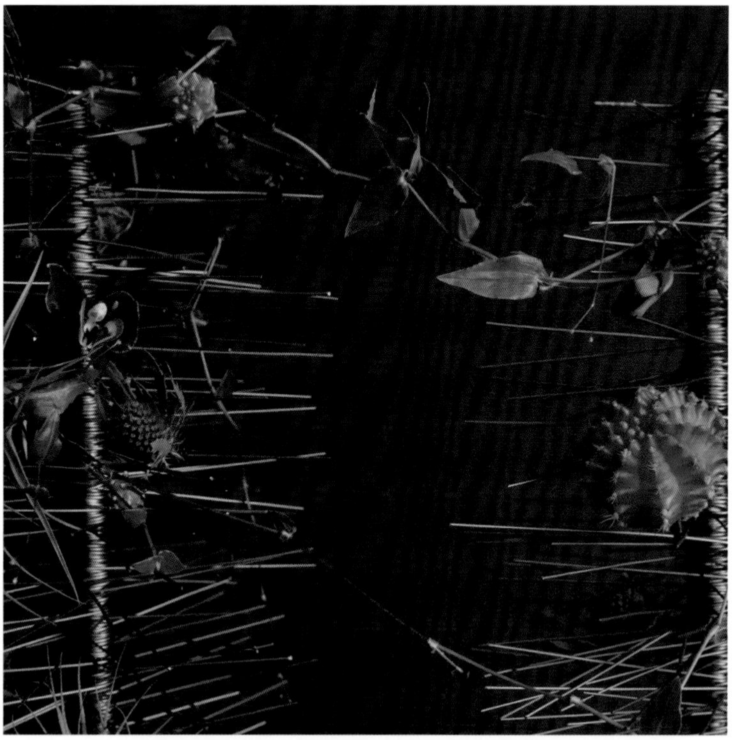

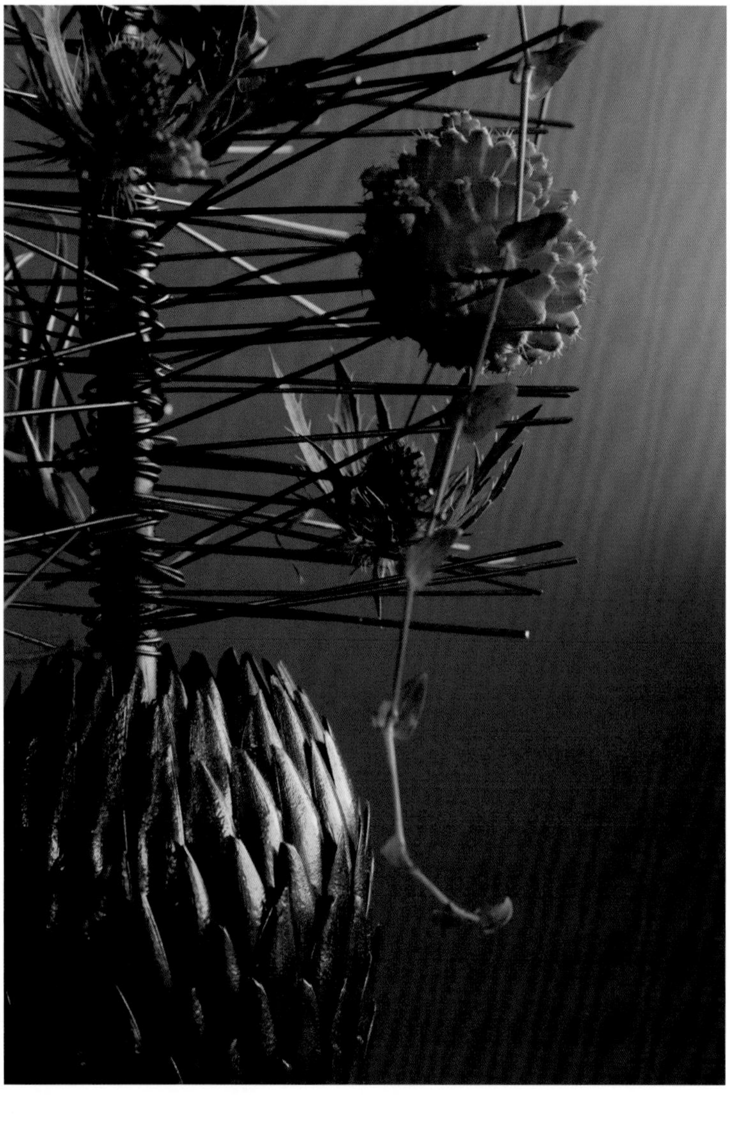

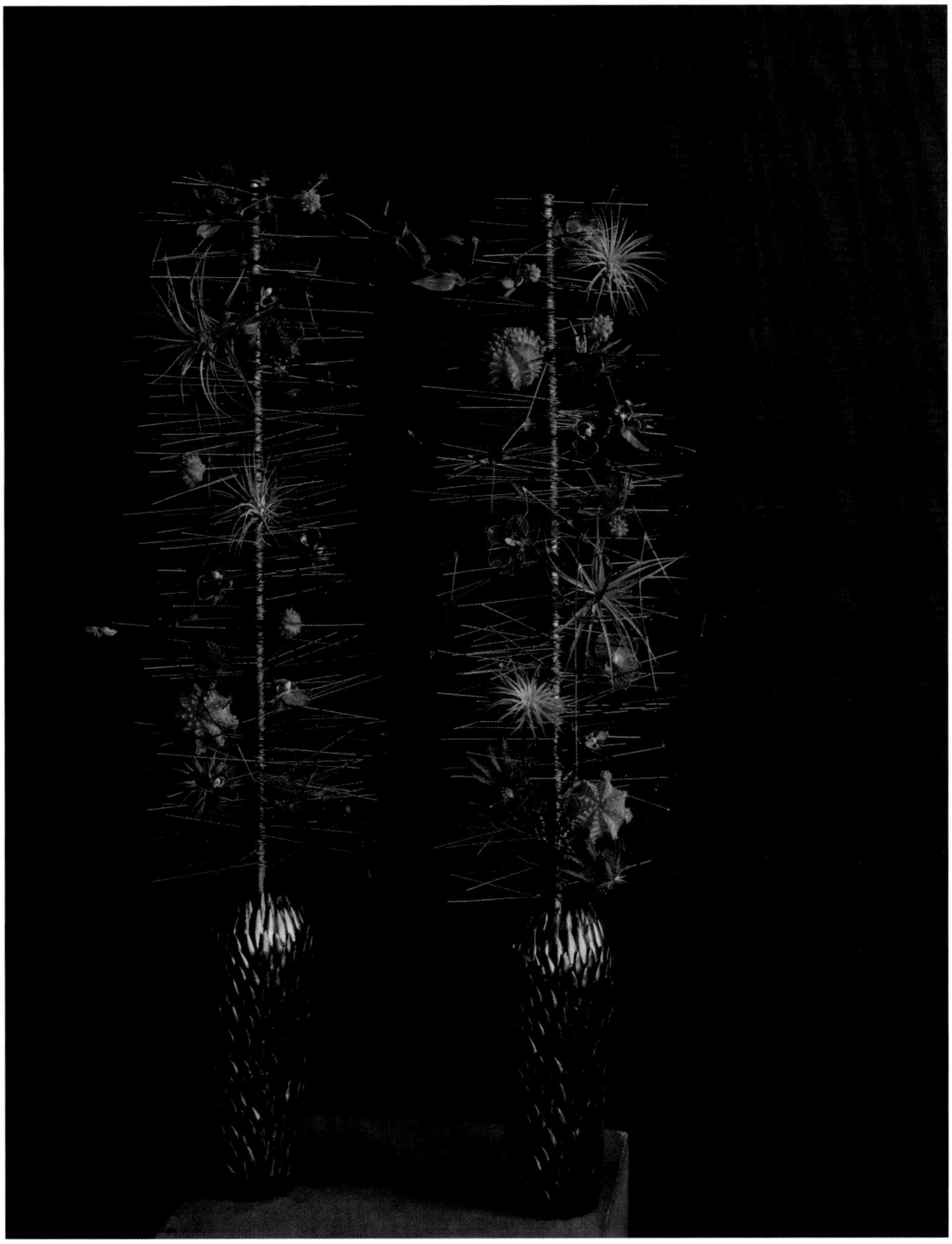

DESIGN BY STACEY BAL | PHOTOGRAPHY BY STACEY BAL

Handmade Sternocera aequisignata vases by Jonas De Vestel

Denver, Colorado | January 2020

METALLINE

"The otherworldly bright and
brilliant metallic elytra of the
Sternocera aequisignata is
the complex color palette
of my dreams."

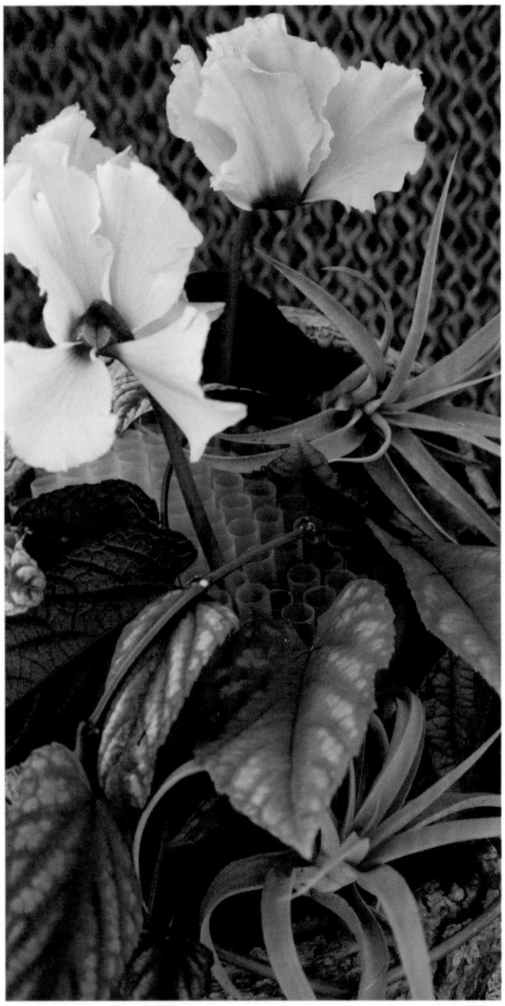

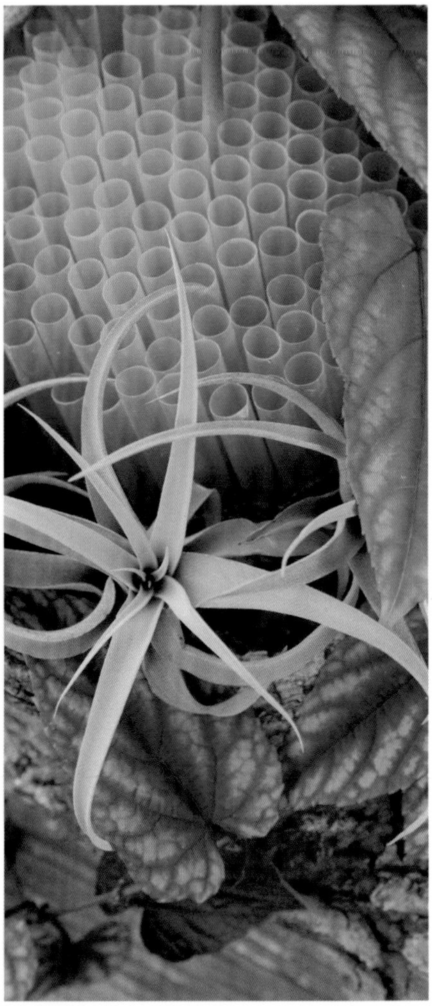

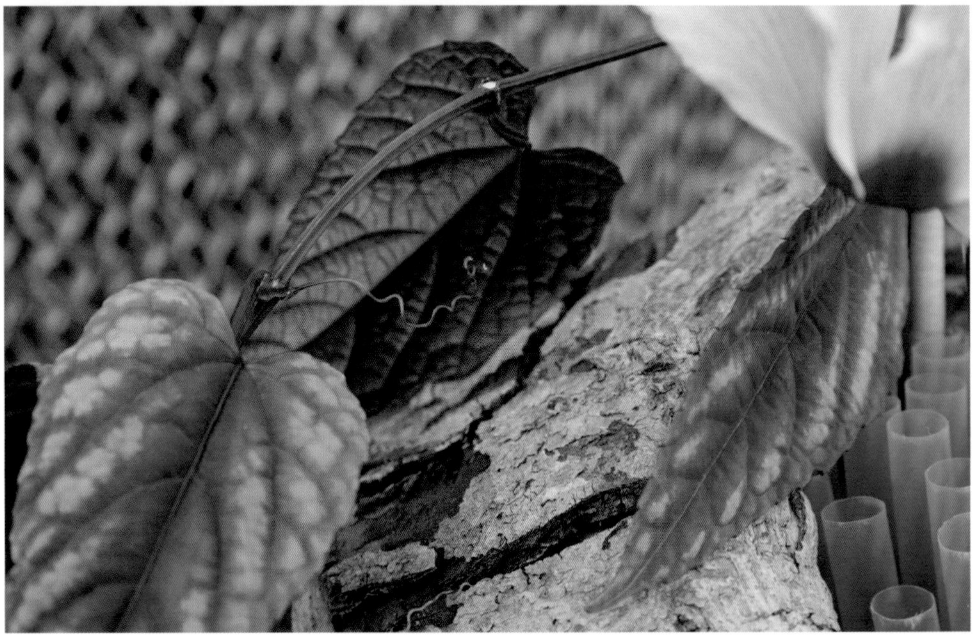

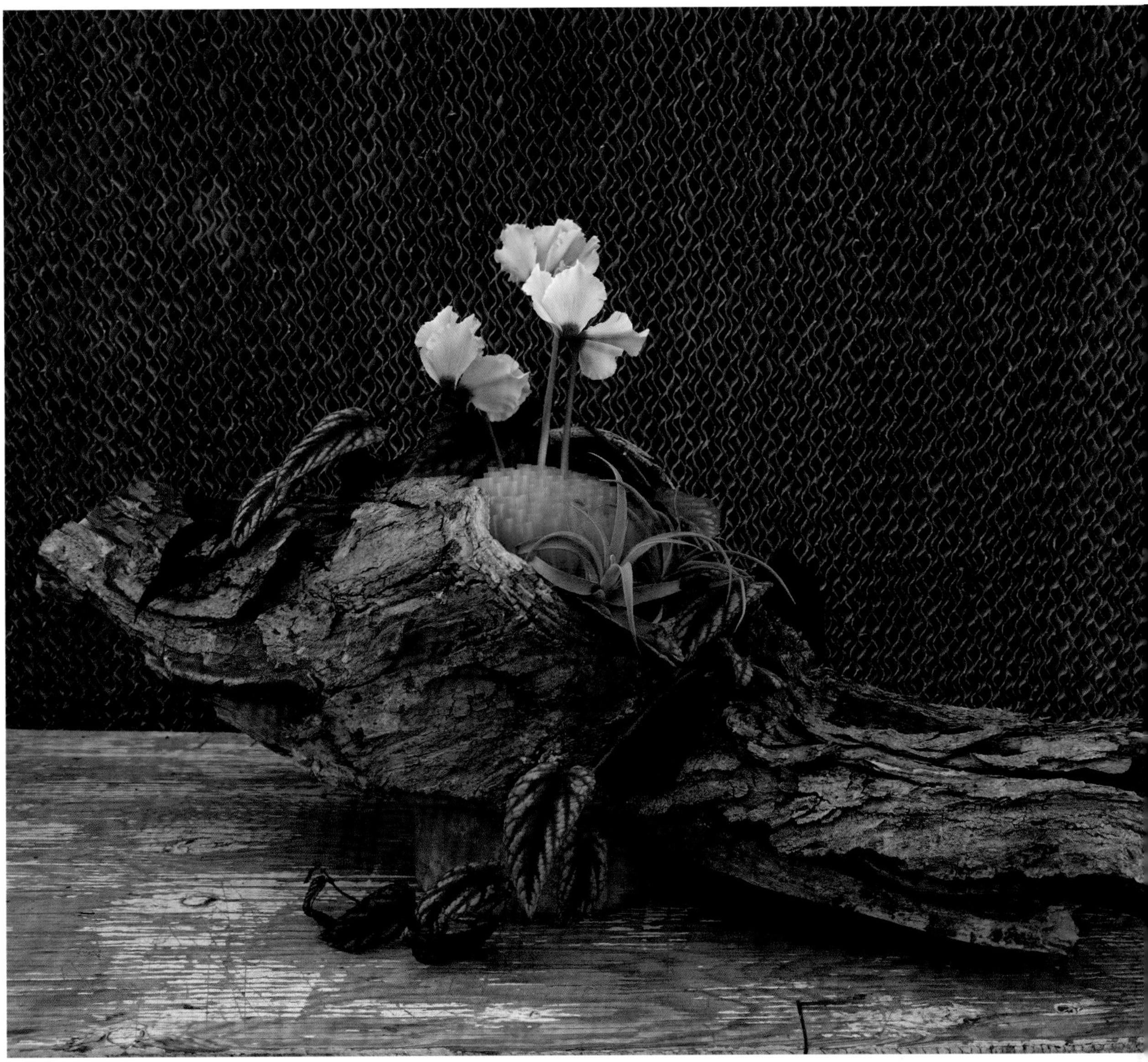

DESIGN BY ARTHUR WILLIAMS | PHOTOGRAPHY BY STACEY BAL
Denver, Colorado | January 2020

MIMIC

"Rethinking waste, using repetition to heal nature's wounds by utilizing the structures that bees use to create honeycomb."

ANDROGYNY

The quality or state of being neither specifically feminine or masculine; the combination of feminine and masculine characteristics.

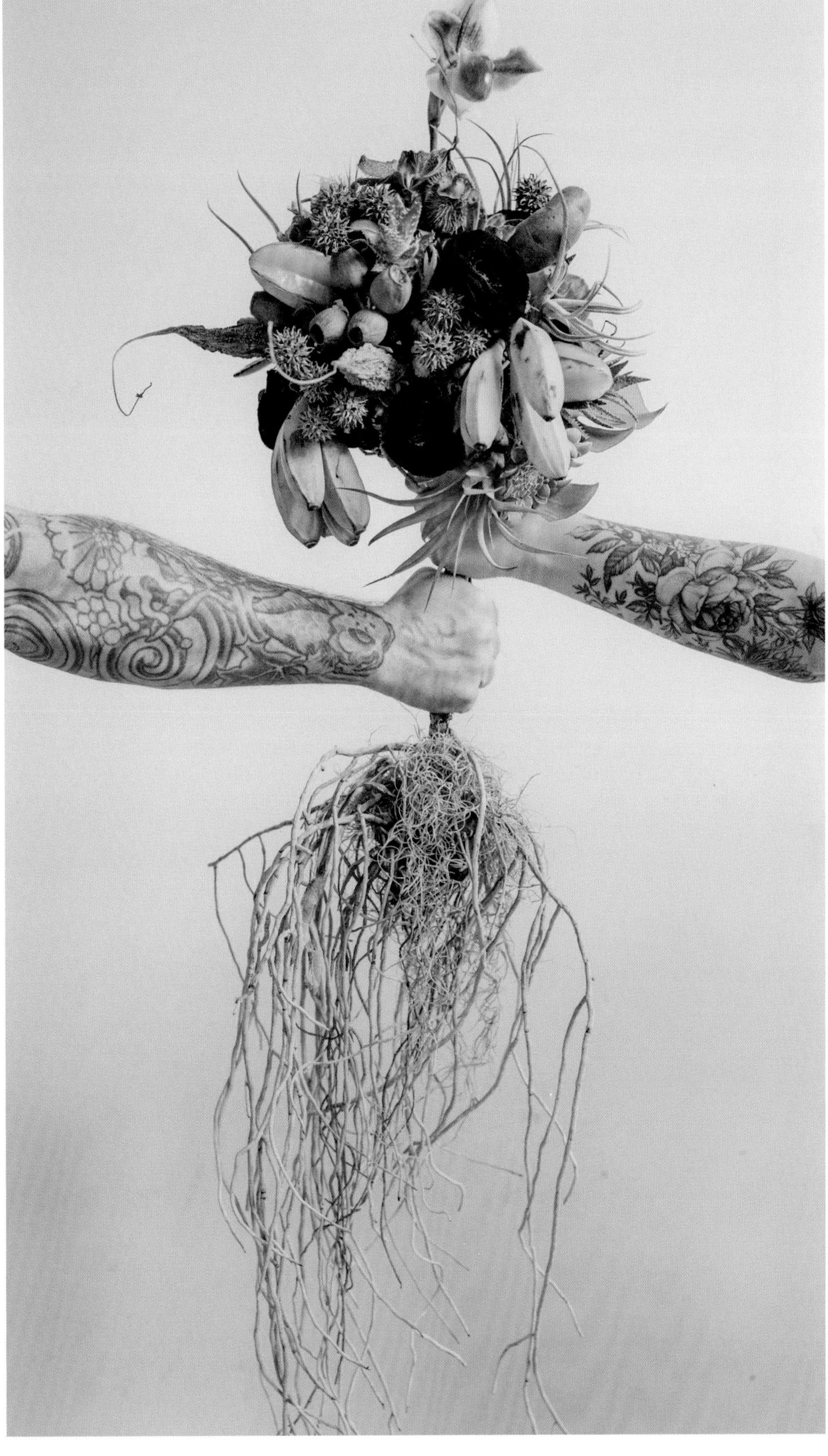

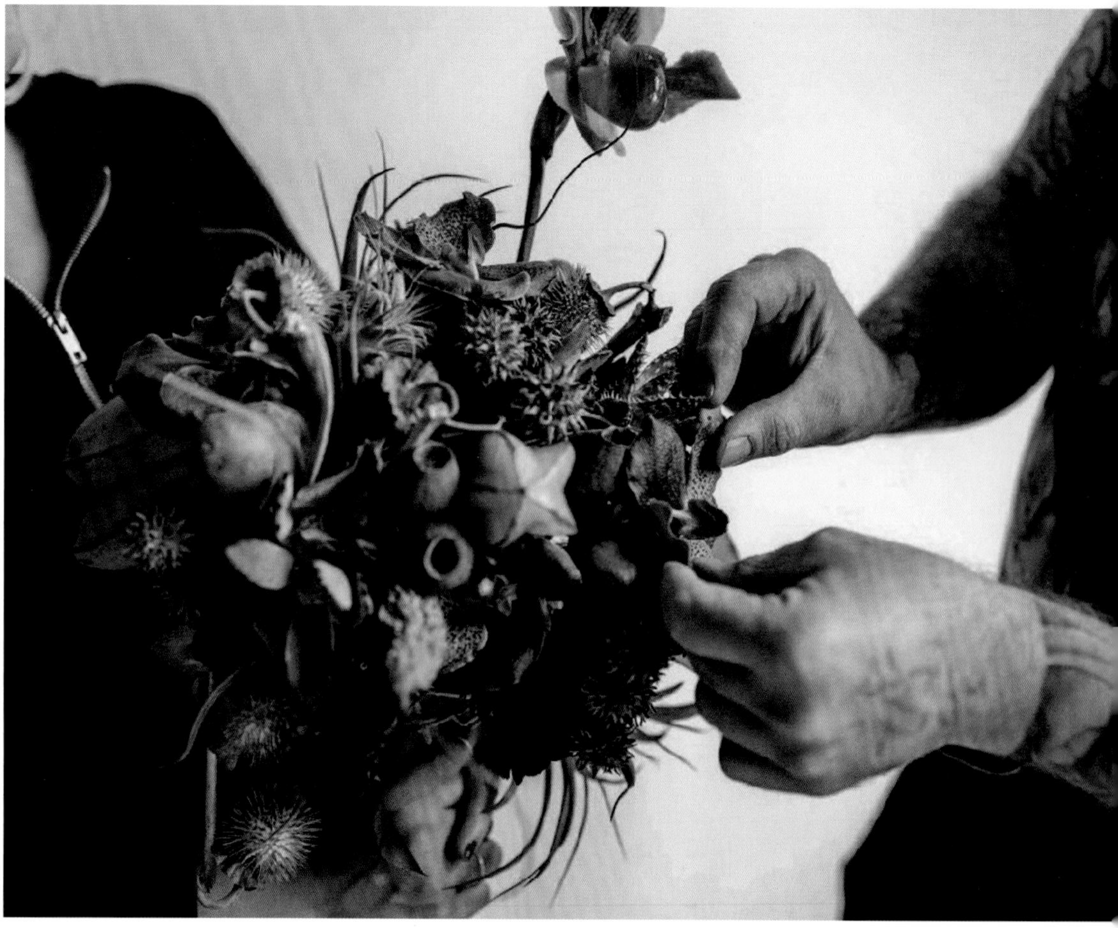

DESIGN BY ARTHUR WILLIAMS + STACEY BAL | PHOTOGRAPHY BY MARIYA BYELIKOVA
Chicago, Illinois | March 2020

AMBIDEXTROUS

"Opposites reconciled.
Duality in design characteristics
provides tension."

Masculine: Static, rough, closed, bold, strong.
Feminine: Dynamic, refined, open, pastel, delicate.

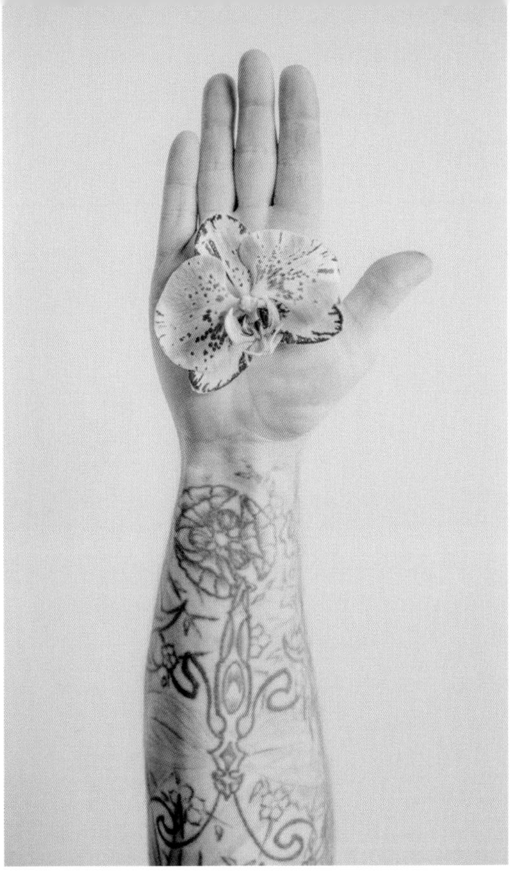

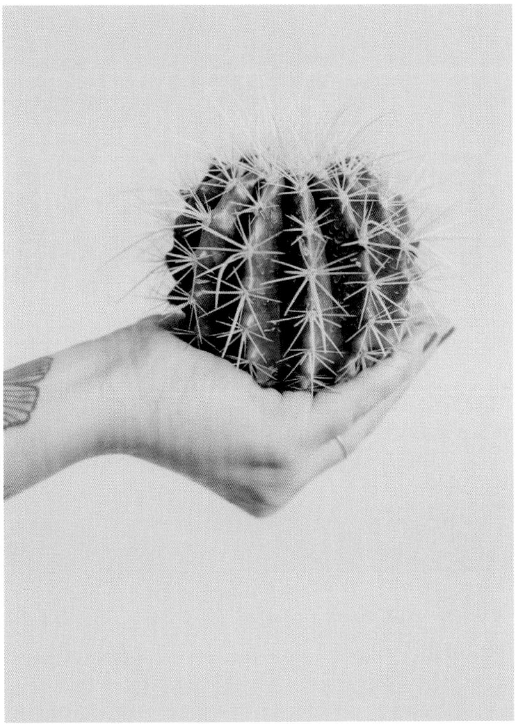

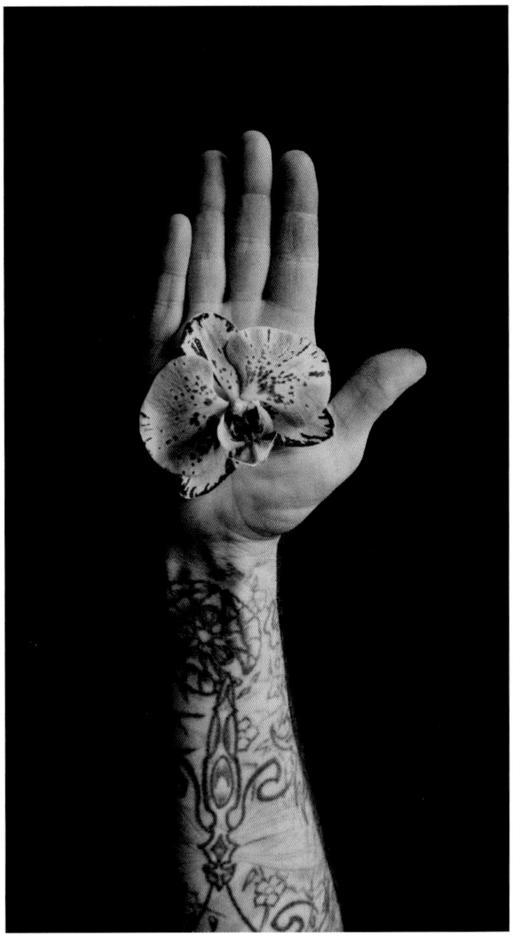

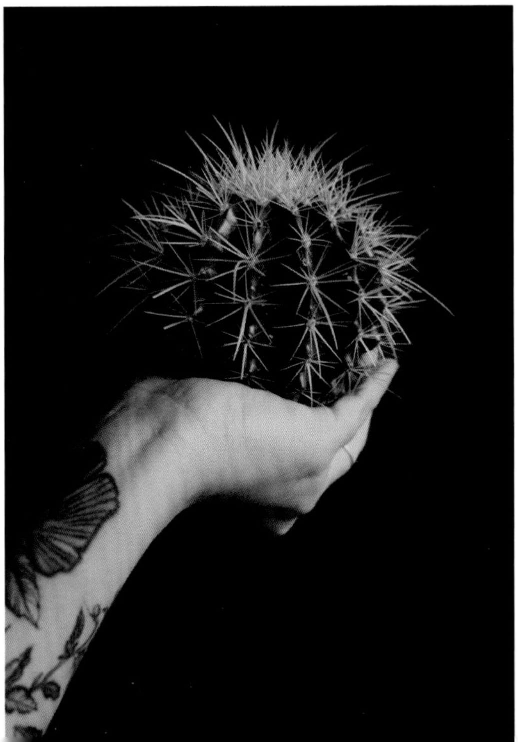

SURREAL

Capturing the hallucinatory
quality of a dream; an artistic
and literary style.

Yang Shaobin, Untitled (1999-4), 1999. Oil on linen.
Gift from Vicki and Kent Loganto the Collection
of the Denver Art Museum, 2001.882A-B. © Yang Shaobin.

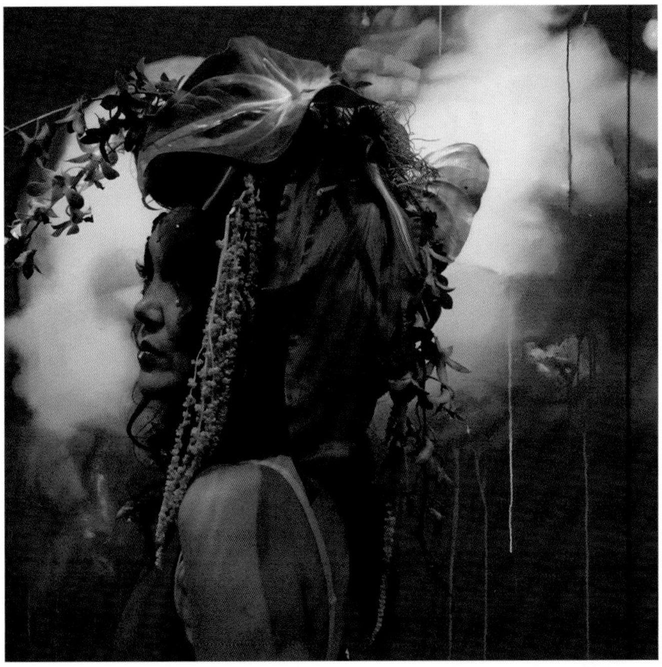

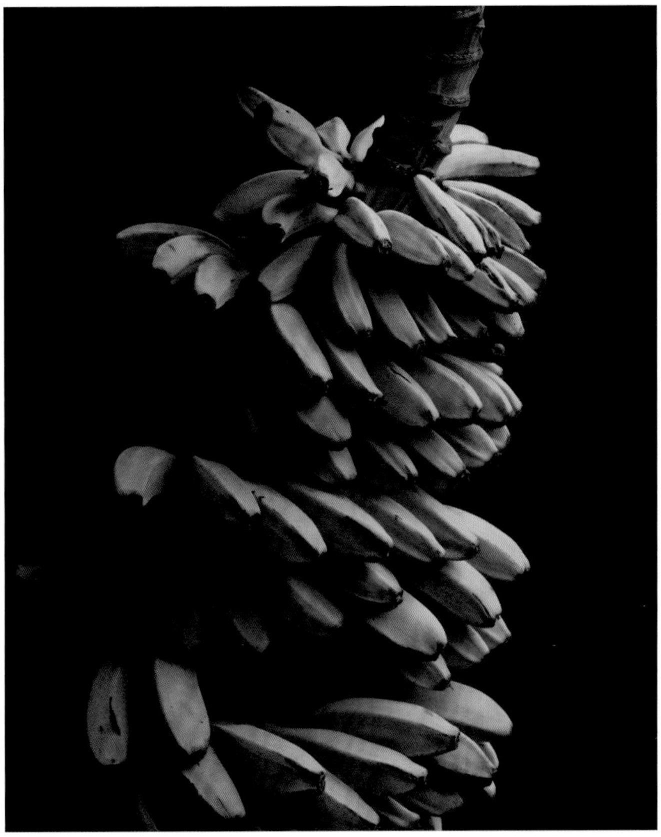

DESIGN BY ARTHUR WILLIAMS | PHOTOGRAPHY BY ARTHUR WILLIAMS

Yang Shaobin, Untitled (1999-4), 1999. Oil on linen. © Yang Shaobin.

Models: Clay Doke, Pamela Wyatt

Denver, Colorado | July 2015

CHANCE MEETING IN A NIGHTMARE

"Nothing is what it seems, just illusions and projections of self."

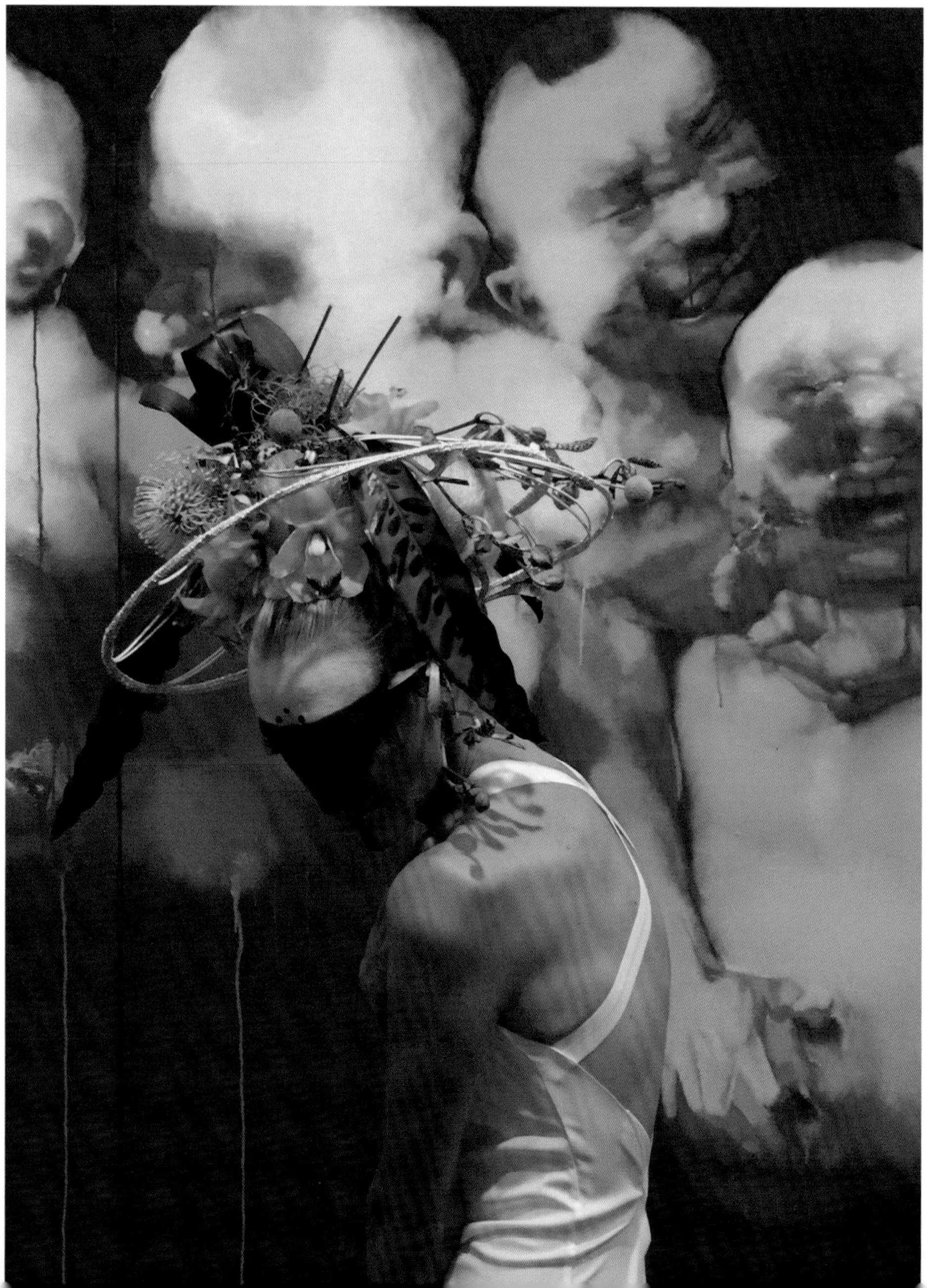

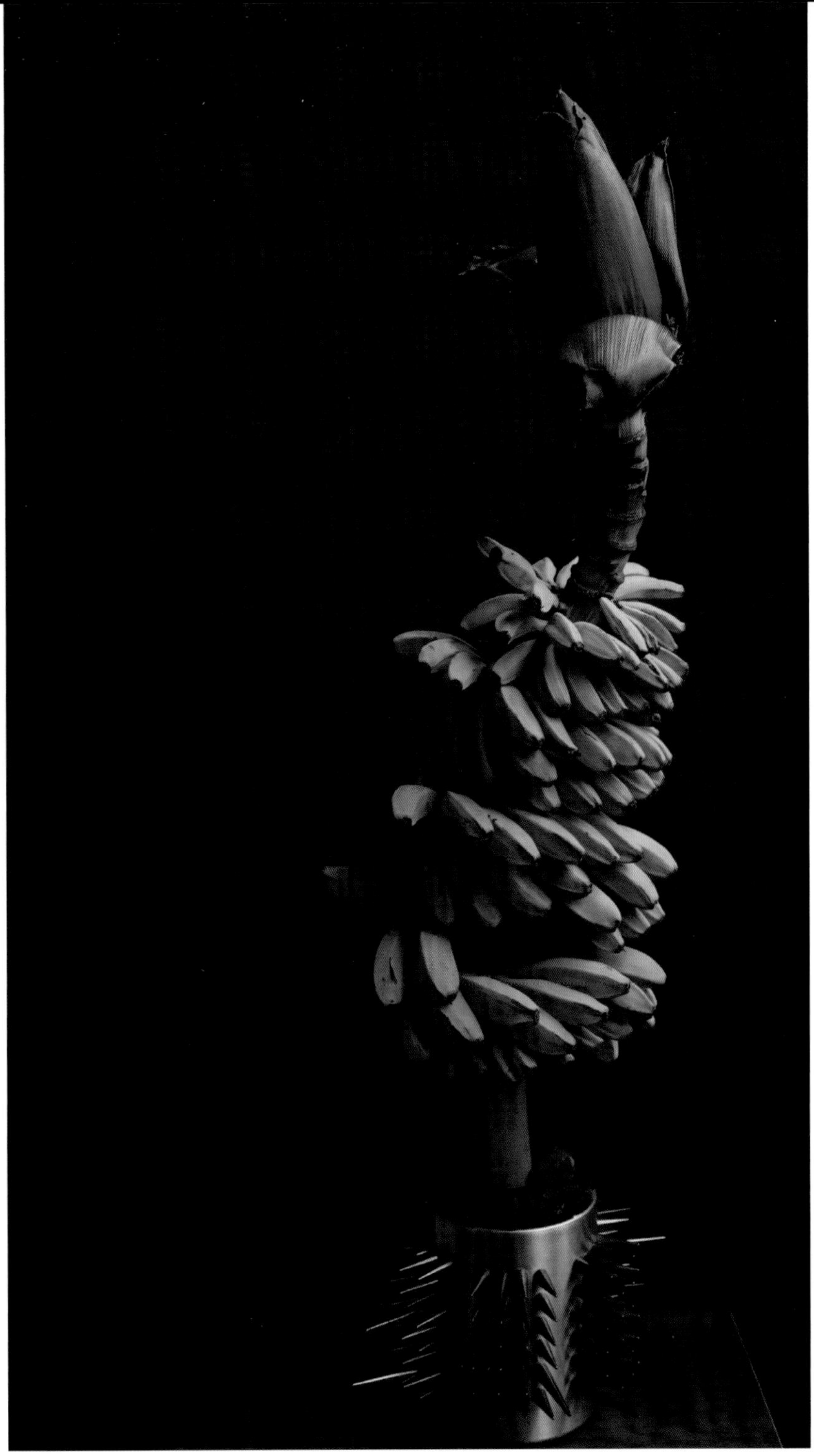

DESIGN BY STACEY BAL | PHOTOGRAPHY BY STACEY BAL
Handmade vessel by Peter Keltz
Chicago, Illinois | March 2020

EXTRATERRESTRIAL

"Limitless vision like omnipotent lucid dreams."

MONO NO AWARE

The Japanese term for the impermanence of things expressed as a gentle sadness at their passing as well as a longer, deeper gentle sadness about this state being the reality of life.

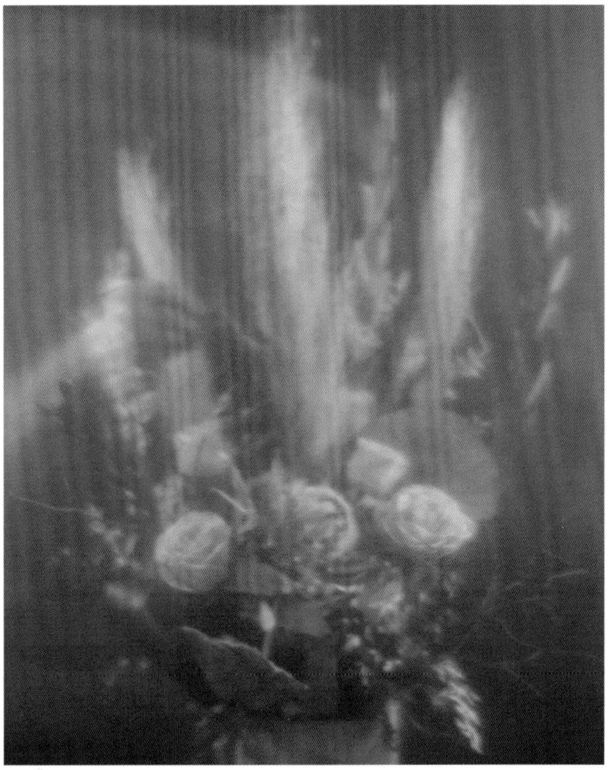

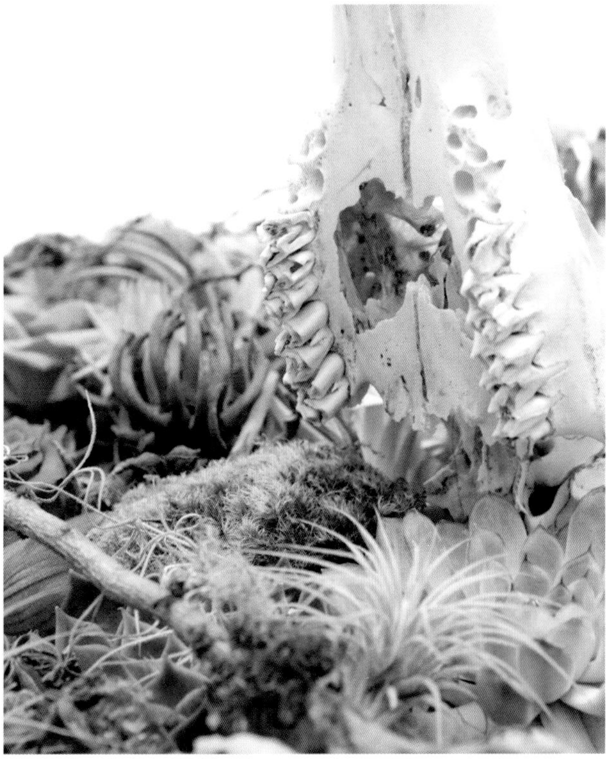

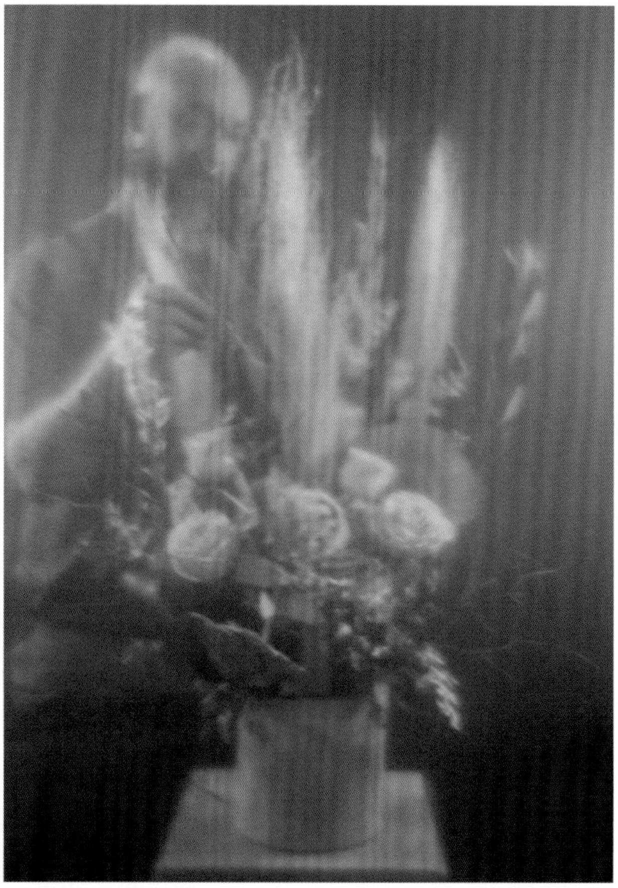

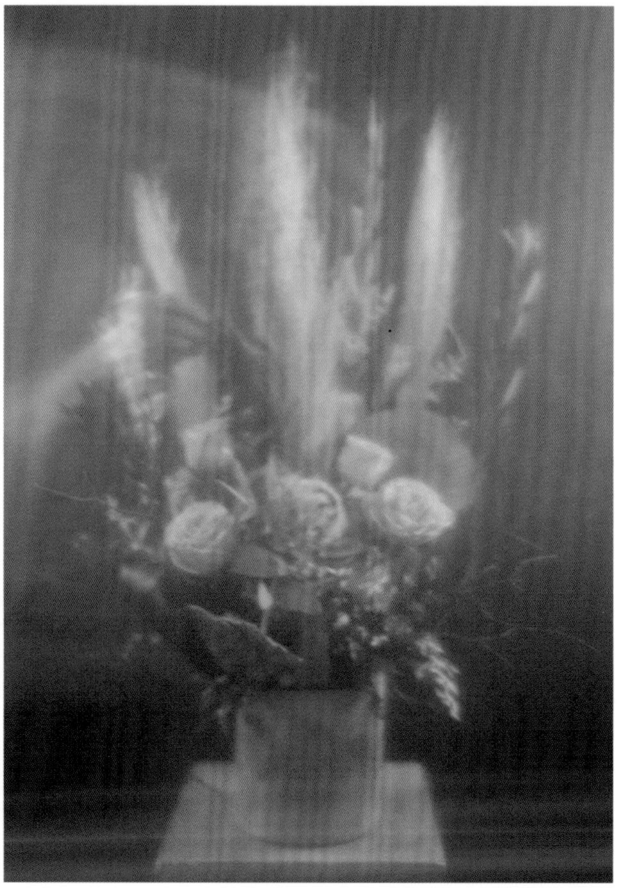

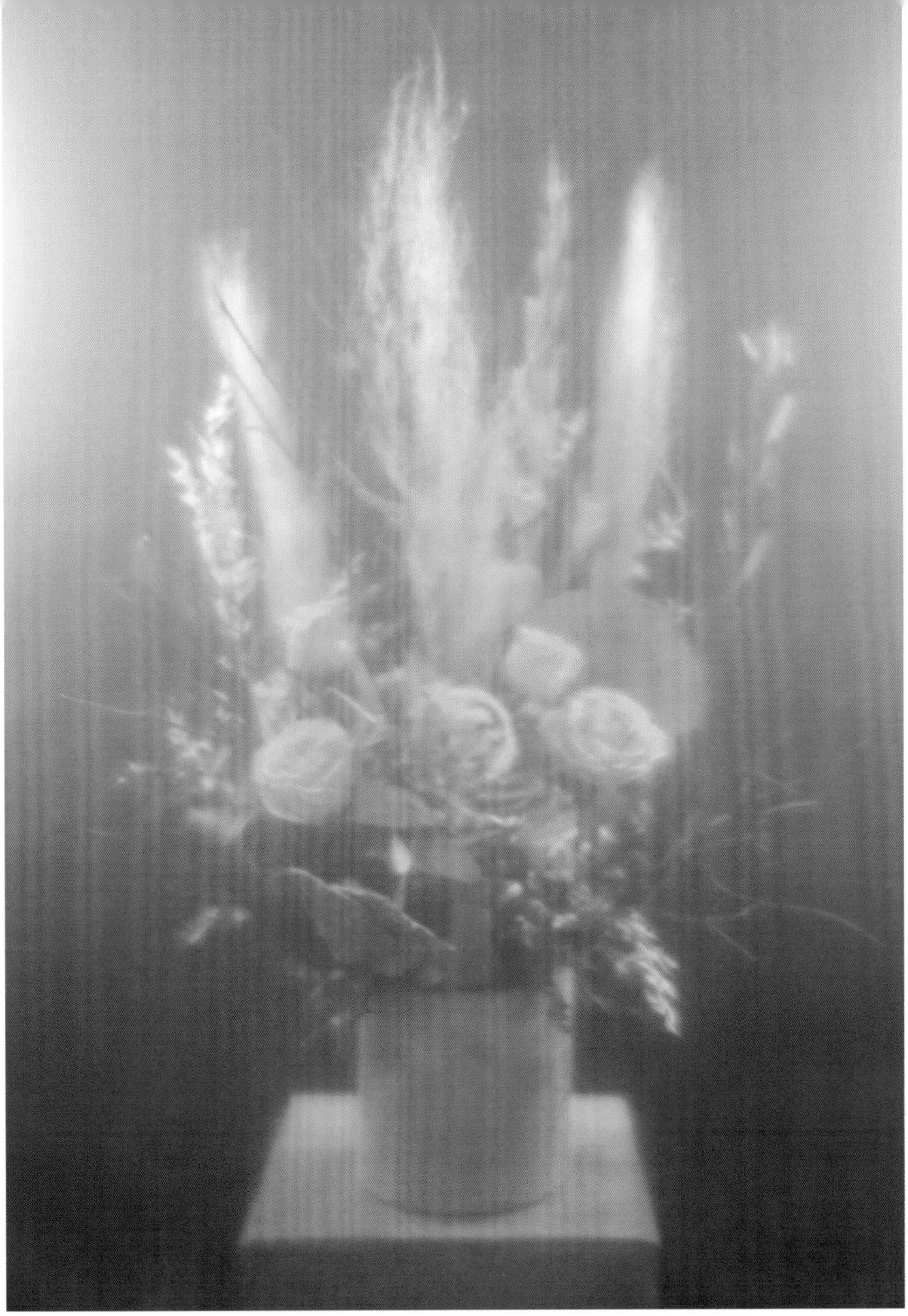

DESIGN BY ARTHUR WILLIAMS | PHOTOGRAPHY BY DAN DE LOS MONTEROS
Denver, Colorado | January 2020

SIGHT

"To regain sight is to realize all the moments of beauty lost to time."

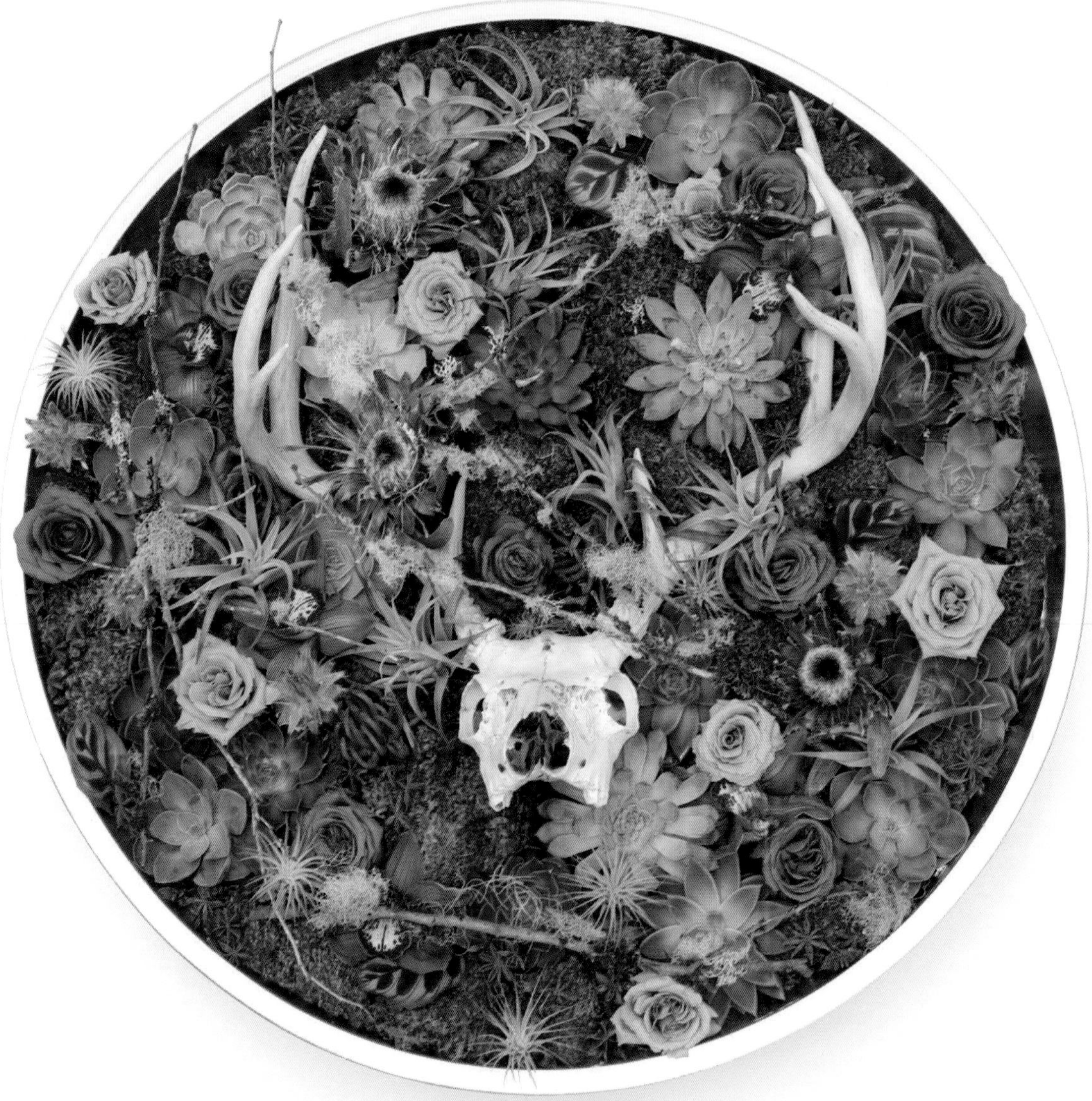

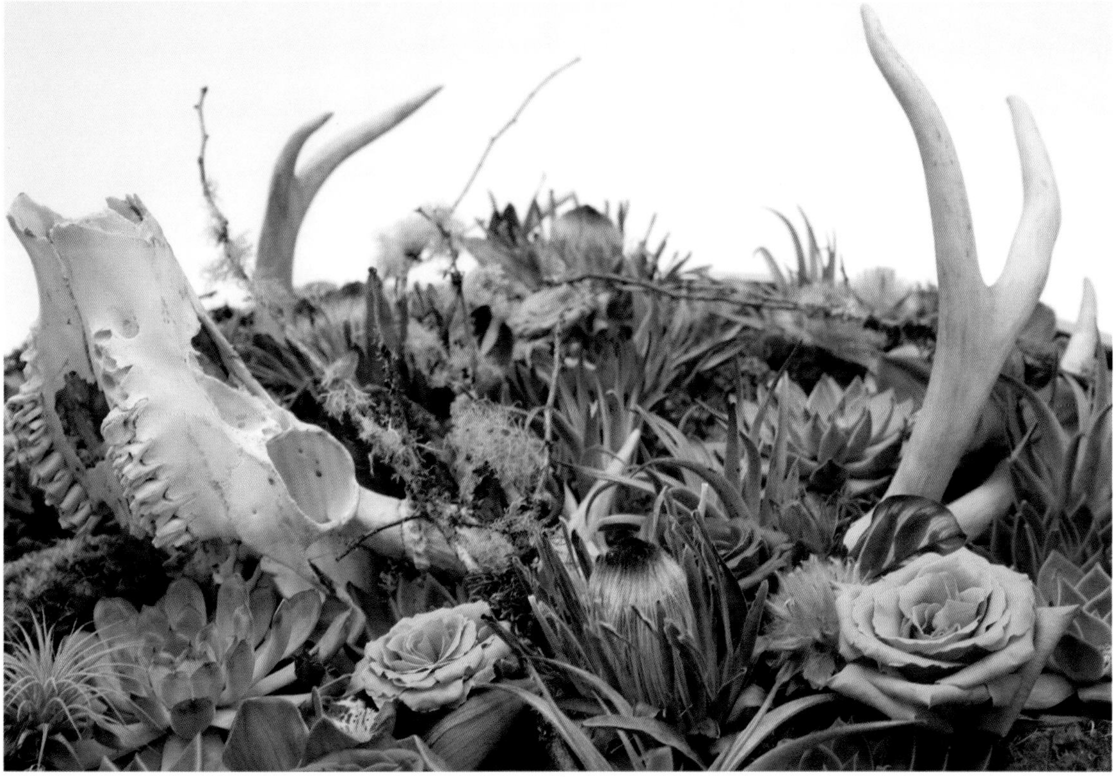

DESIGN BY STACEY BAL | PHOTOGRAPHY BY STACEY BAL

Denver, Colorado | January 2020

CONSCIOUS CONSUMPTION

"Driven by a personal connection to moral vegetarianism: representing the collective impact on the environment and honoring the memory of the defenseless animal kingdom in relation to human participation."

POSSESSION

The state of having, owning, or controlling something.

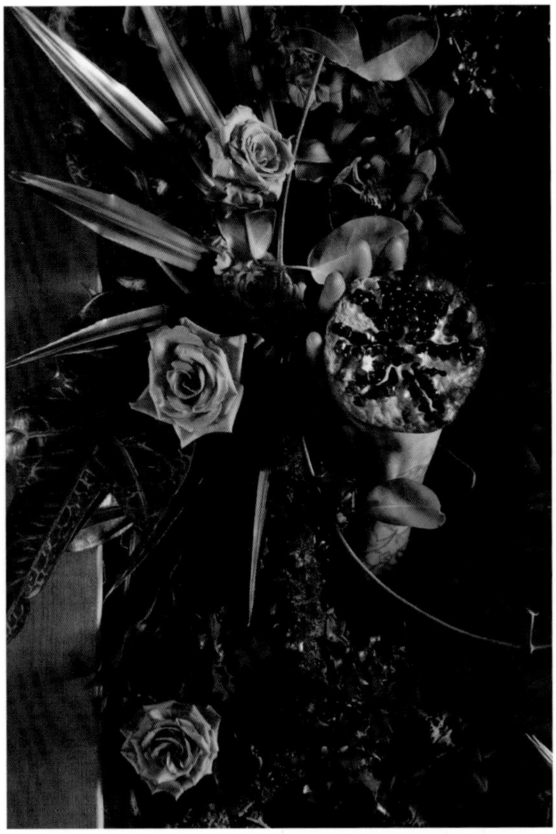

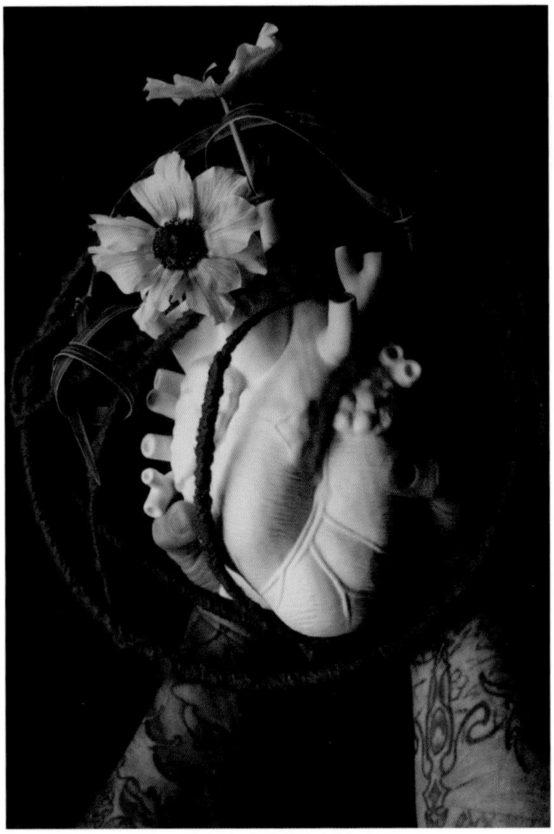

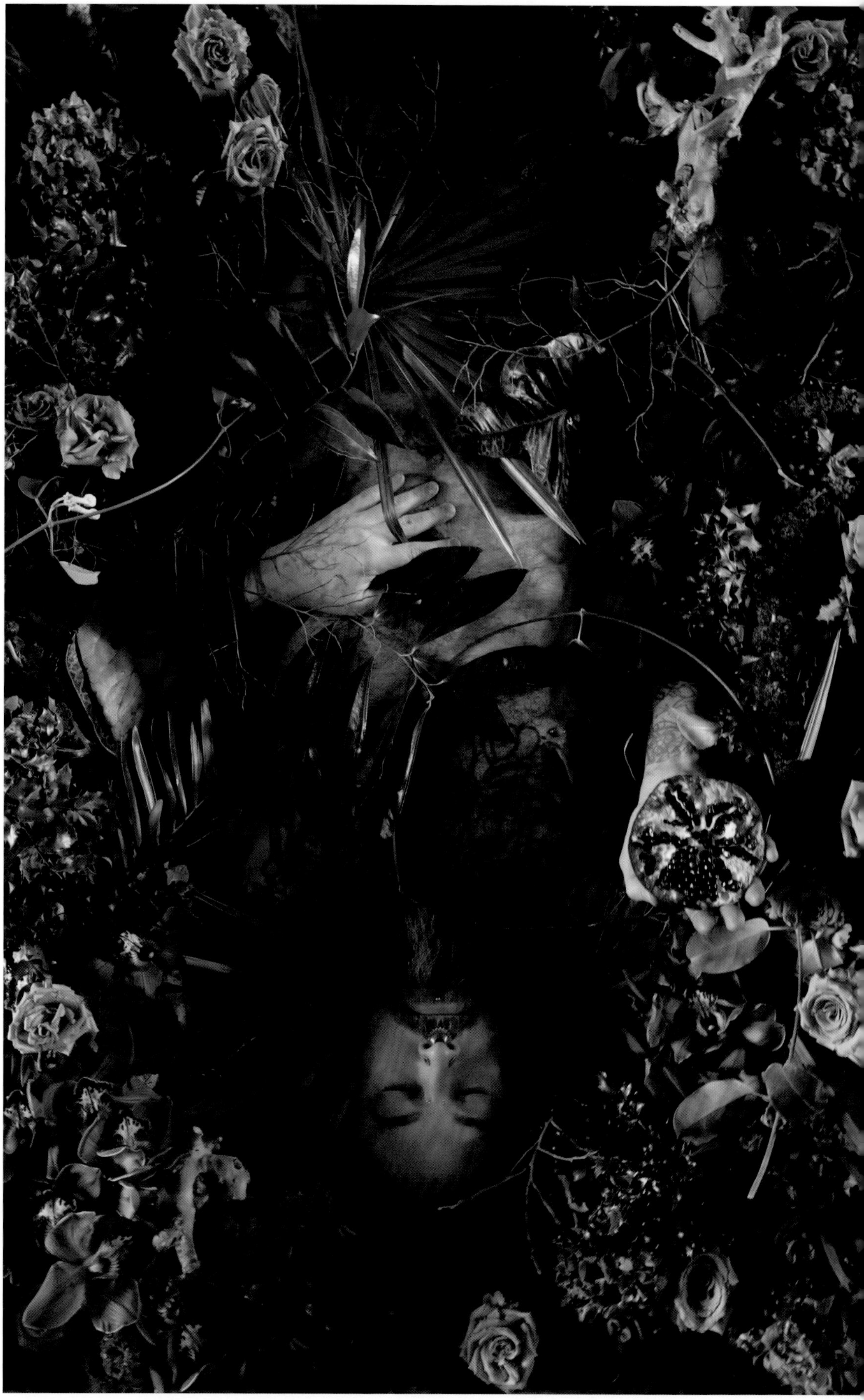

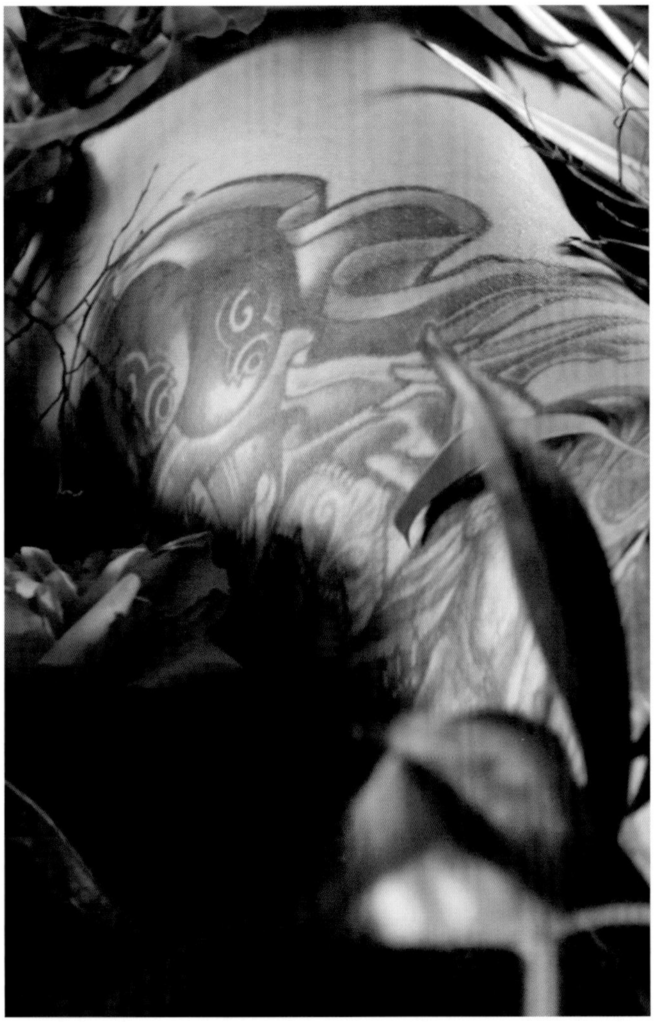

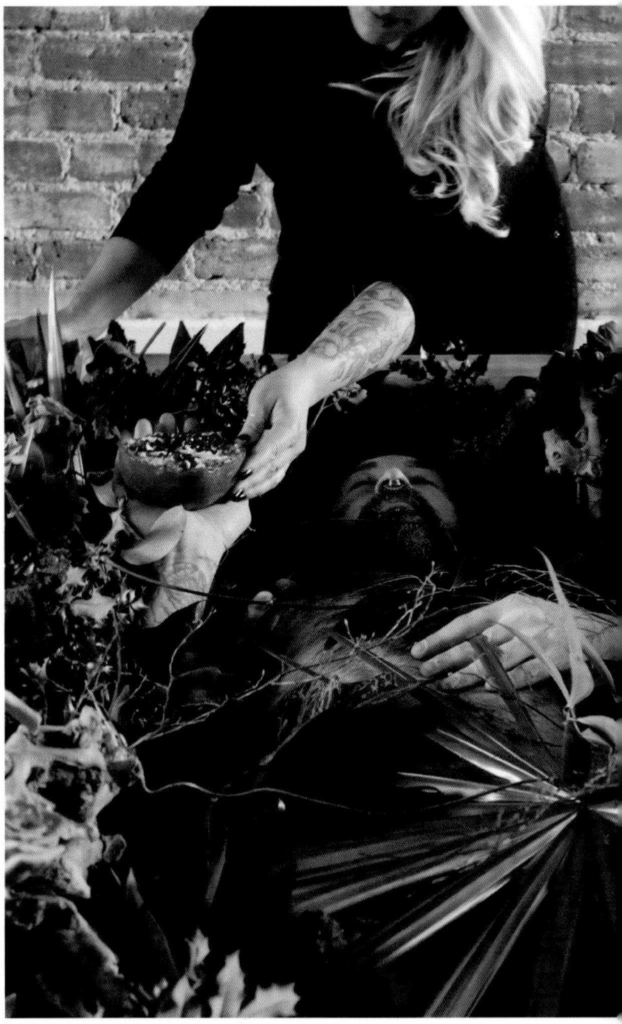

DESIGN BY STACEY BAL | PHOTOGRAPHY BY STACEY BAL + CHUCK HUTSON

Muse: Arthur Williams

Denver, Colorado | January 2020

HADES

"The act, fact, or condition of having control of something."

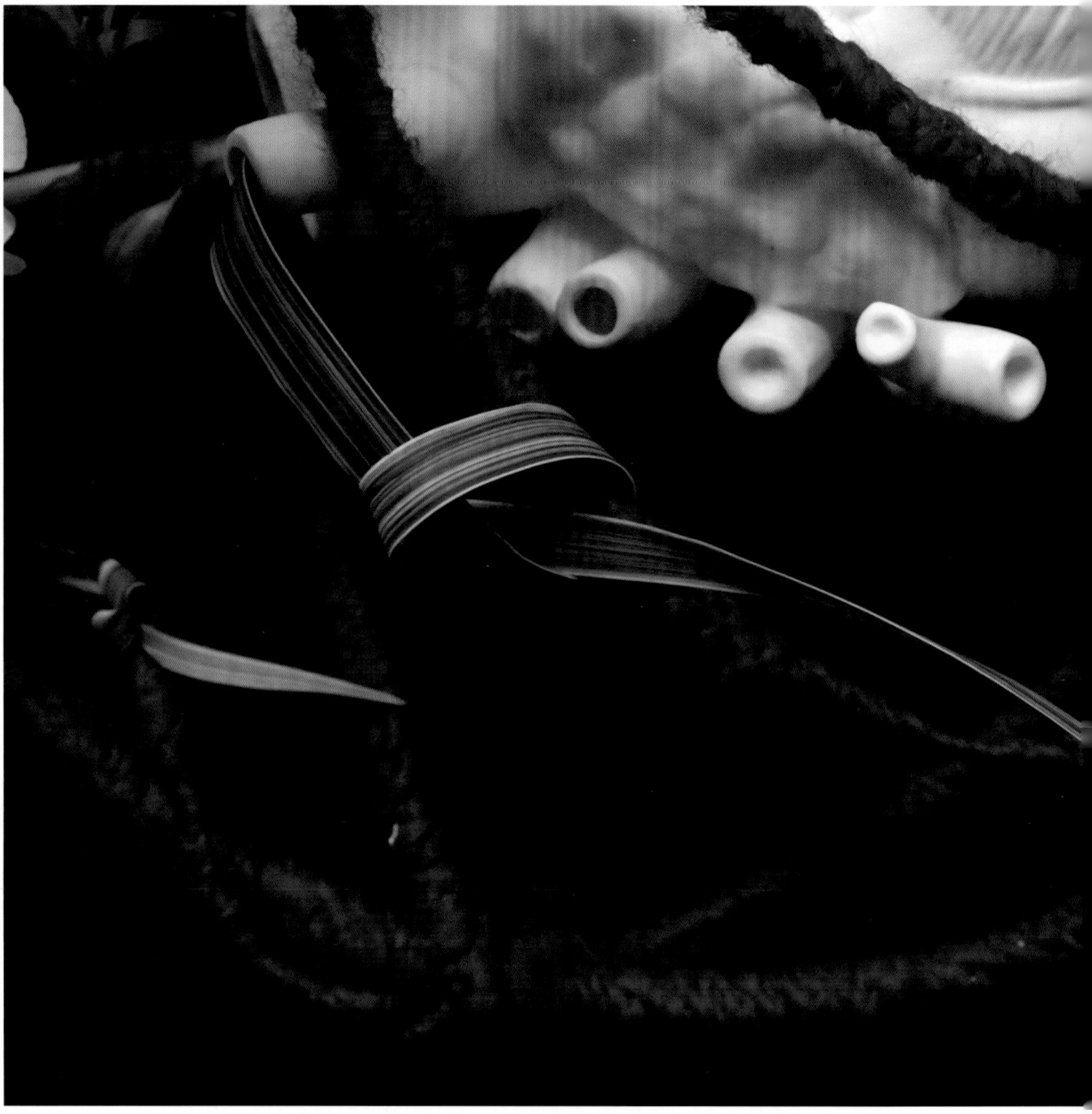

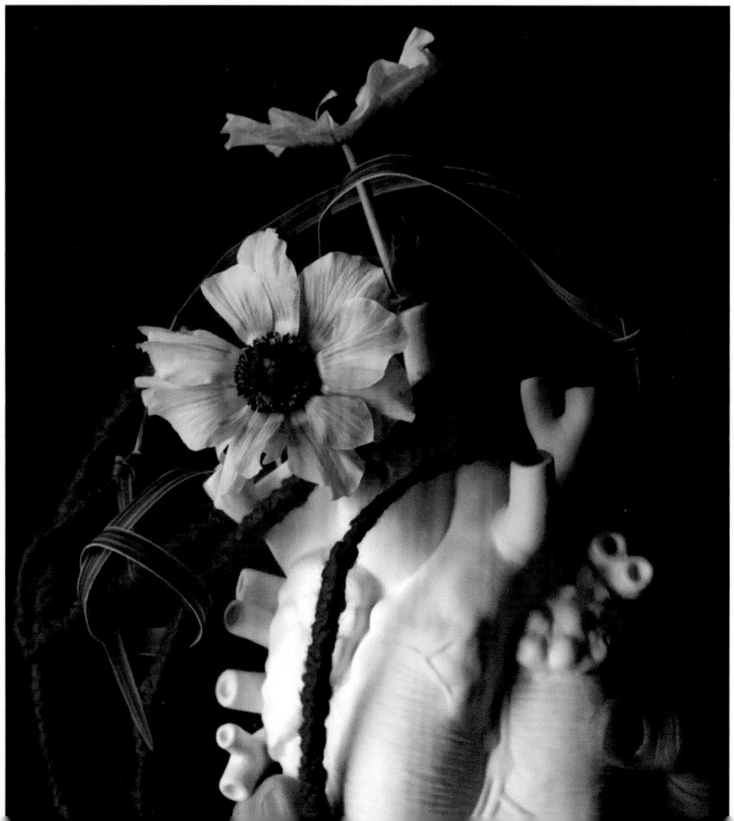

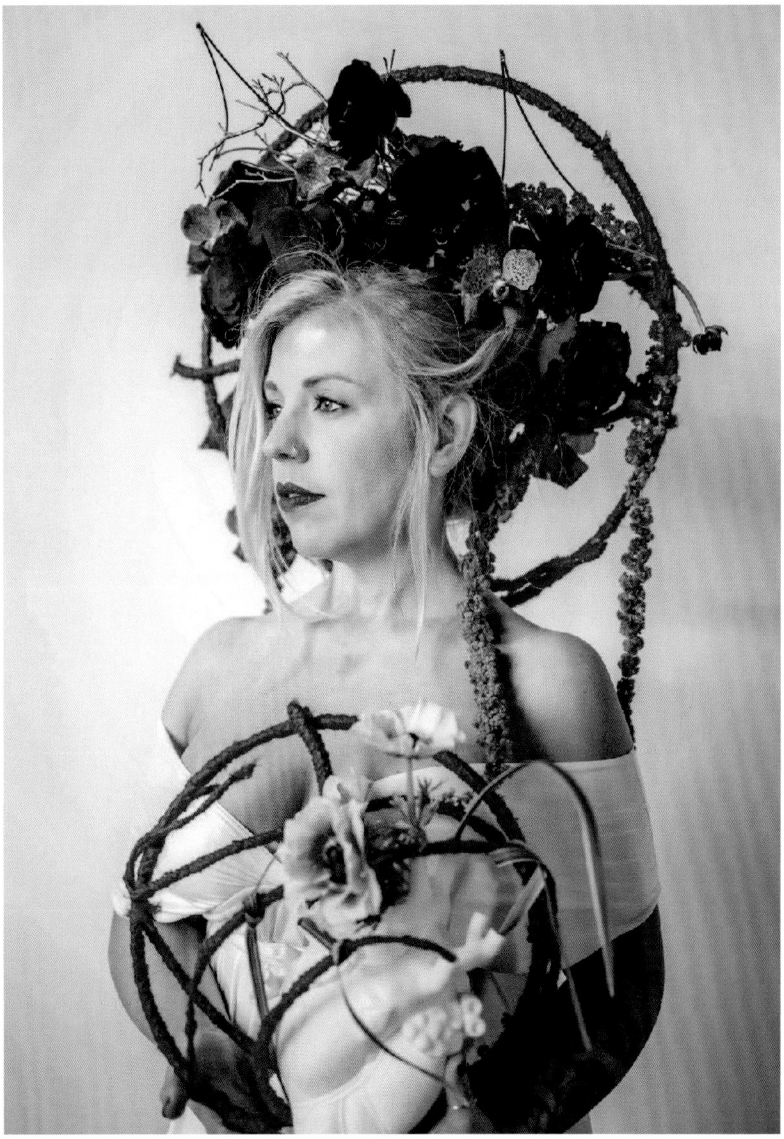

DESIGN BY ARTHUR WILLIAMS | PHOTOGRAPHY BY STACEY BAL + MARIYA BYELIKOVA

Muse: Stacey Bal

Chicago, Illinois | March 2020

ANIMUS

"The state of being controlled
by a demon or spirit."

TENSION

An integrated pattern
of thoughts, actions,
values, customs,
and beliefs that
connect us.

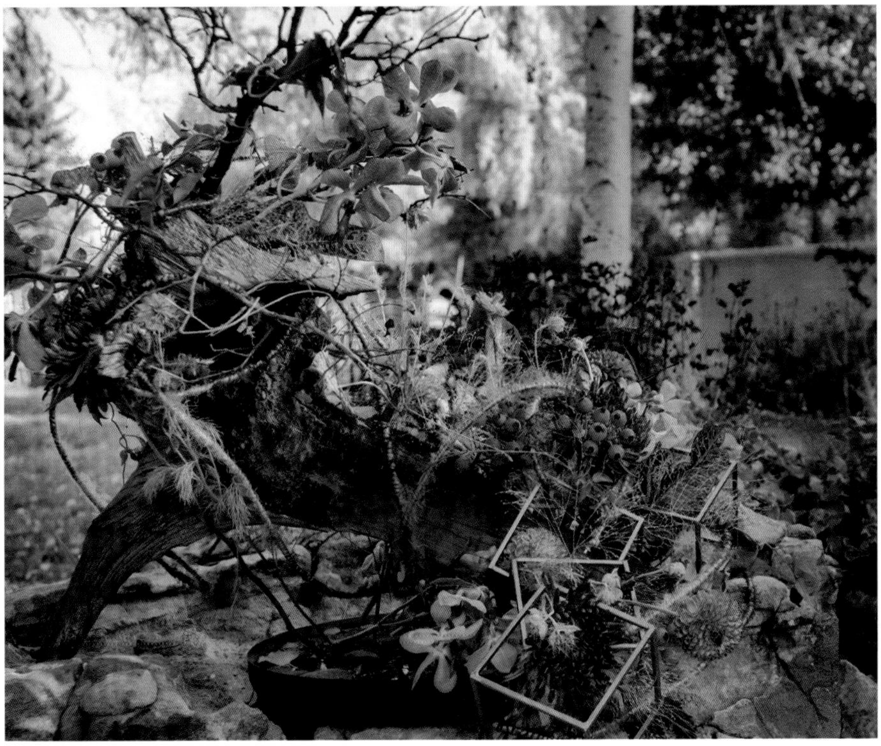

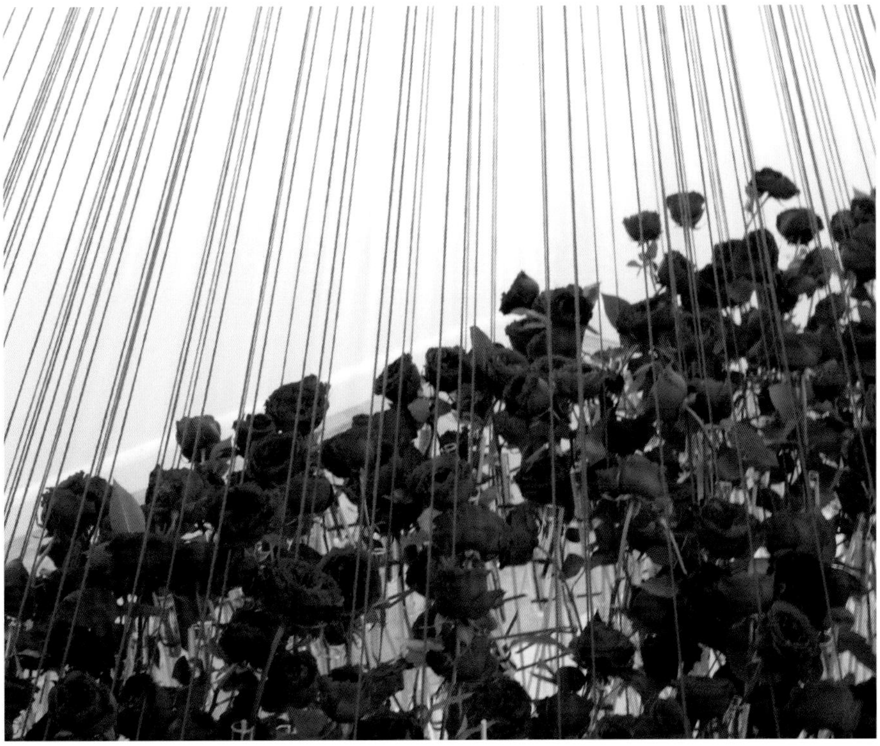

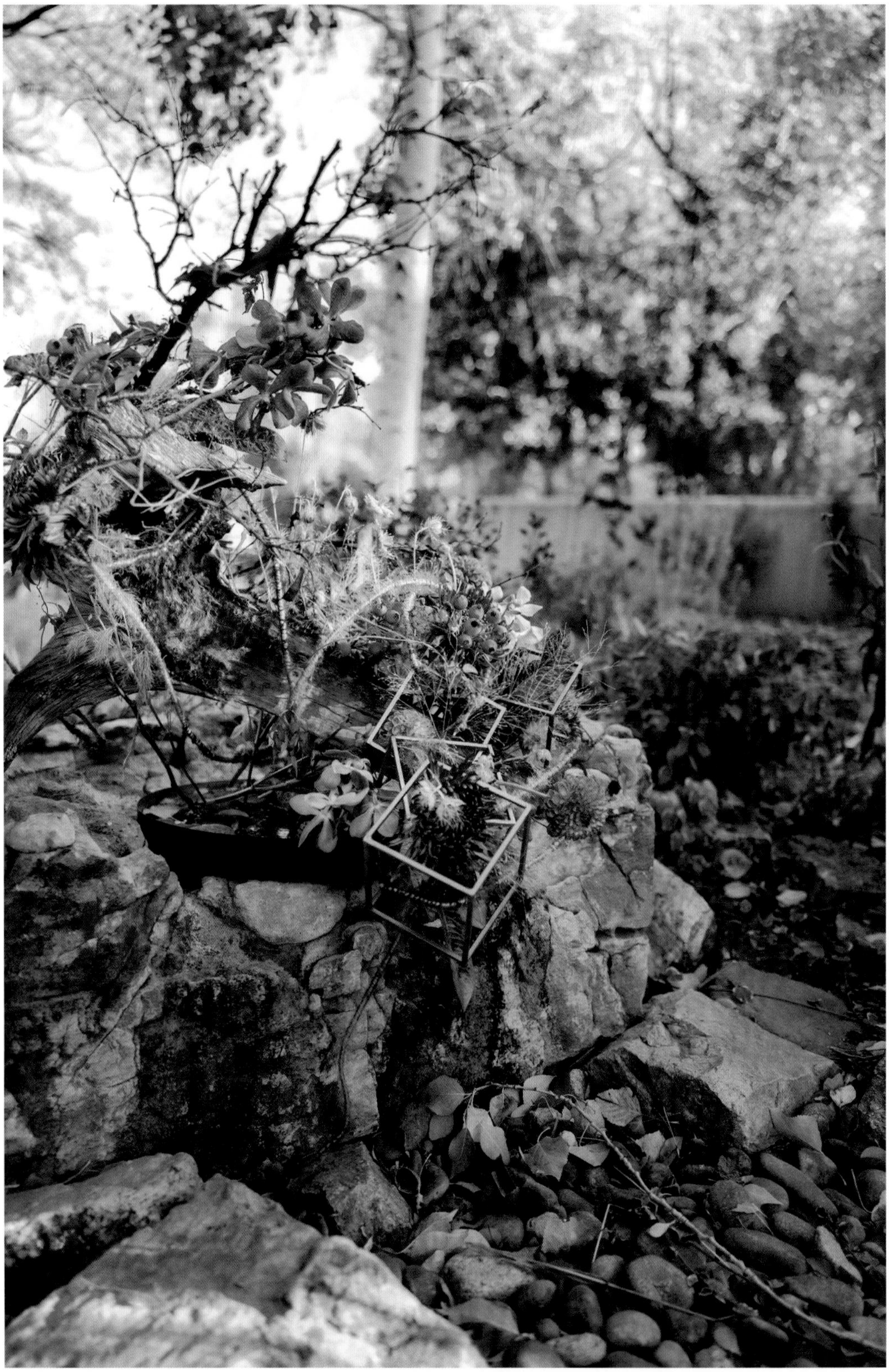

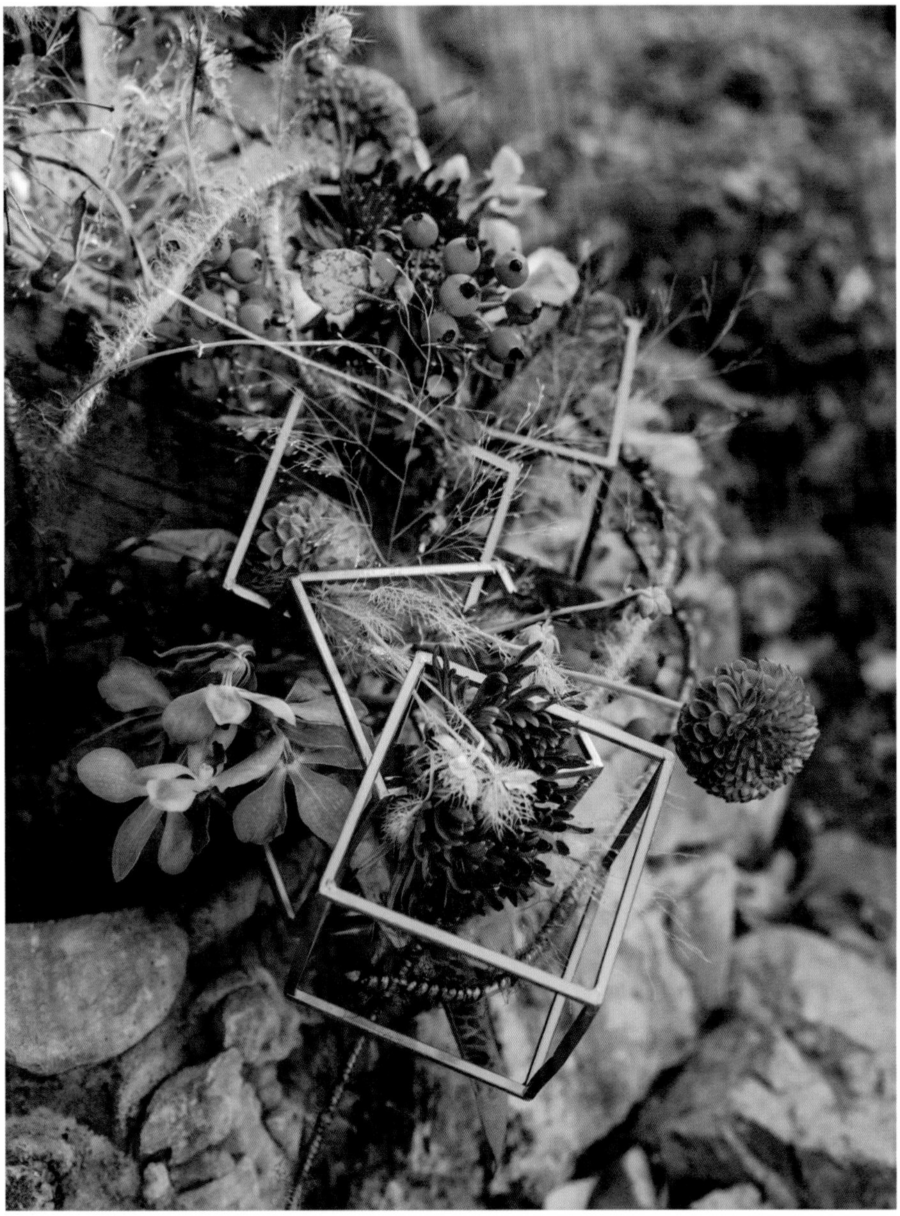

DESIGN BY ARTHUR WILLIAMS | PHOTOGRAPHY BY COLIN GILLIAM

Taos, New Mexico | October 2019

ENCASE

"We struggle to define and contain nature in the struggle to create order and to reinforce our false belief that we are separate from our surroundings."

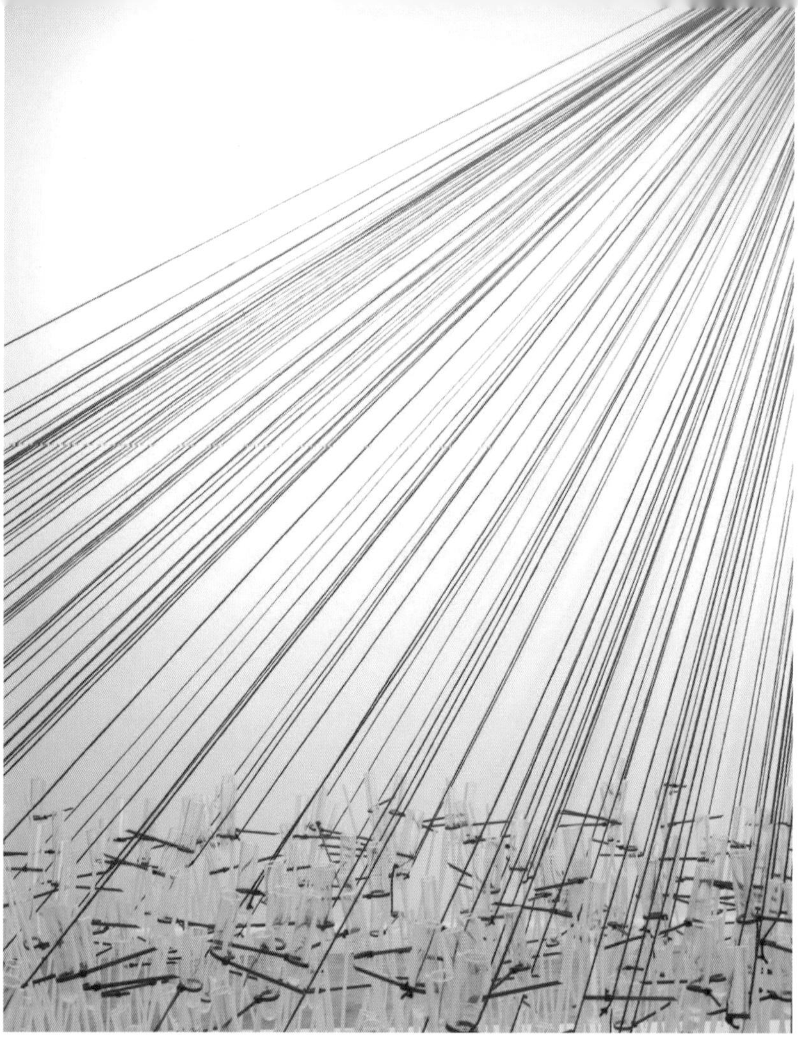

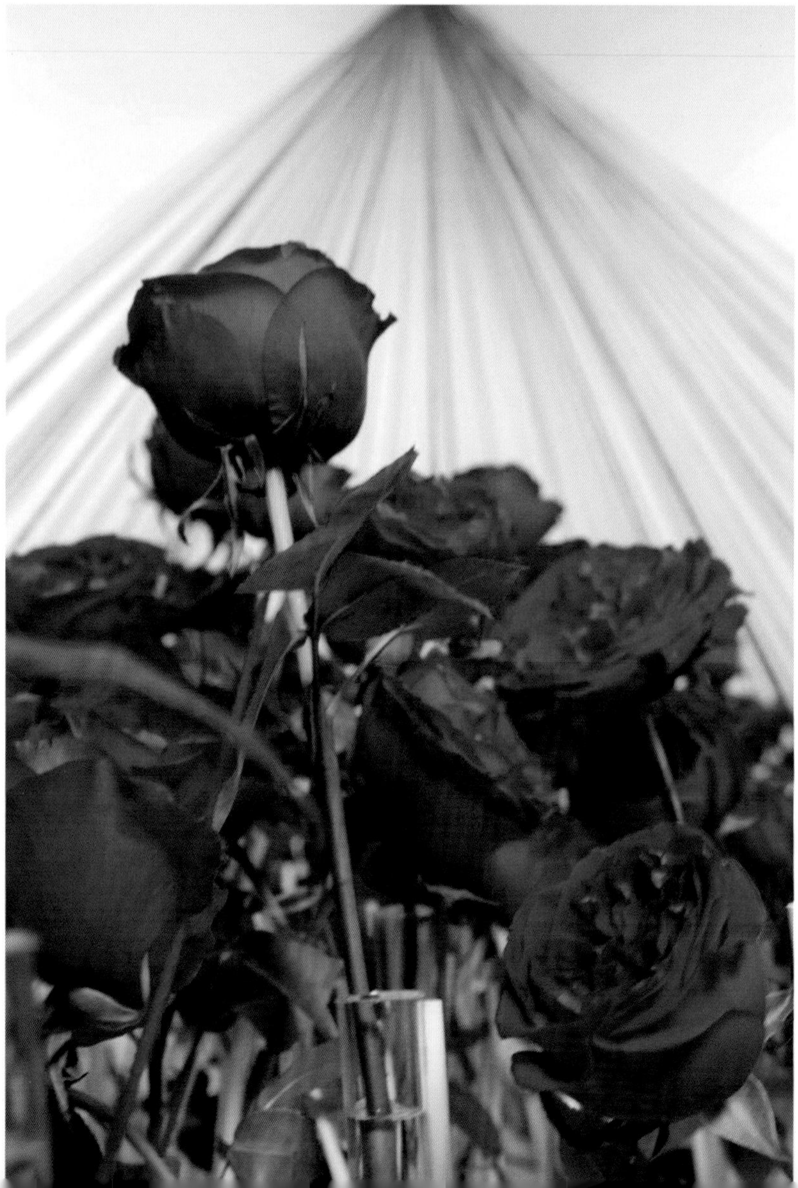

IMPERMANENT

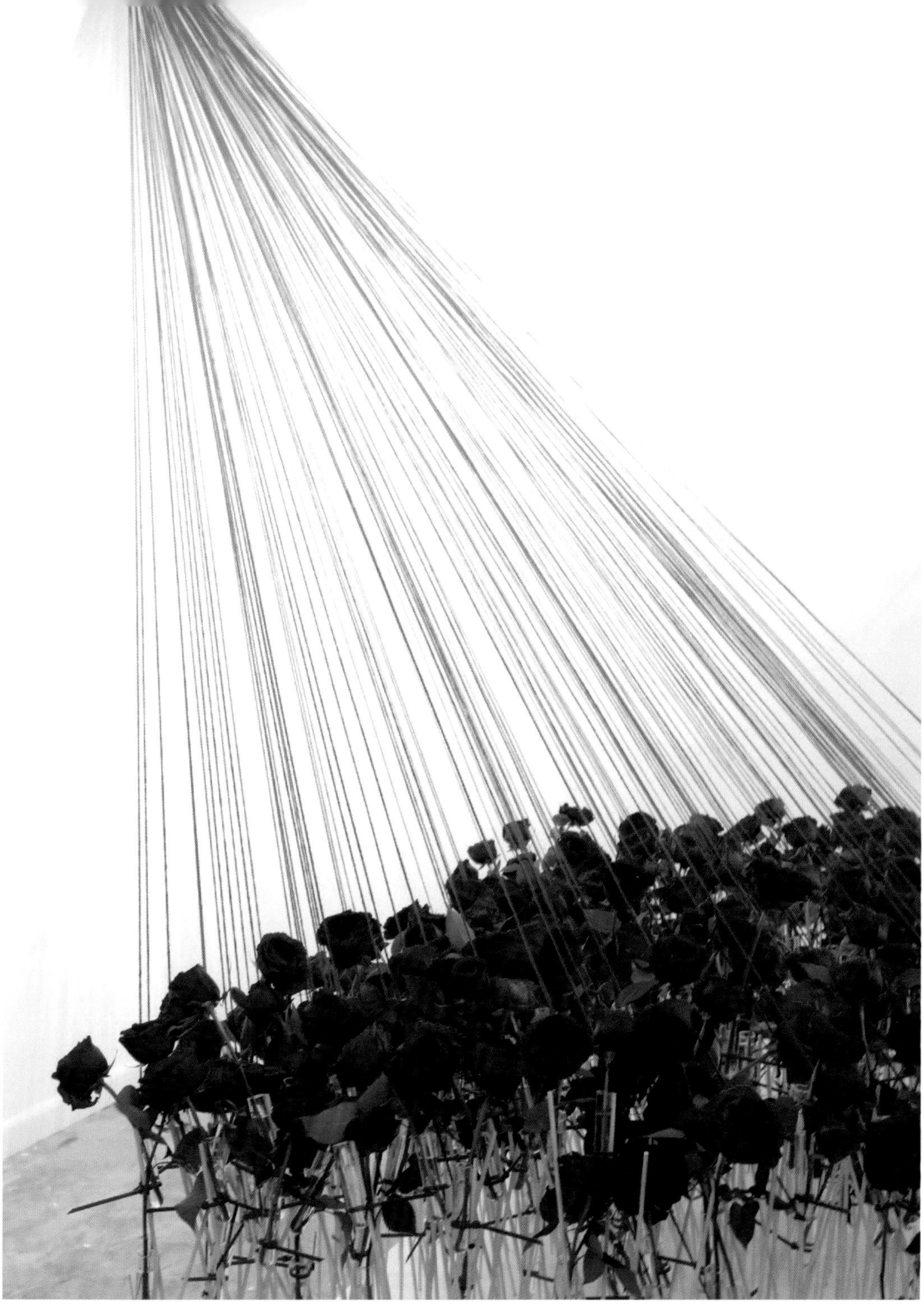

DESIGN BY STACEY BAL | PHOTOGRAPHY BY STACEY BAL
Art Basel; Miami, Florida | December 2019

STRINGS ATTACHED

"A satirical visual and olfactory expression representing conditions that humans place on one another in relation to love, affection, and commitment."

CHIMERA

CHI-MI-RA

A single organism composed of
two or more different populations
of genetically distinct cells.

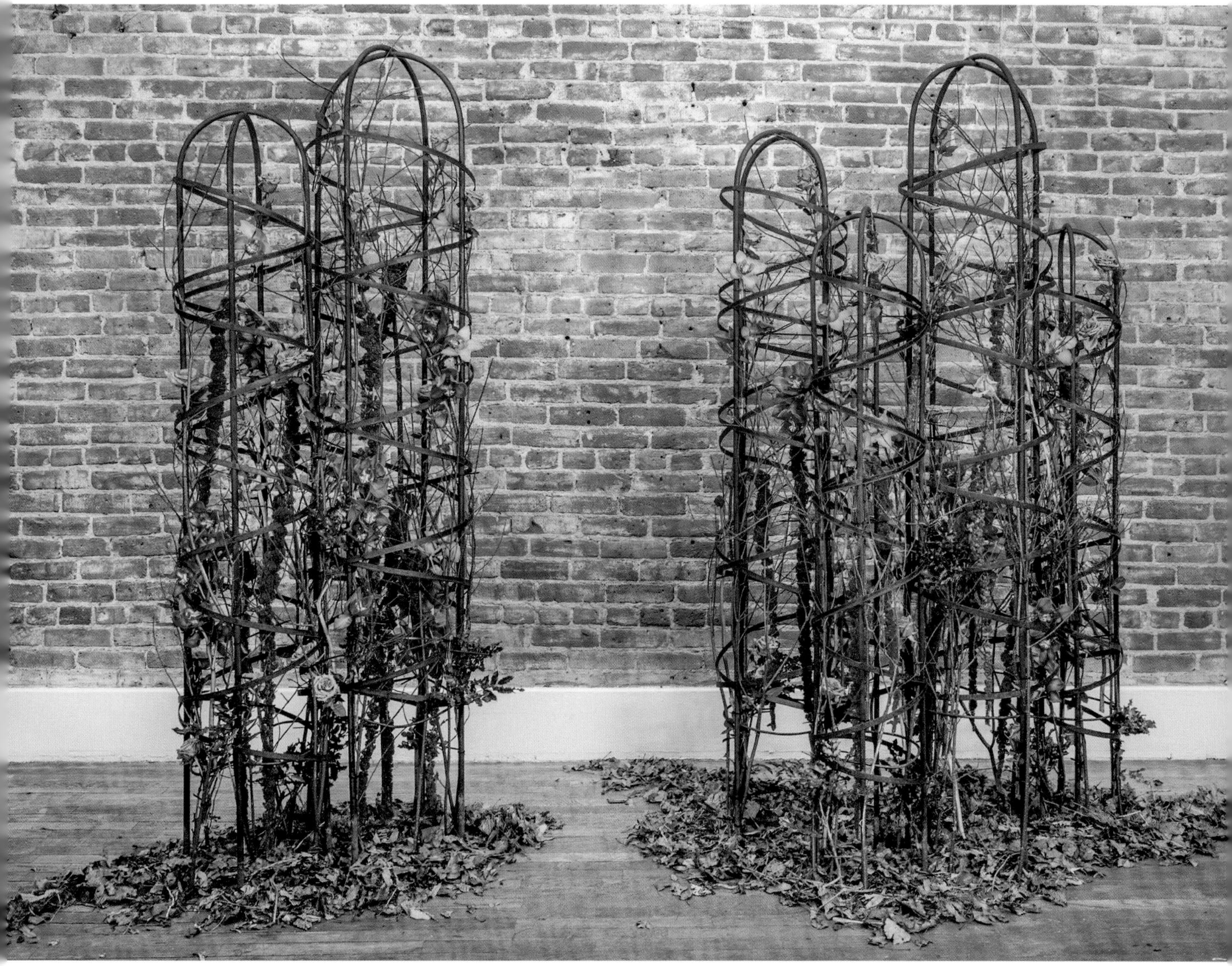

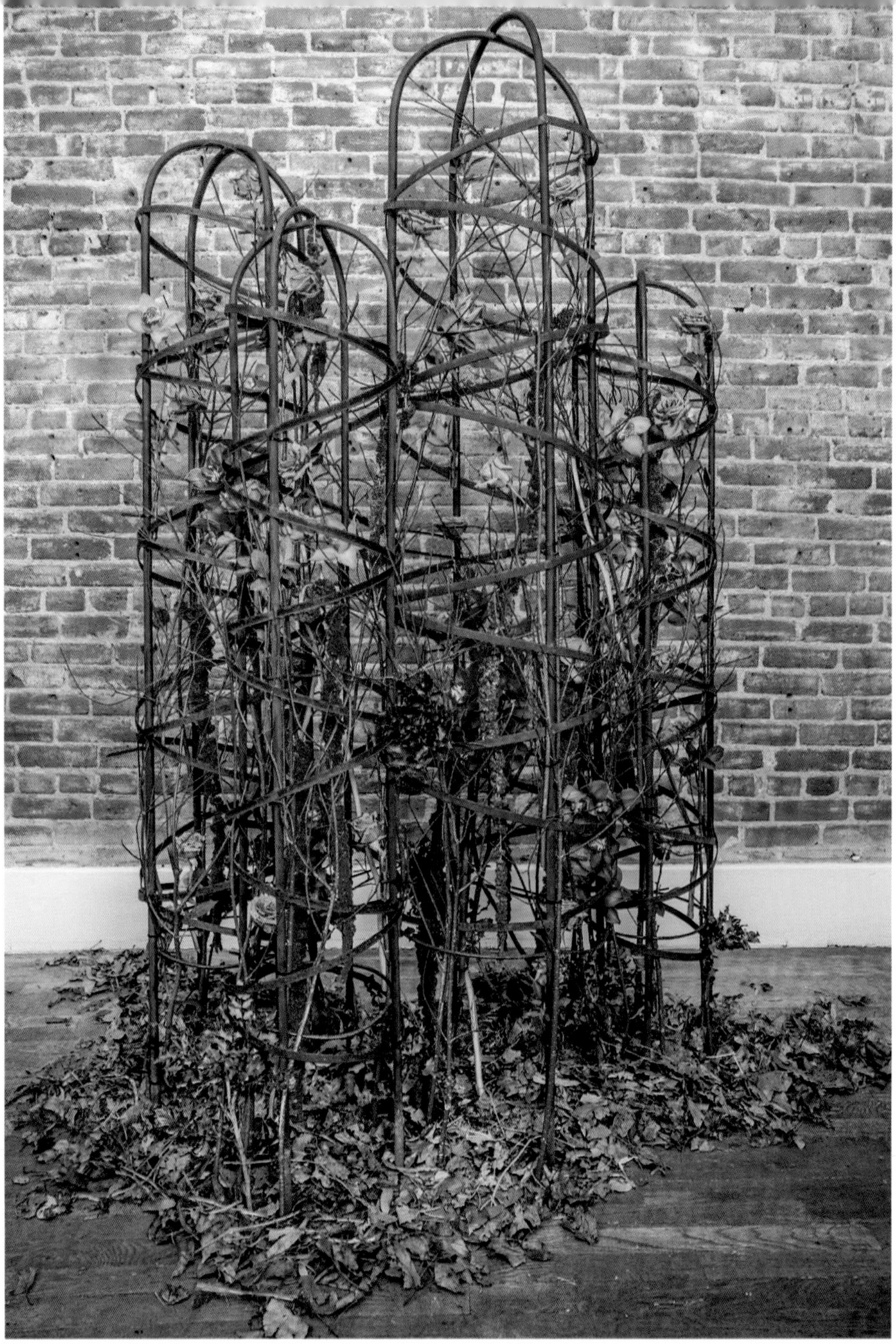

DESIGN BY ARTHUR WILLIAMS, STACEY BAL, KARI SMITH, CHUCK HUTSON, DAN DEVLIN, MARY PAPPAS
PHOTOGRAPHY BY DAN DE LOS MONTEROS + STACEY BAL
Leon Gallery; Denver, Colorado | January 2020

CONDUIT

"Collaboration in art requires mutual respect, the awareness that the work belongs to those involved, and that all involved with the creation of the piece will benefit from the exposure accumulated when it is exhibited."

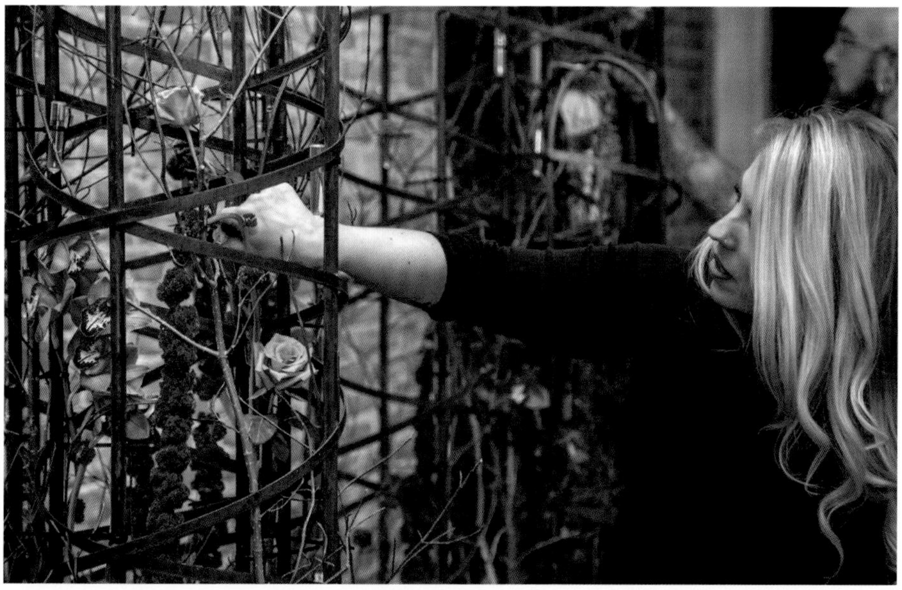

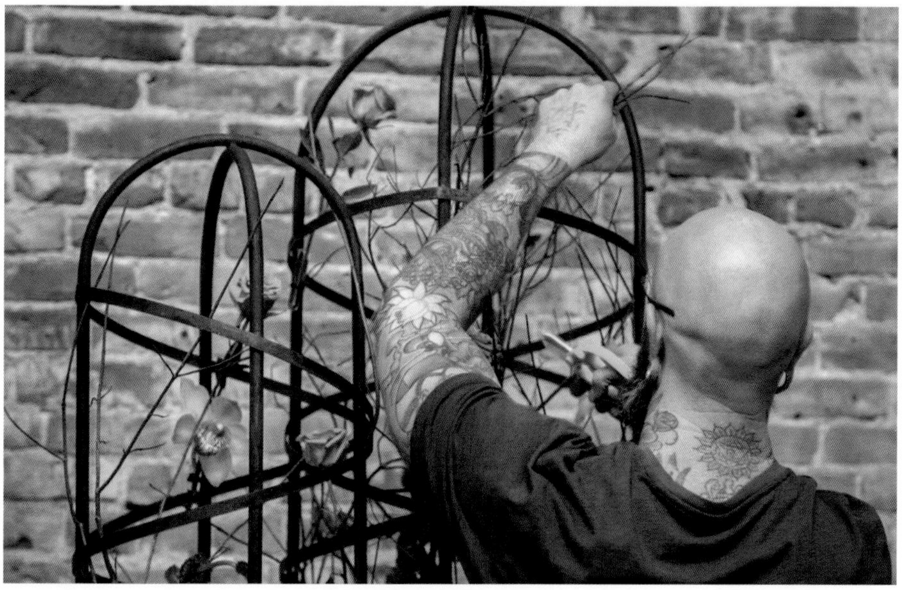

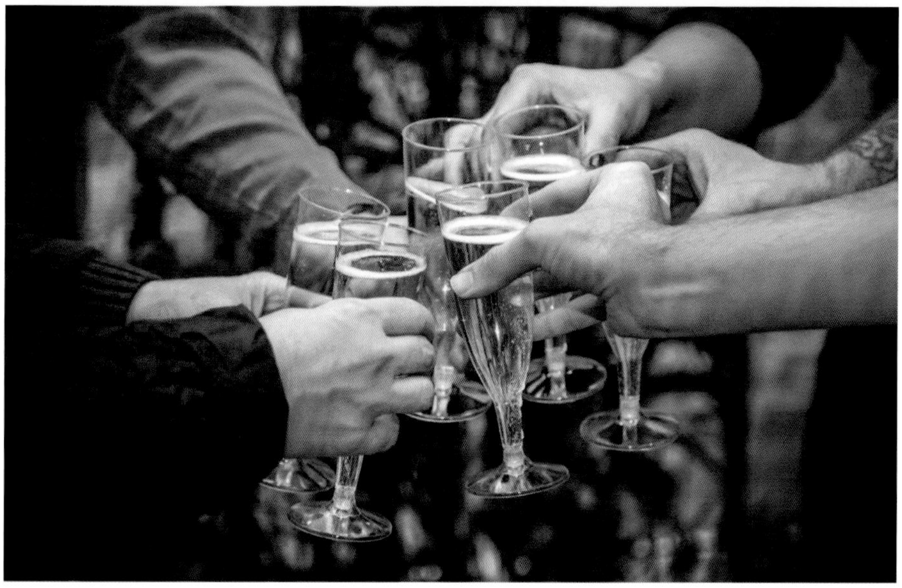

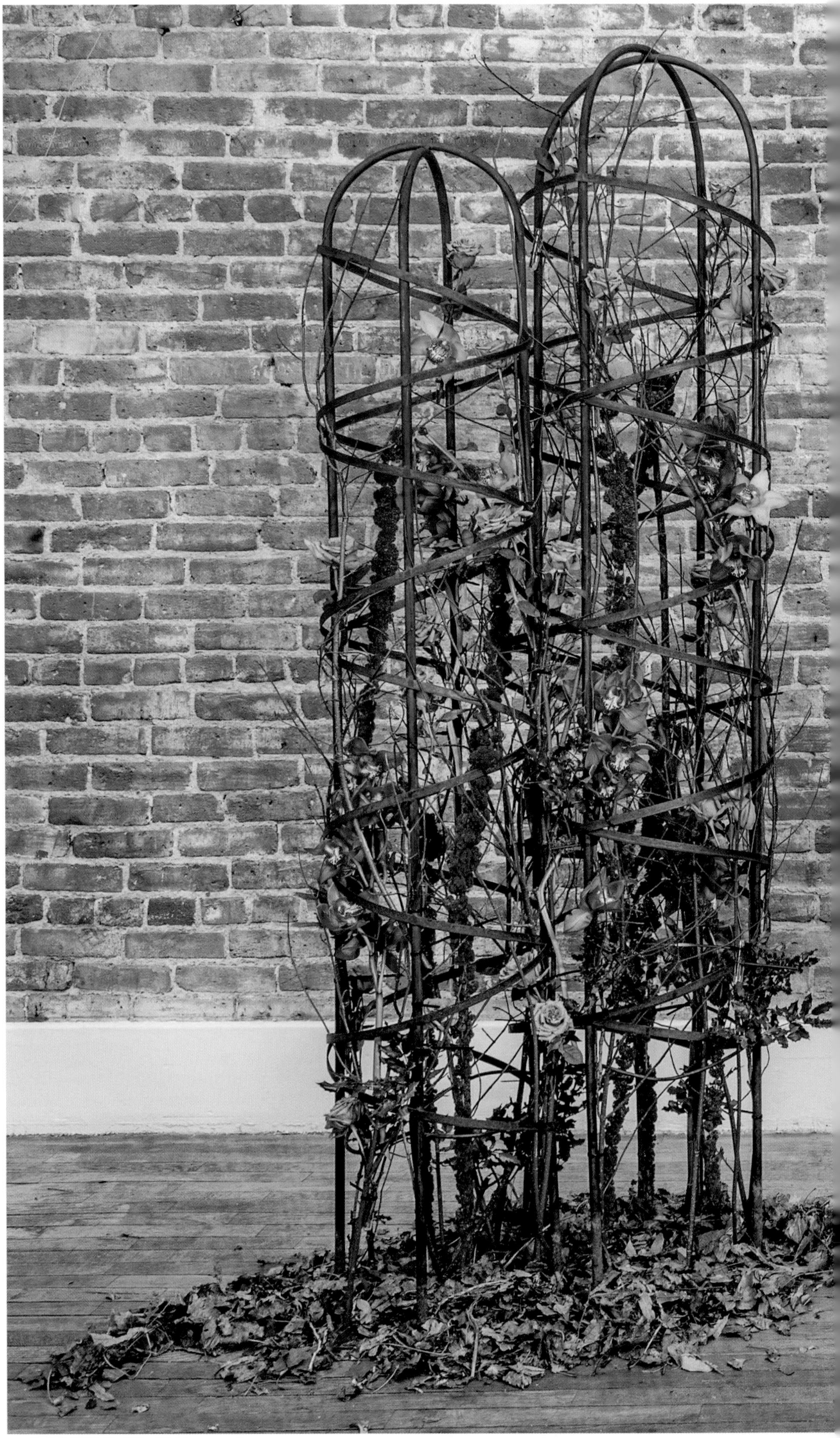

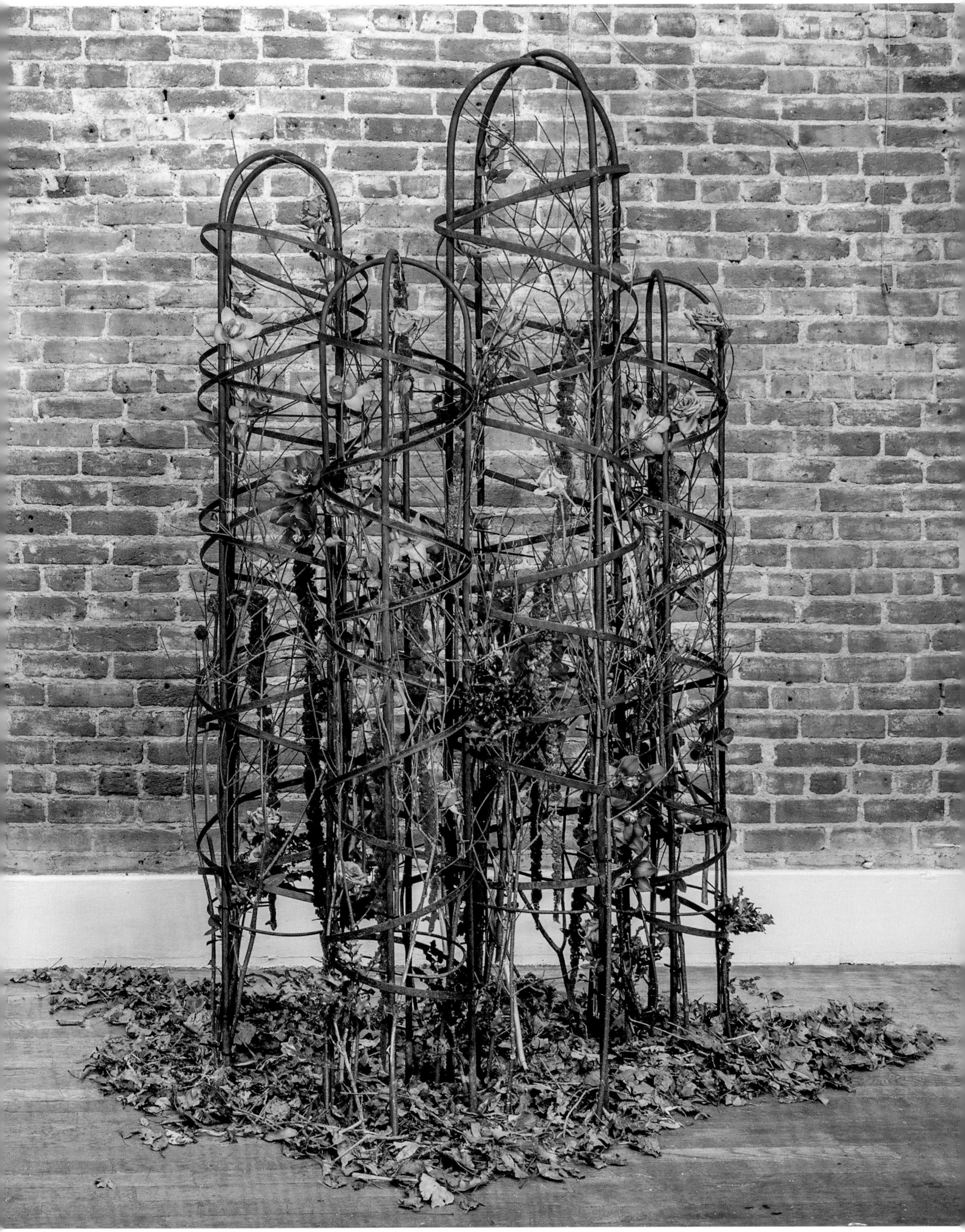

NOCTURNE

A composition inspired by,
or evocative of, the night.

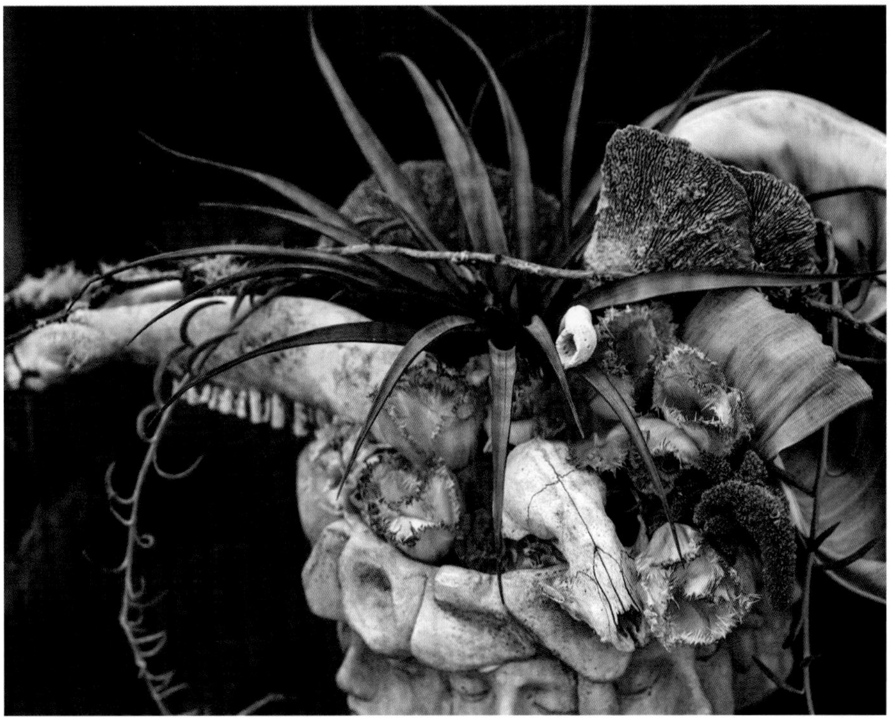

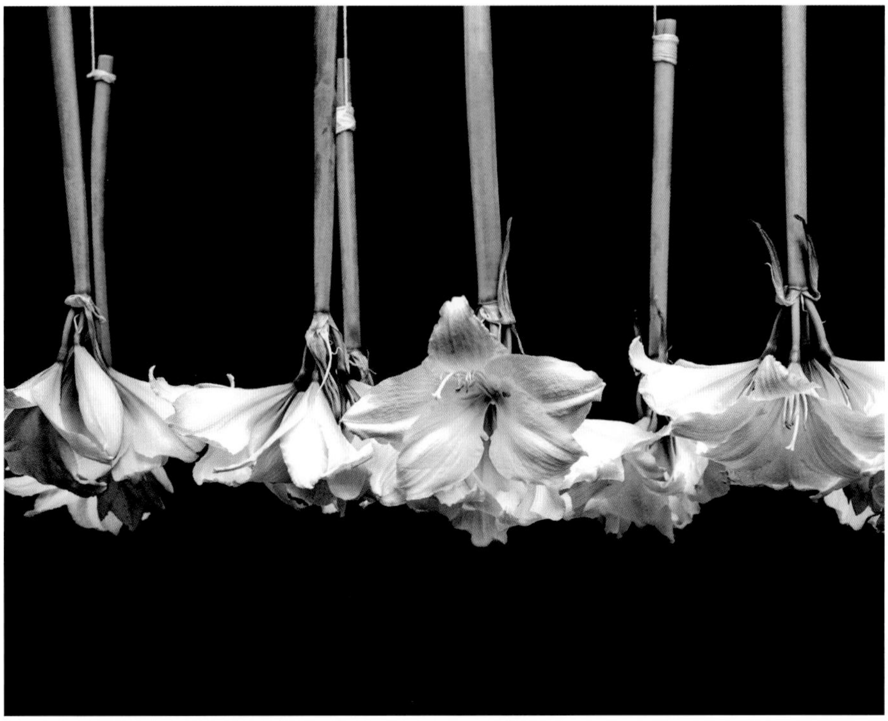

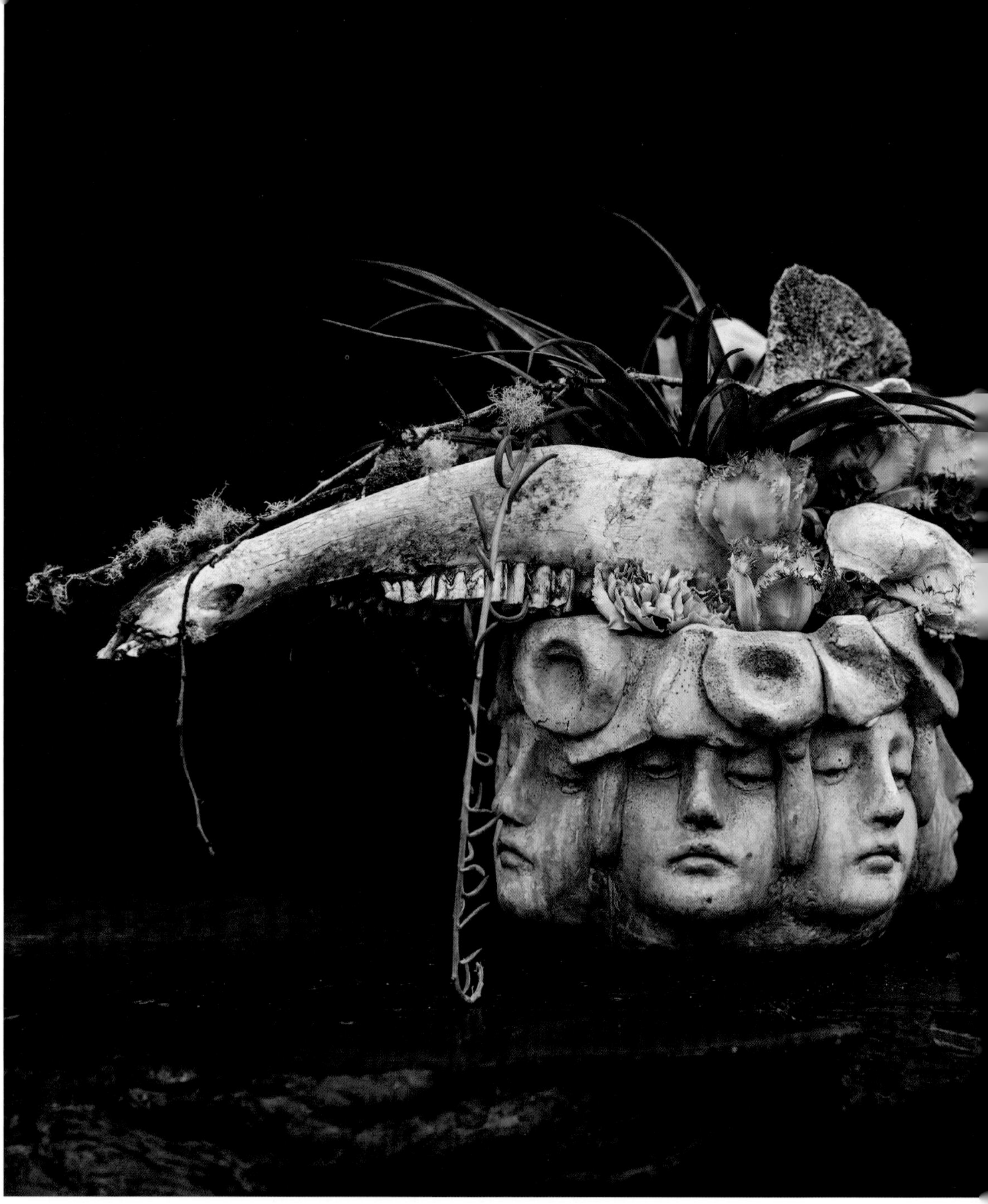

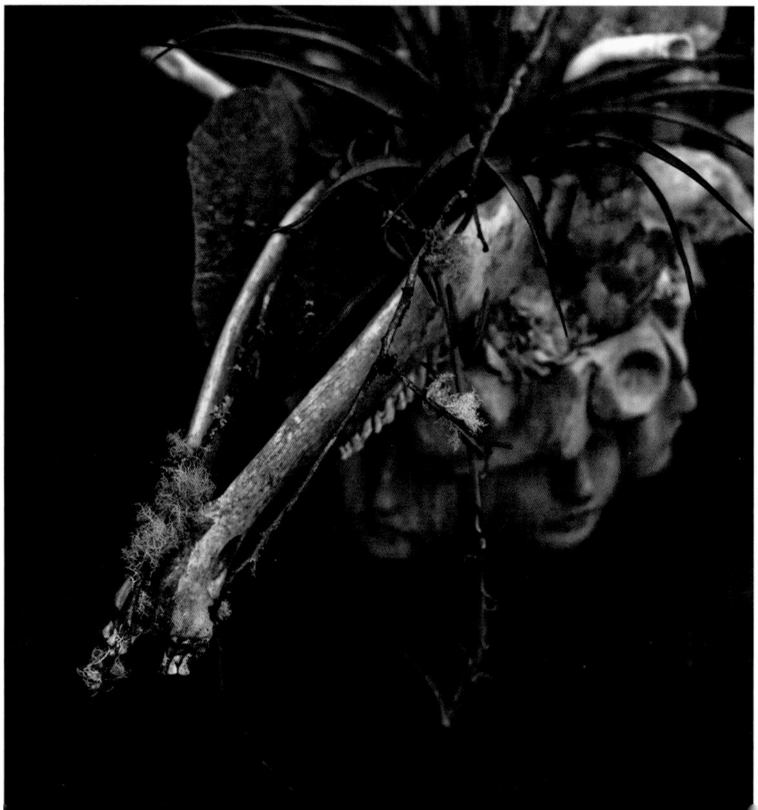

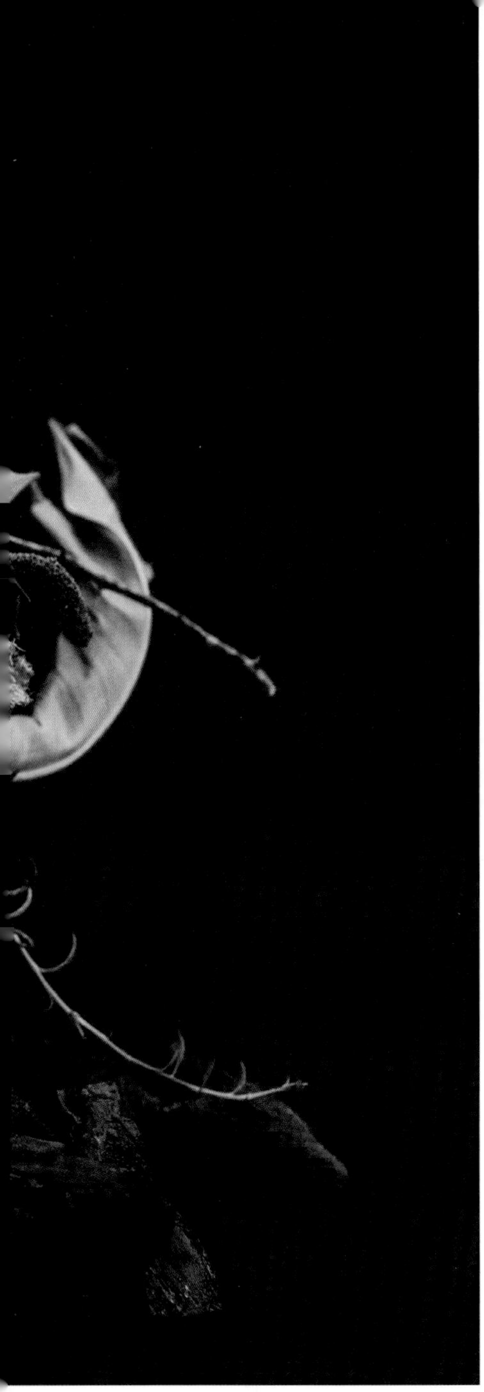

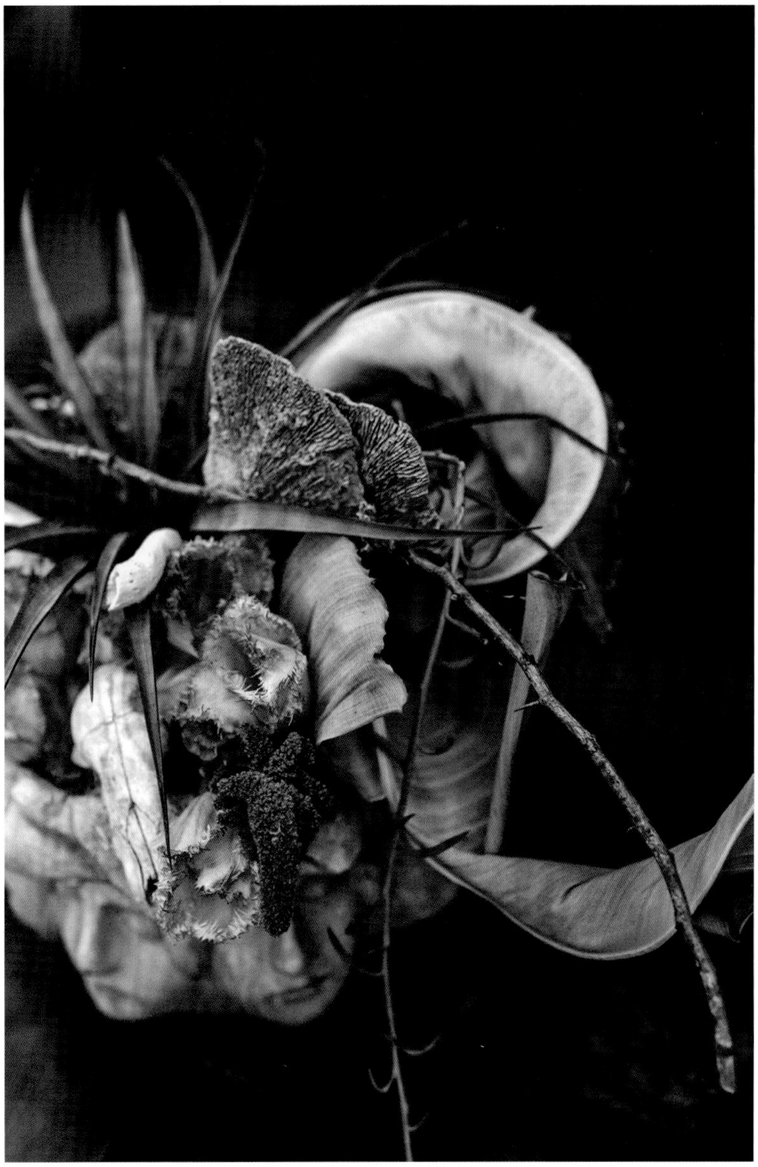

DESIGN BY ARTHUR WILLIAMS | PHOTOGRAPHY BY NICOLE PEREZ

Denver, Colorado | February 2020

HECATE

"An offering left to the threefold Goddess of Witchcraft, the Moon and Crossroads. Night is her domain, and she bridges the seen and unseen worlds."

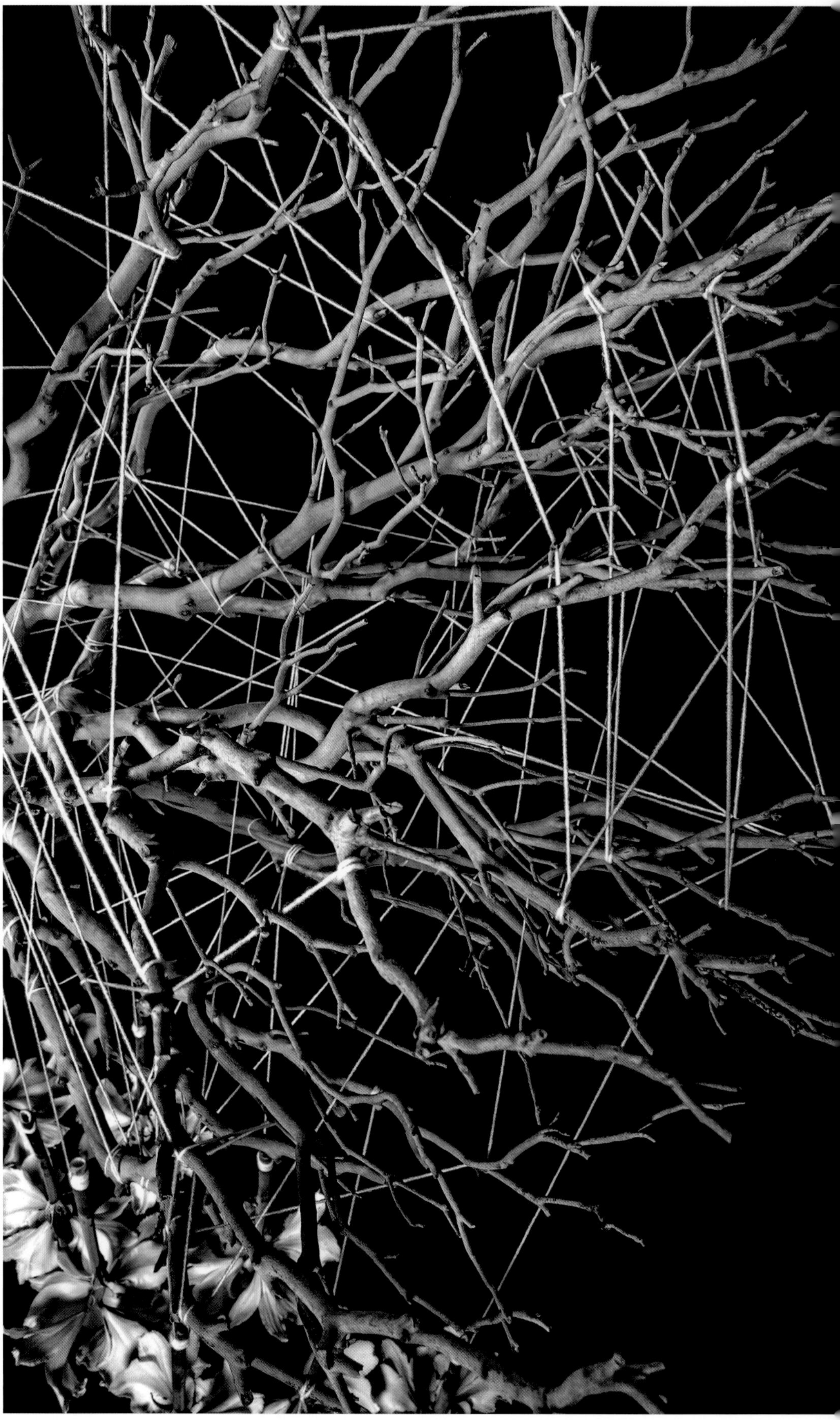

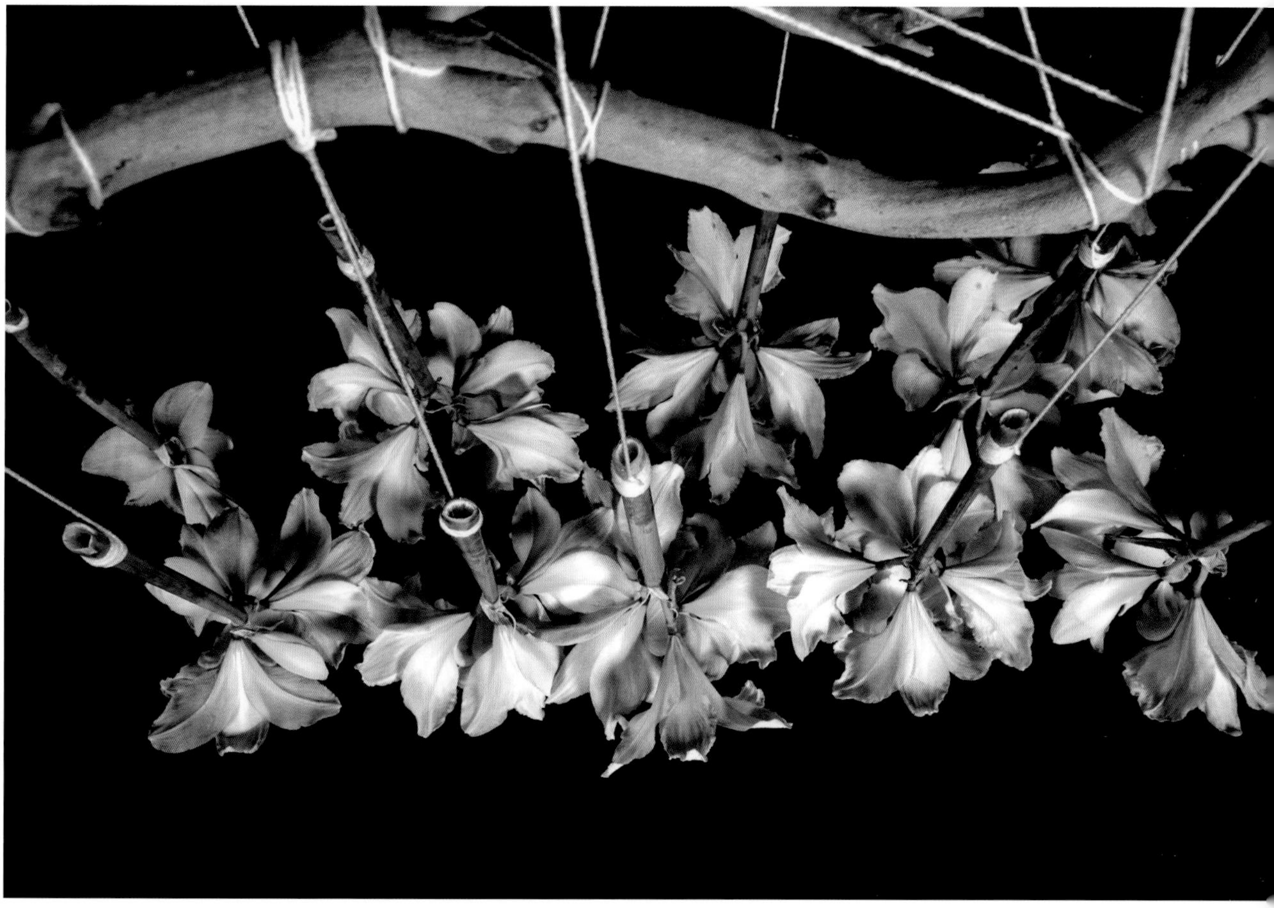

DESIGN BY STACEY BAL | PHOTOGRAPHY BY DAN DE LOS MONTEROS + STACEY BAL

Denver, Colorado | January 2020

INSOMNIA

"When unwelcome wakefulness
becomes an oasis glowing with
flashes of creative genius."

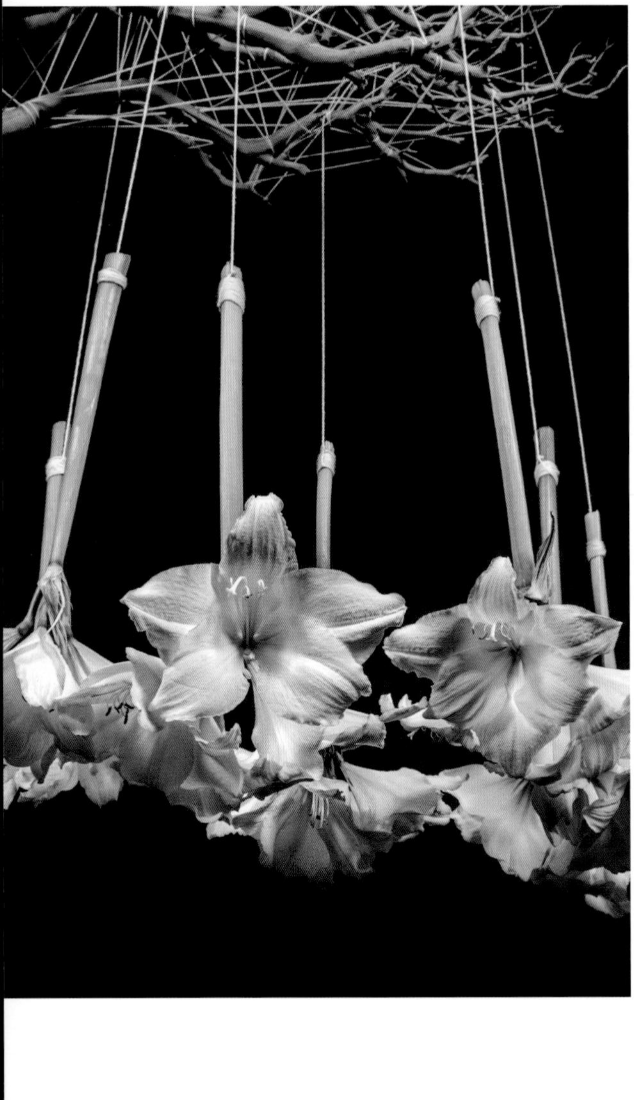

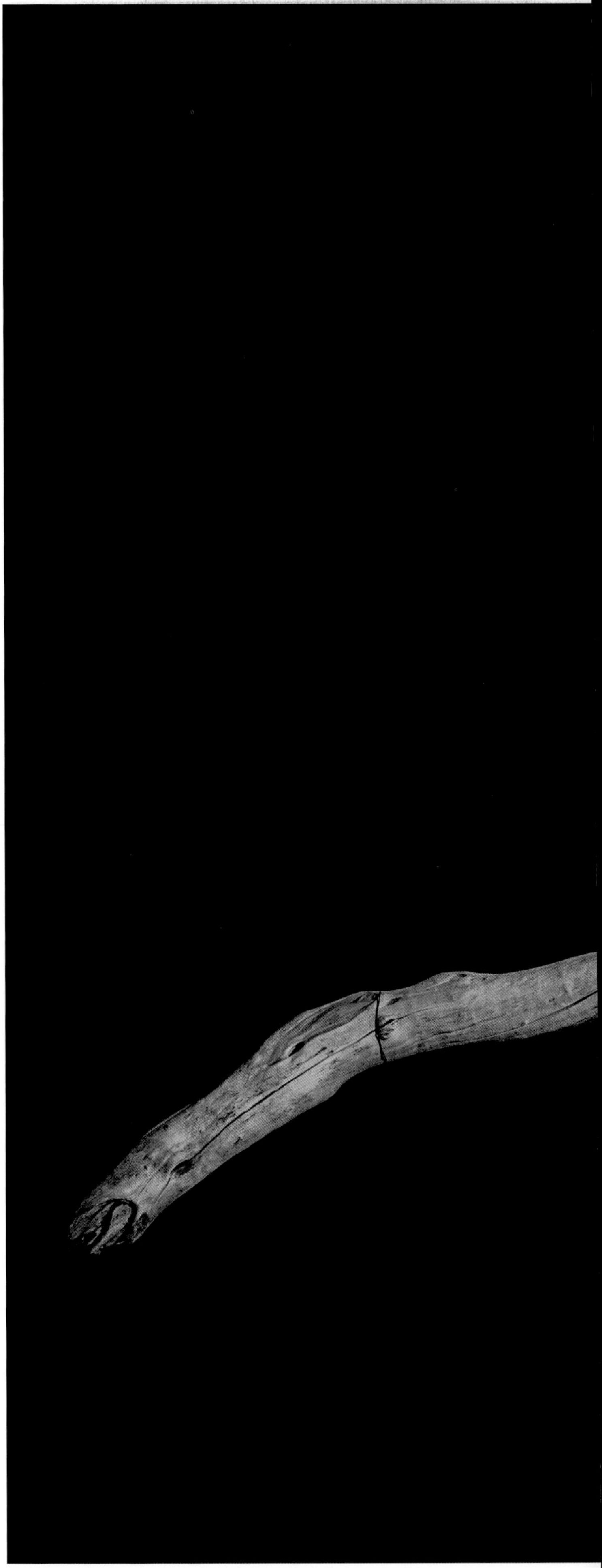

IMPERMANENT

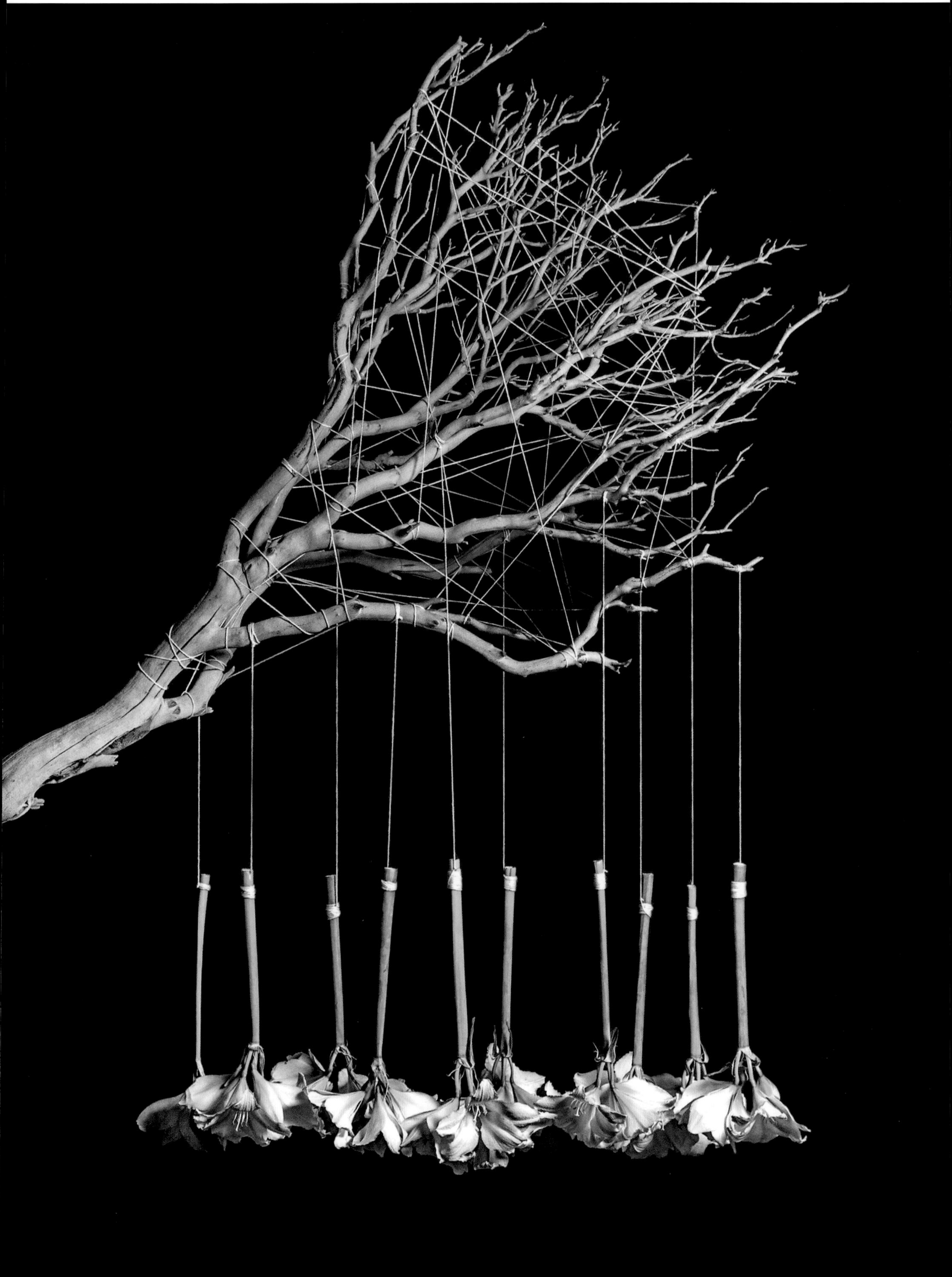

PROJECTION

A plan for an
anticipated course
of action.

Deborah Butterfield, Willy, Argus, and Lucky, 1996-97. Painted and patinated bronze.
Denver Art Museum: Funds from the Enid and Crosby Kemper Foundation,
UMB Bank Trustees, 1996.198.1-3. © Deborah Butterfield

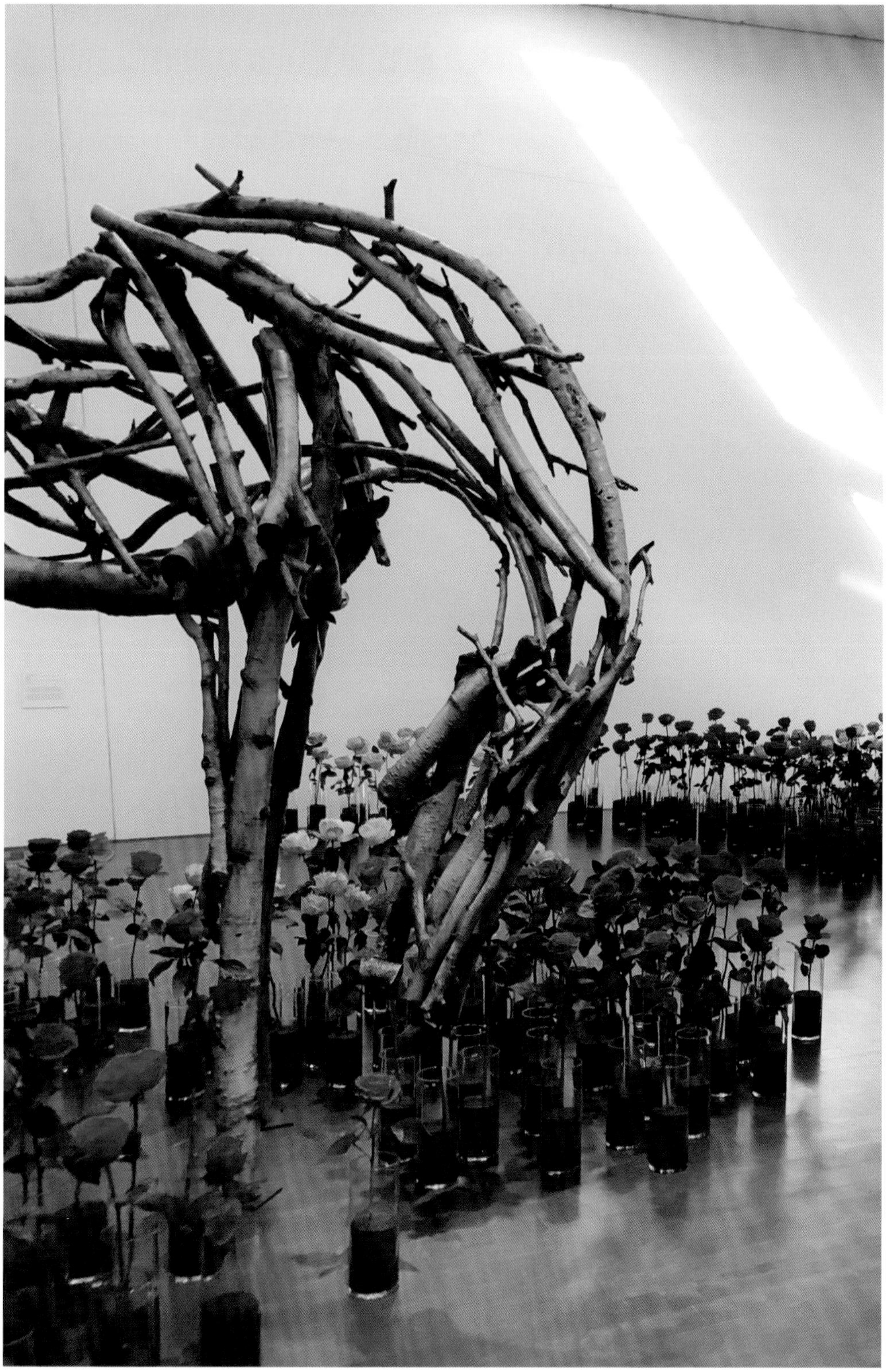

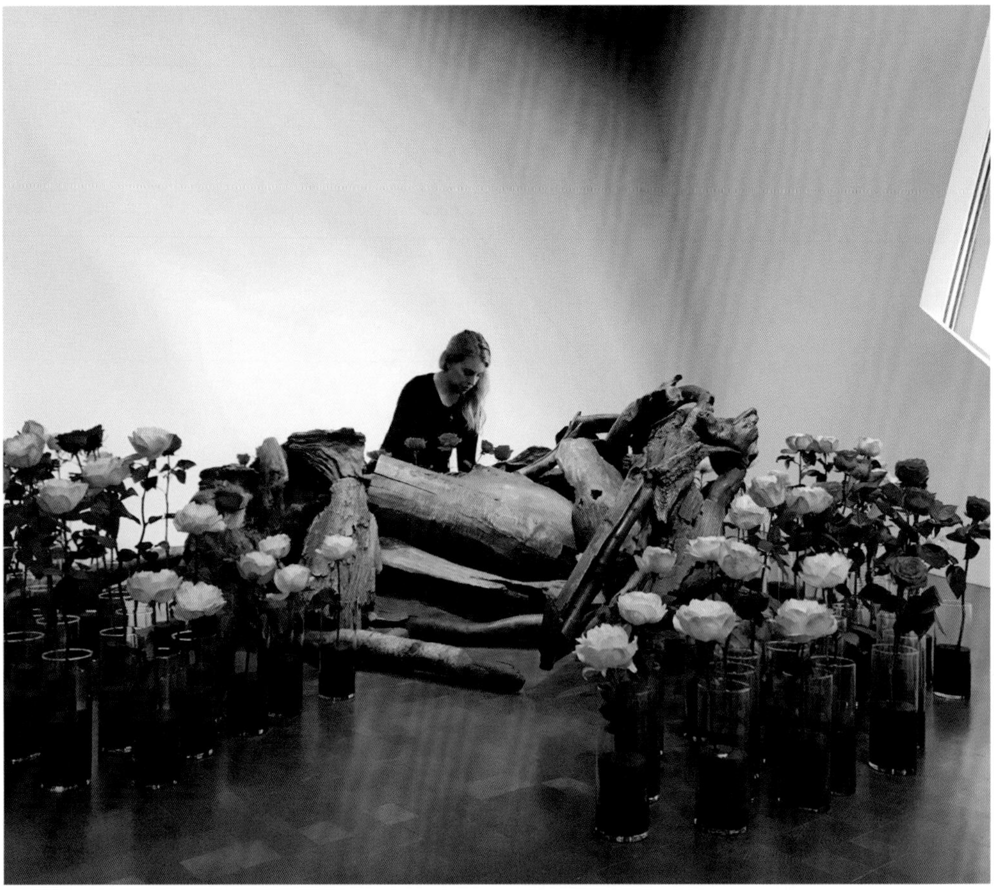

DESIGN BY ARTHUR WILLIAMS + STACEY BAL | PHOTOGRAPHY BY STACEY BAL
Deborah Butterfield, Willy, Argus, and Lucky, 1996-97.
Painted and patinated bronze. © Deborah Butterfield
Denver, Colorado | September 2018

PERSEPHONE'S FINAL BREATH

An installation based around Deborah Butterfield's horse sculptures "Willy, Argus and Lucky" for the Denver Art Museum's Untitled Creative in Residence program.

"The Law of Cause and Effect states that whatever you send into the universe comes back. Every cause has its effect, and every effect its cause."

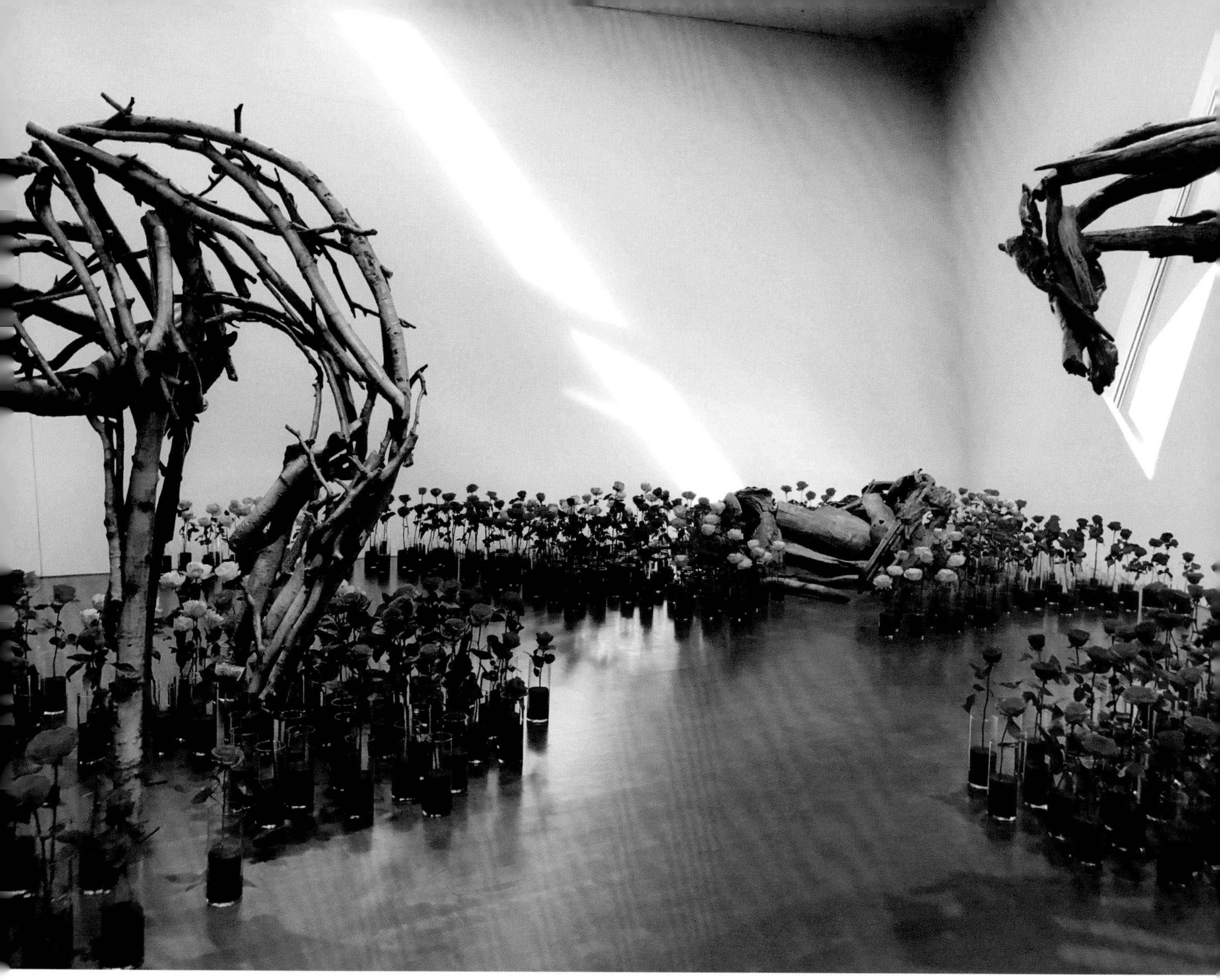

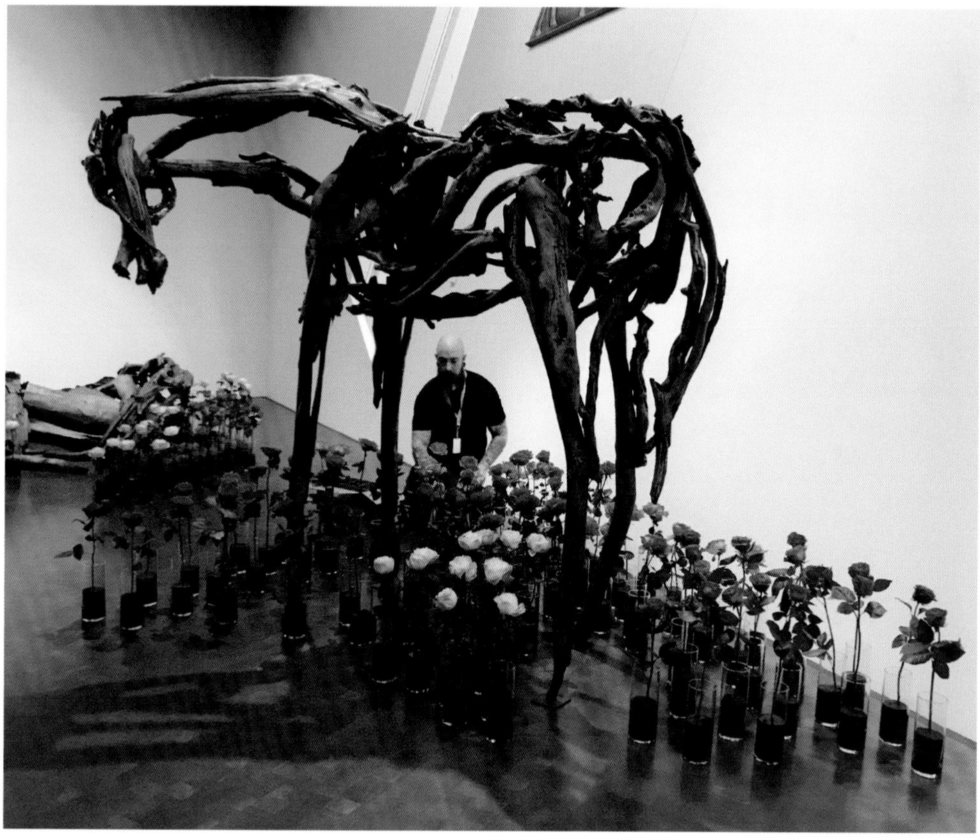

NOMADIC

Living the life of a nomad;
someone who lives by traveling
from place to place, a wanderer.

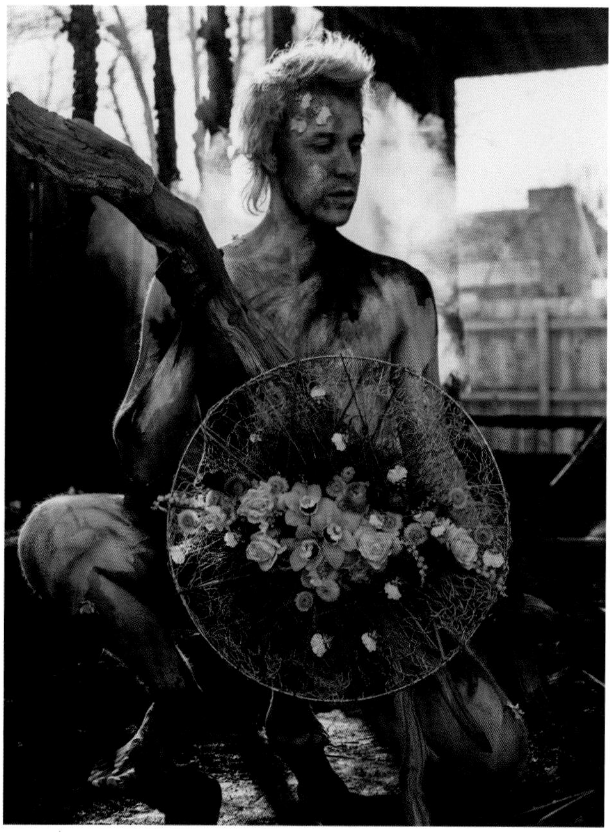

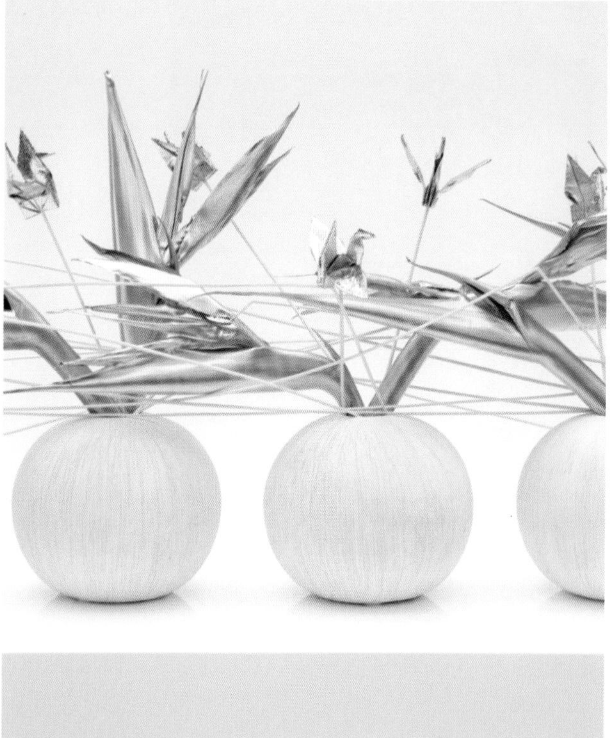

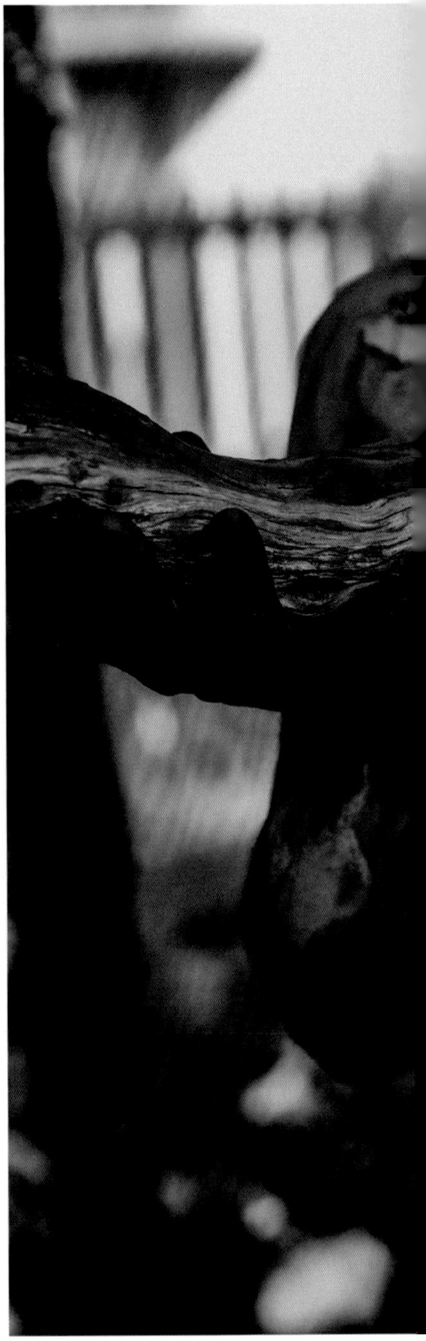

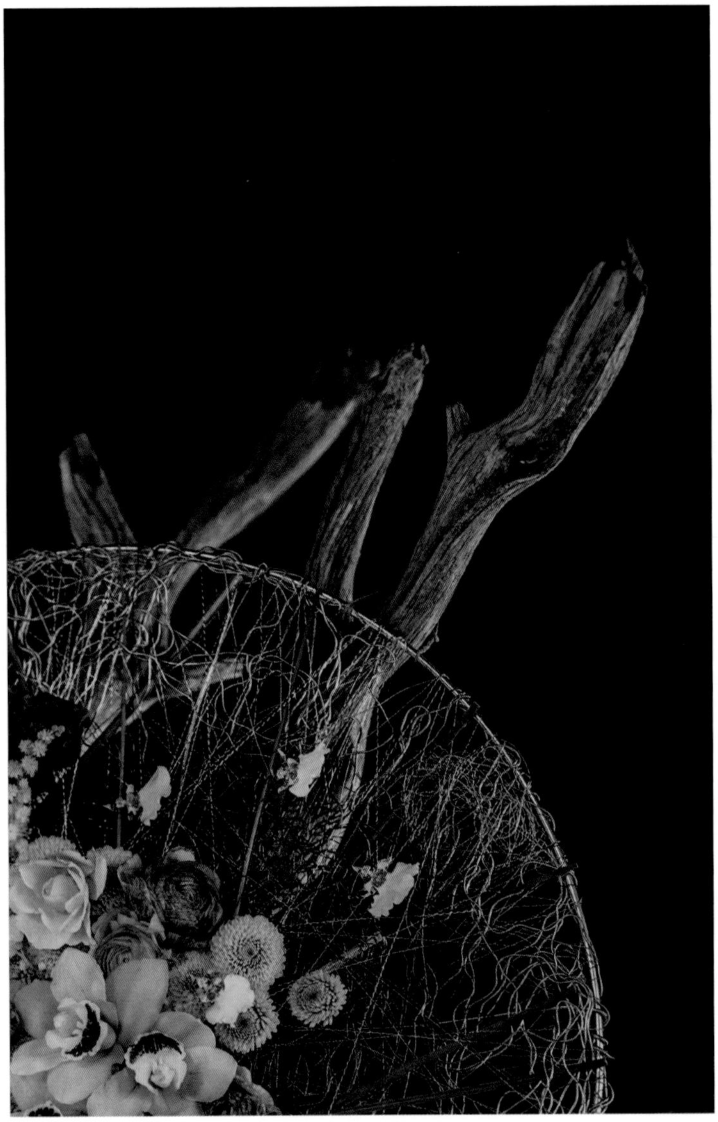

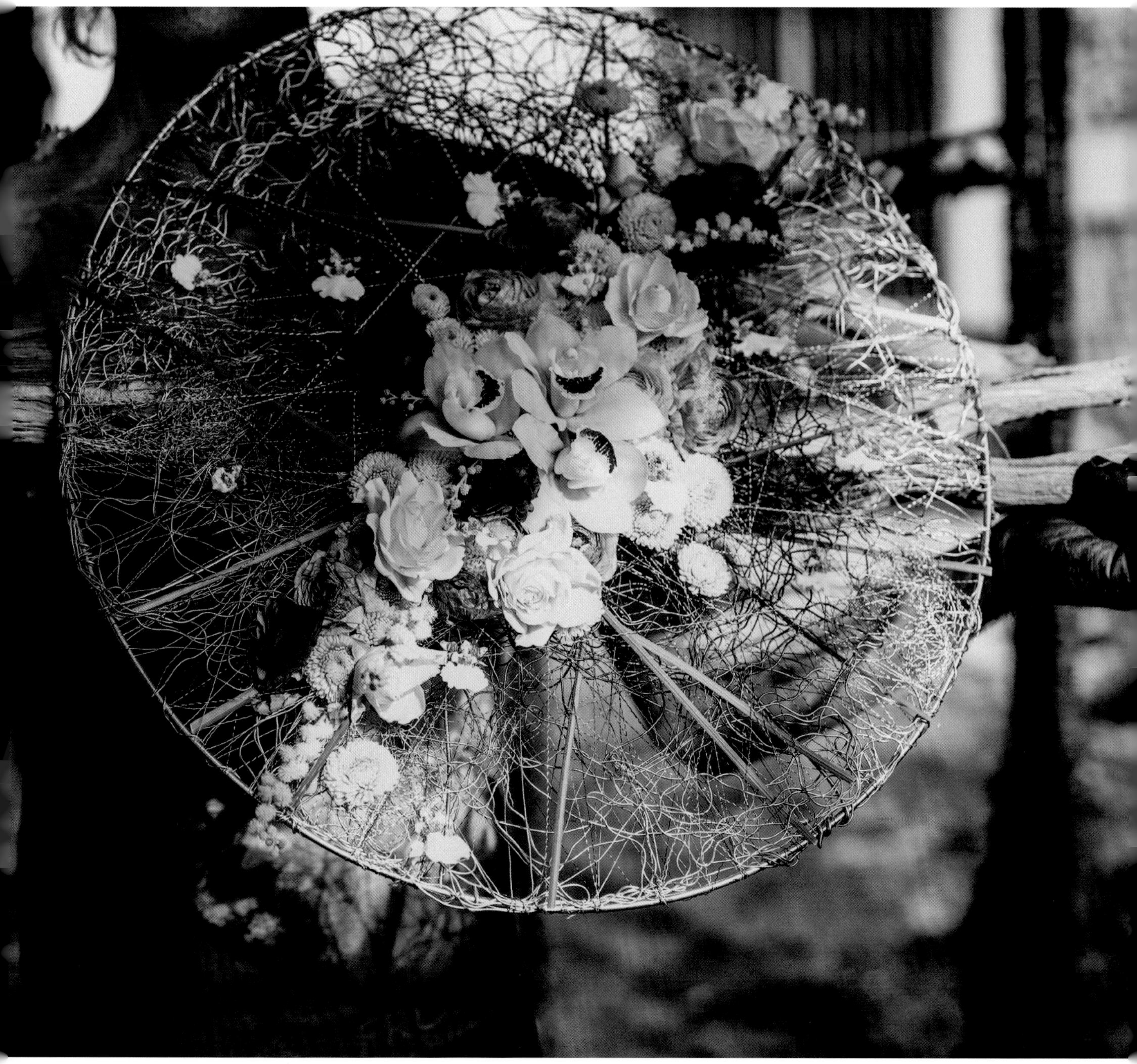

DESIGN BY ARTHUR WILLIAMS | PHOTOGRAPHY BY NICOLE PEREZ

Model: Skyler Heck

Denver, Colorado | February 2020

BEACON

"Out of the ashes, nature shines a bright beacon of hope guiding wanderers to a sustainable future."

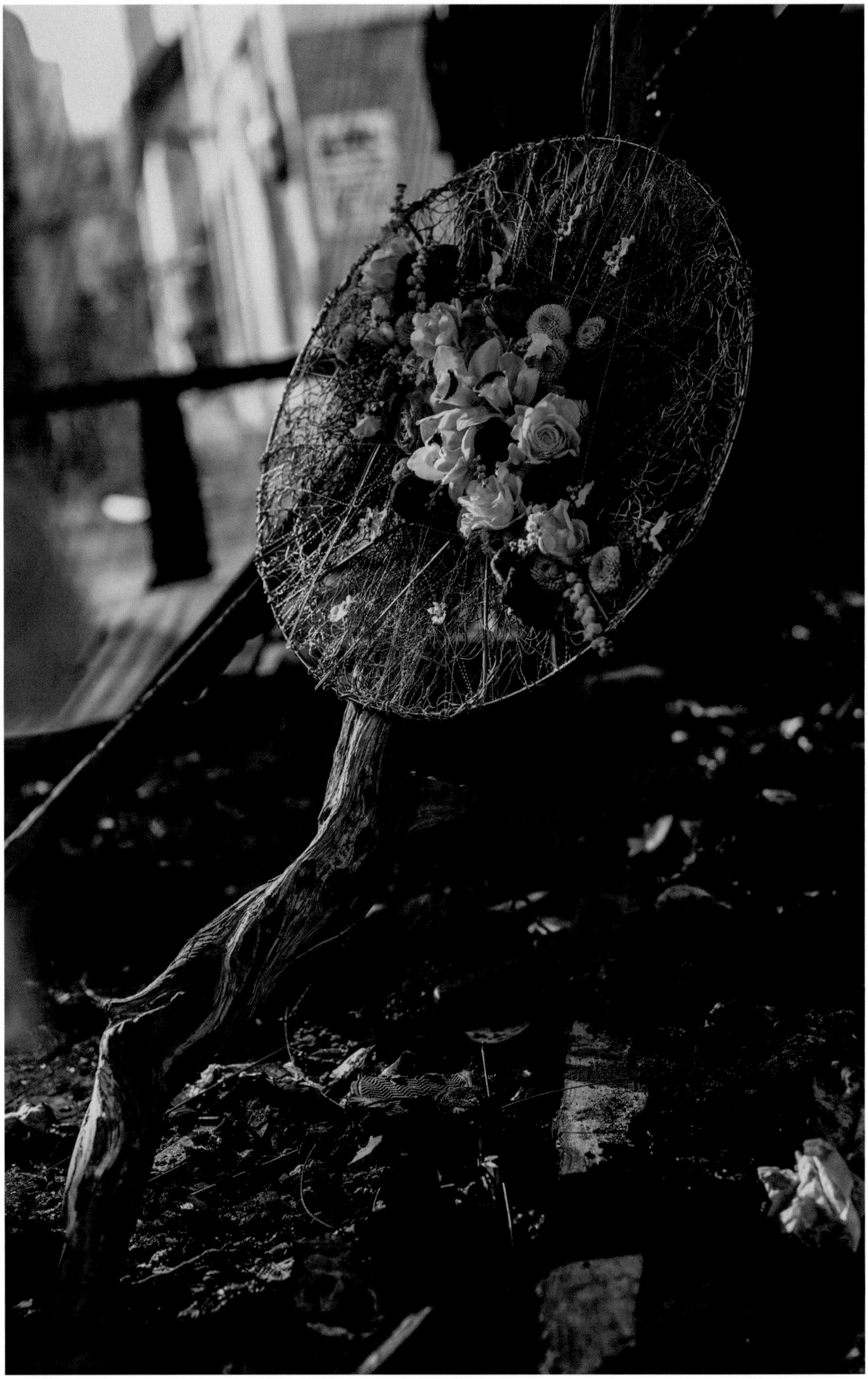

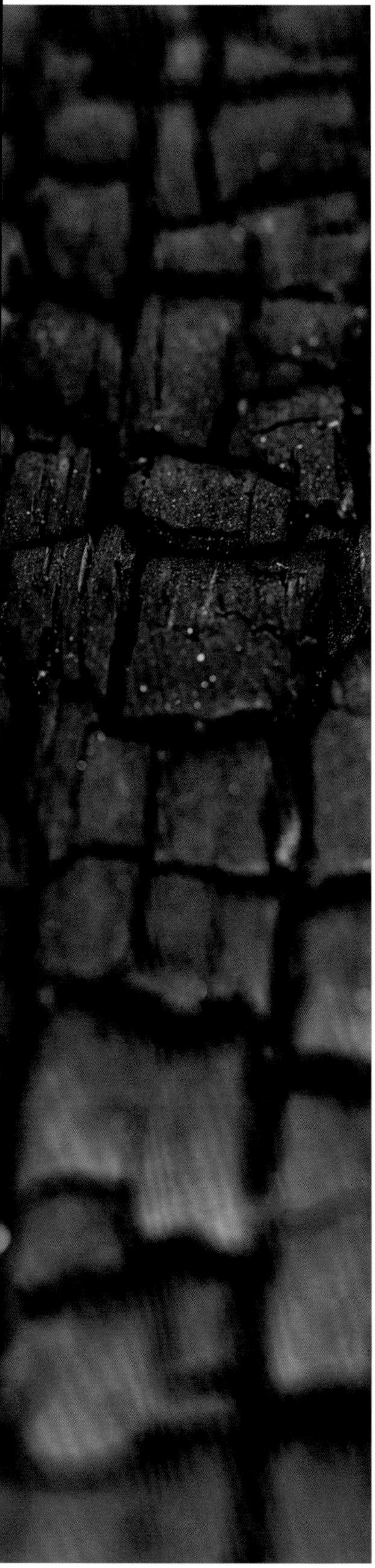

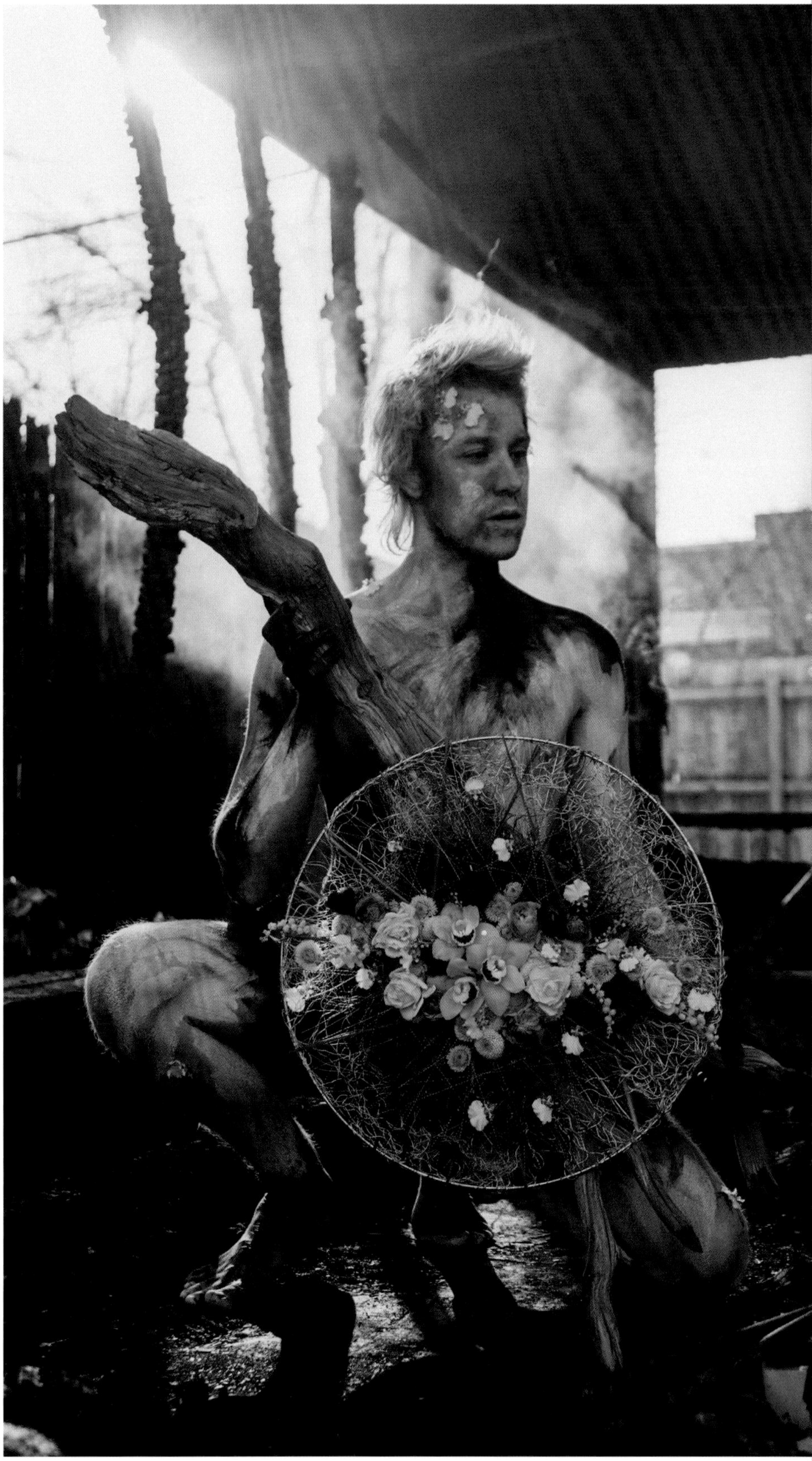

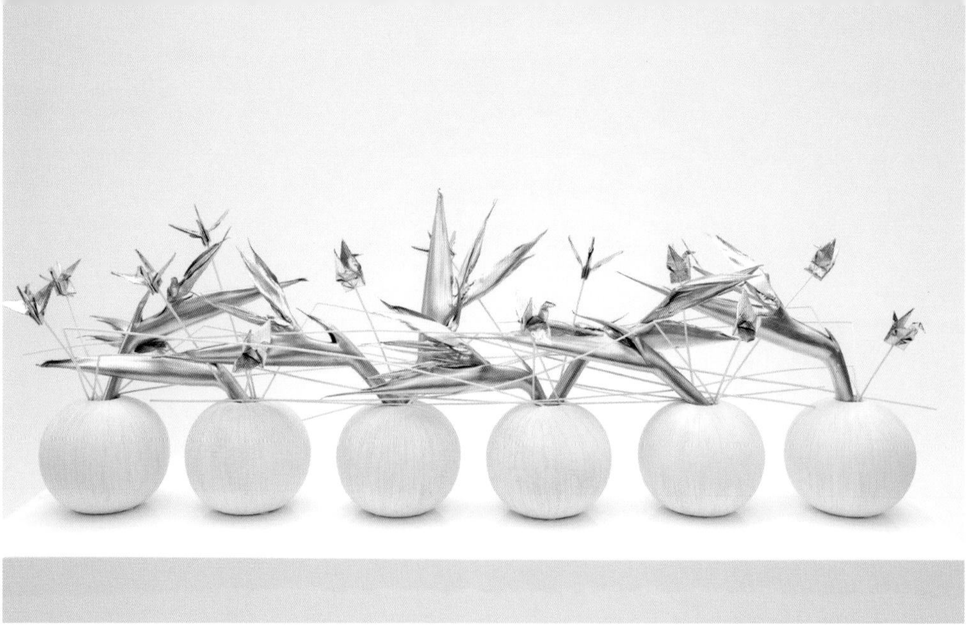

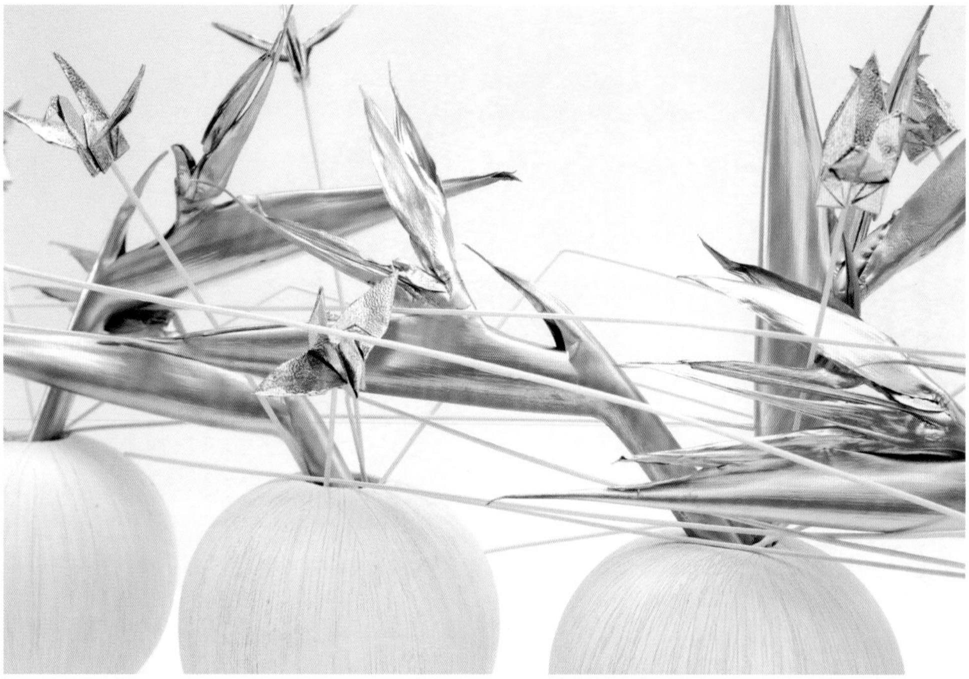

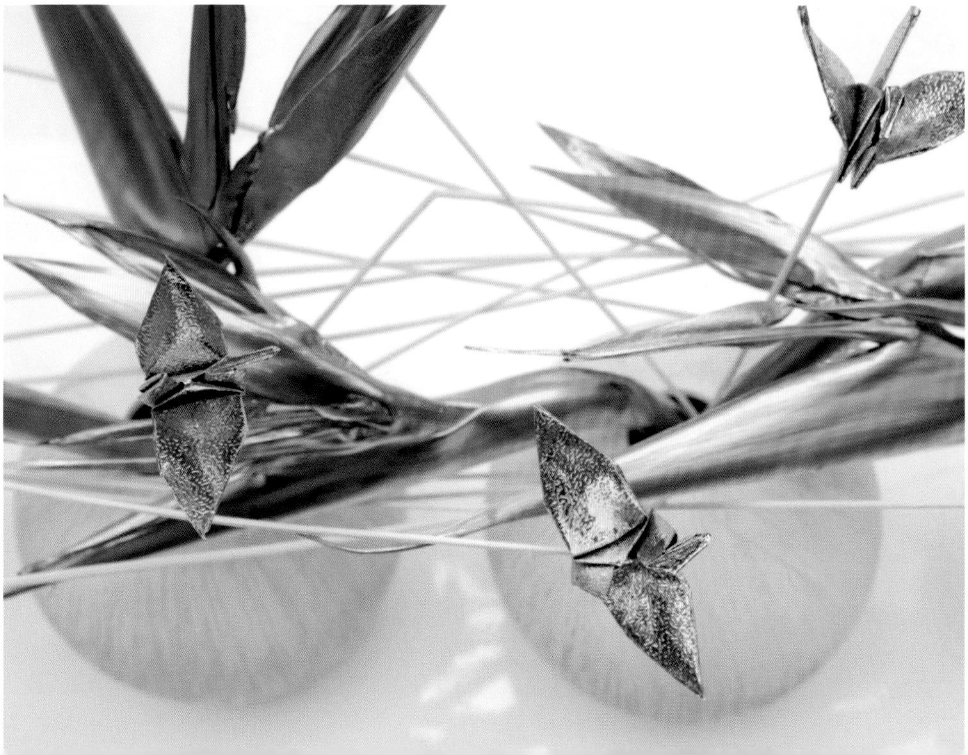

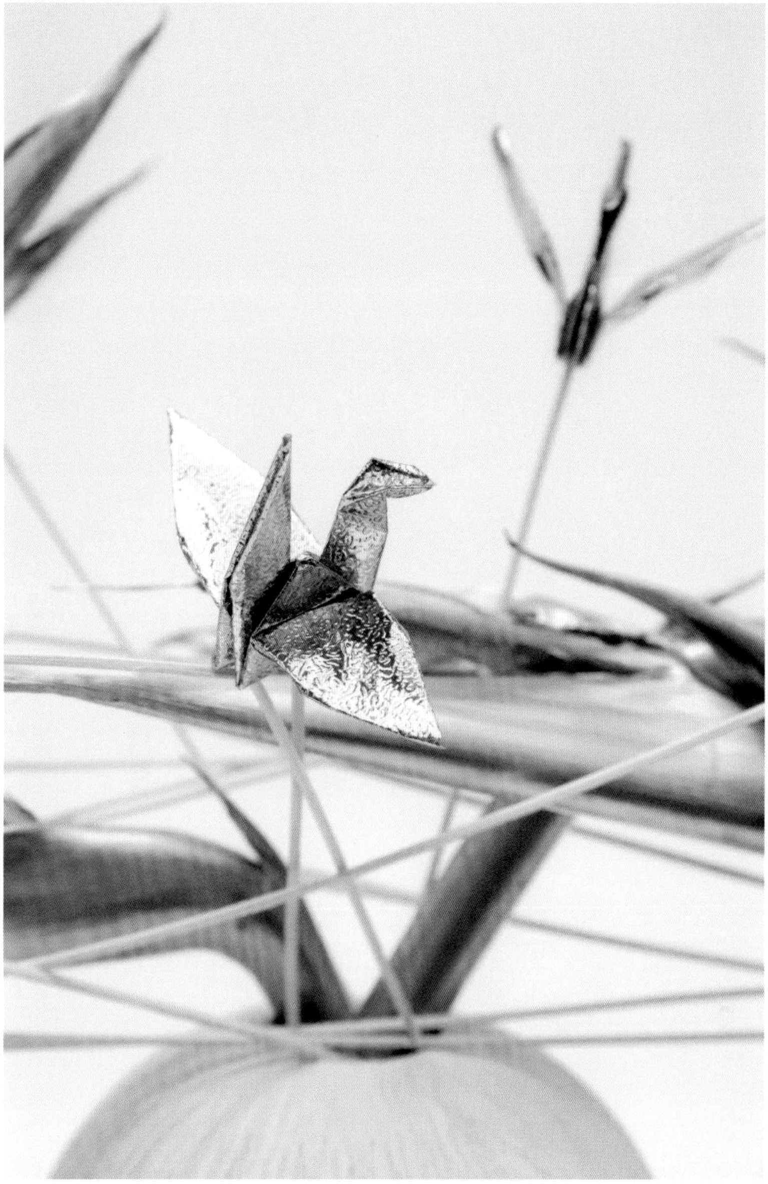

DESIGN BY STACEY BAL | PHOTOGRAPHY BY STACEY BAL
Denver, Colorado | January 2020

FLIGHT

"Peace, tranquility, off the grid.
At home in the sky."

KAMI

KA-ME

From the Shinto belief meaning
deity or spirit. Everything is
imbued with spirit, all
nature has an associated
Kami or energy.

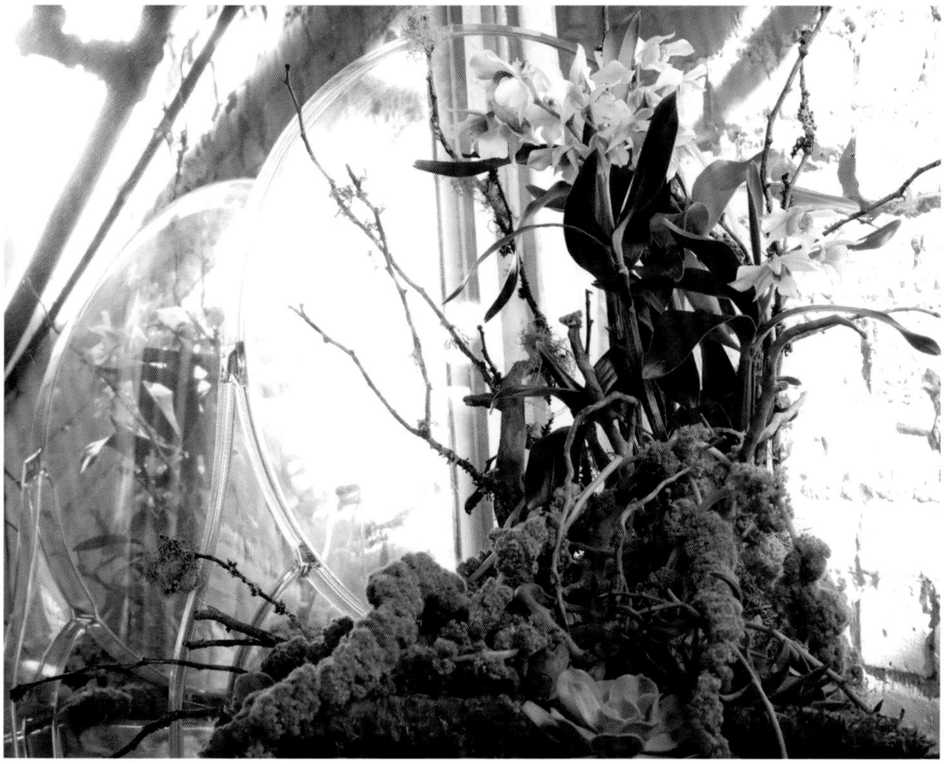

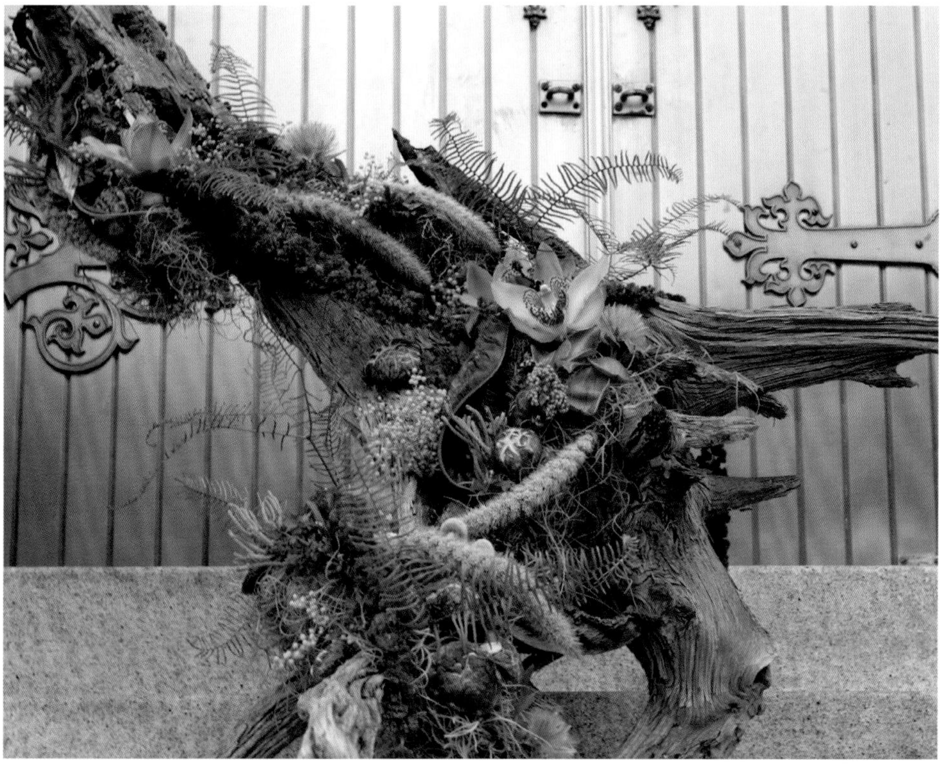

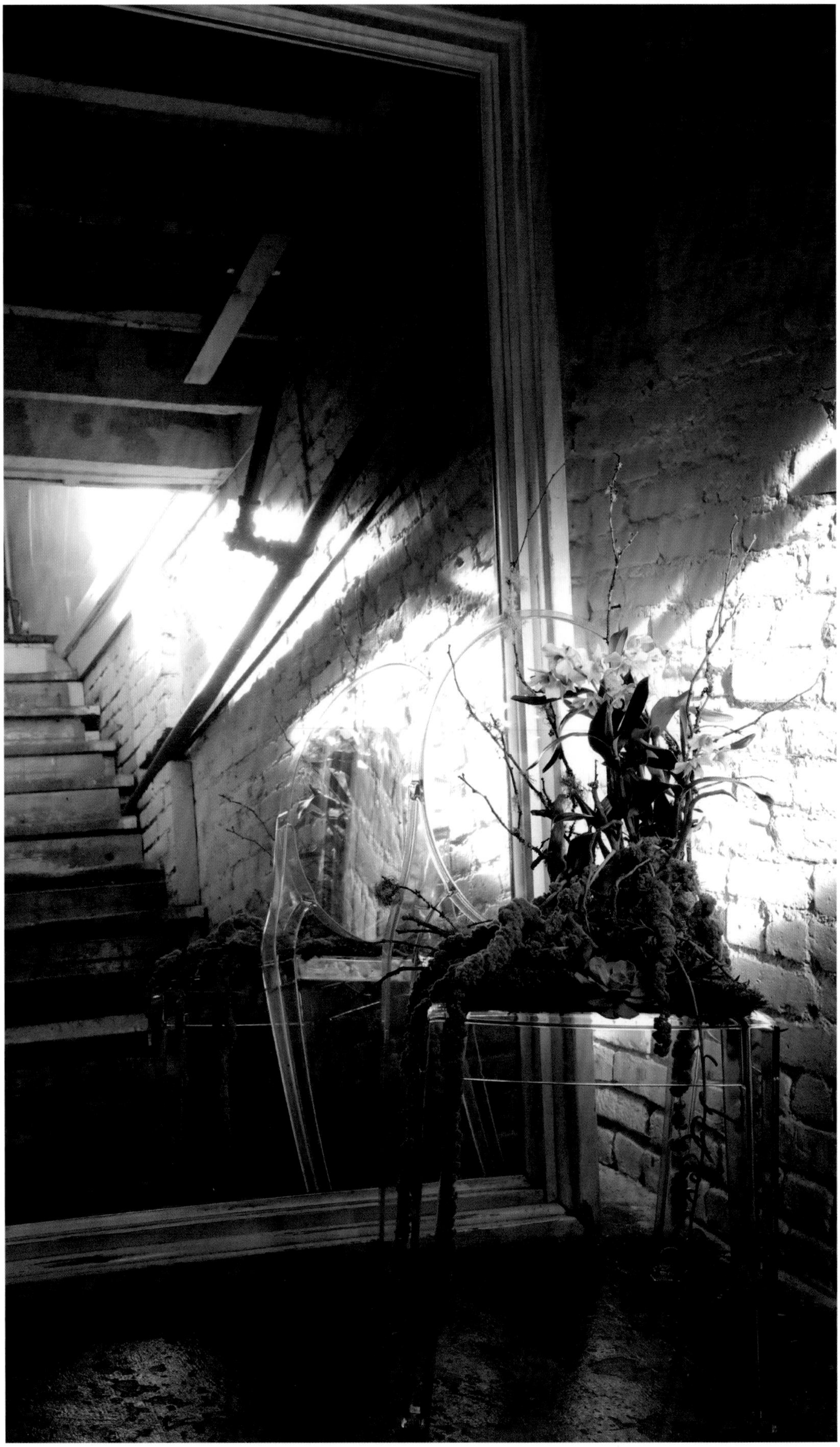

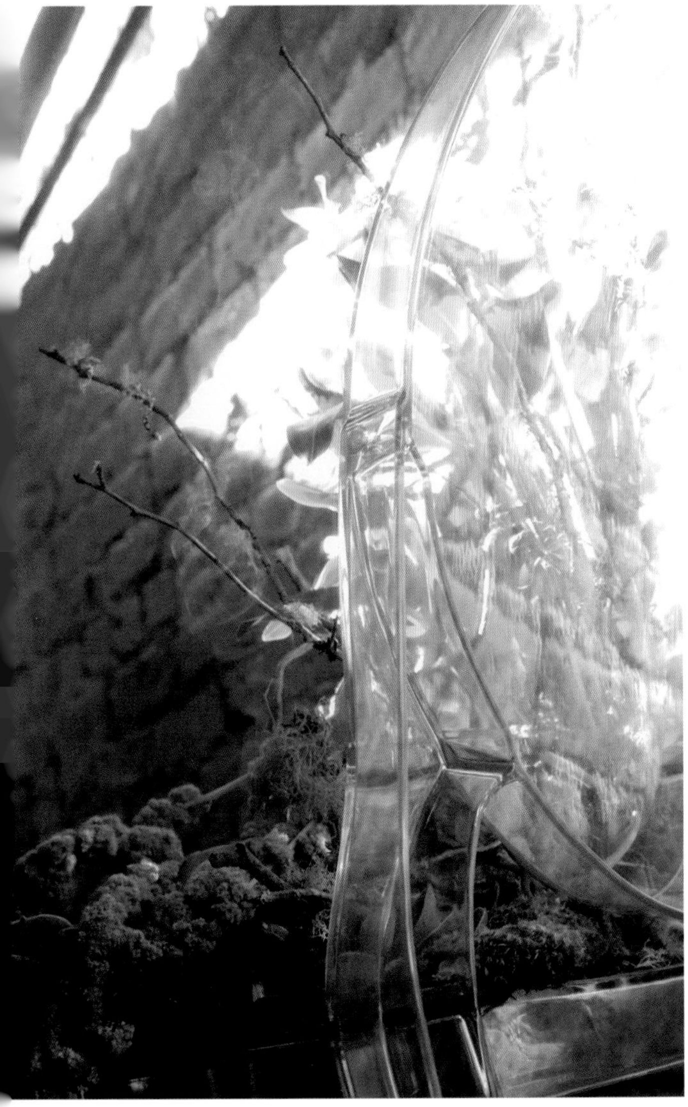 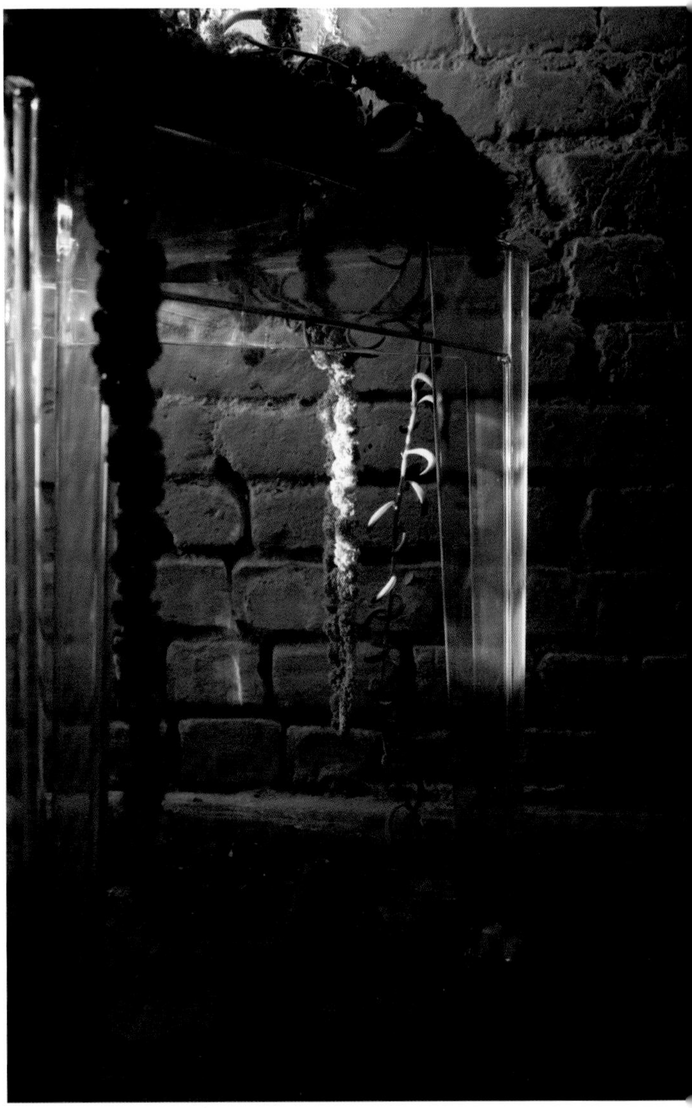

DESIGN BY STACEY BAL | PHOTOGRAPHY BY STACEY BAL
Denver, Colorado | January 2020

PHANTOM

"Physical space held for lost and departed souls."

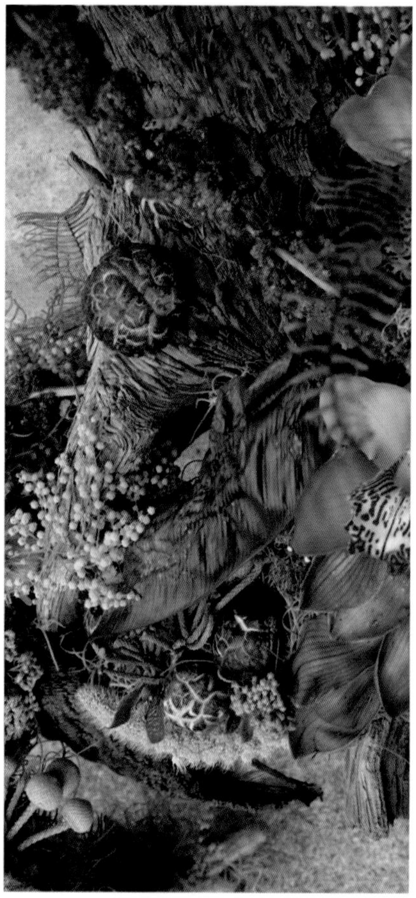

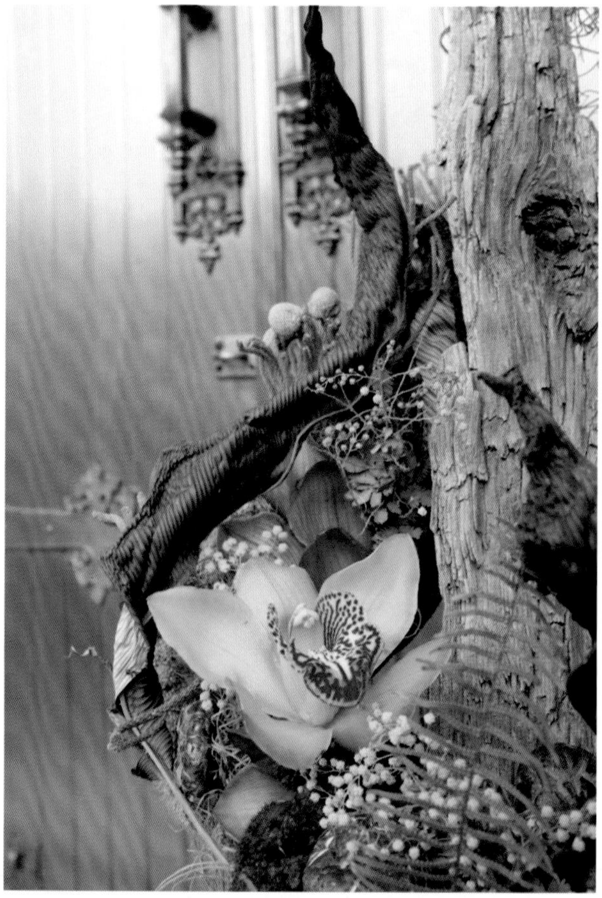

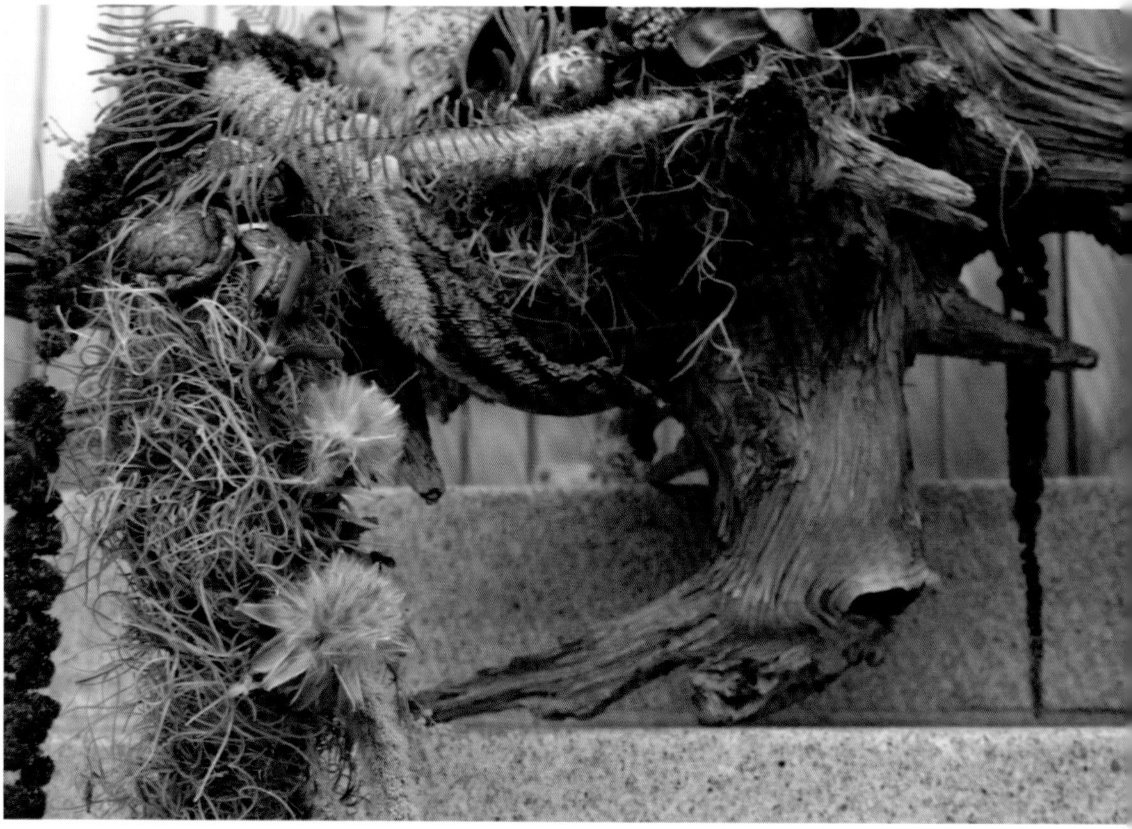

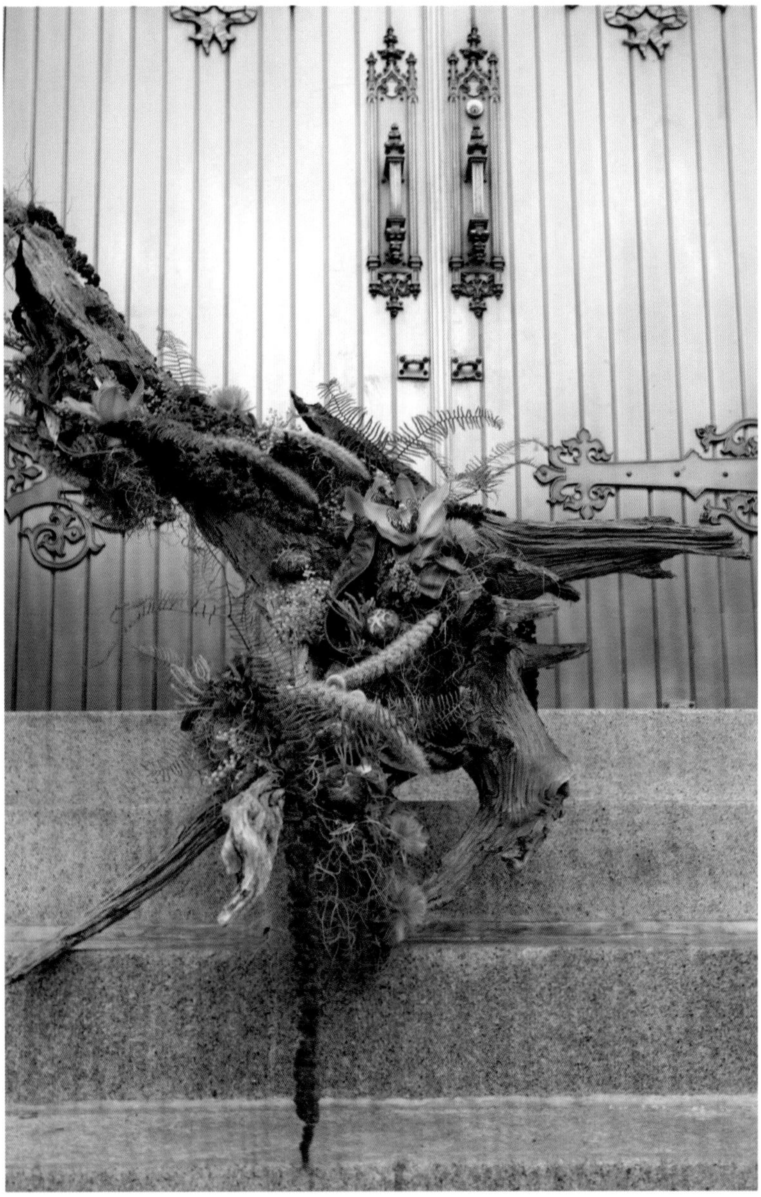

DESIGN BY ARTHUR WILLIAMS | PHOTOGRAPHY BY STACEY BAL

Denver, Colorado | January 2020

YORISHIRO

"Such selfish beings we are to foolishly give "God" a human form. We are merely temporary vessels of spirit."

PANDORA

Pandora is the first mortal woman, according to Greek mythology, who dared to open a box containing all the bad things that could happen to humans and let them out.

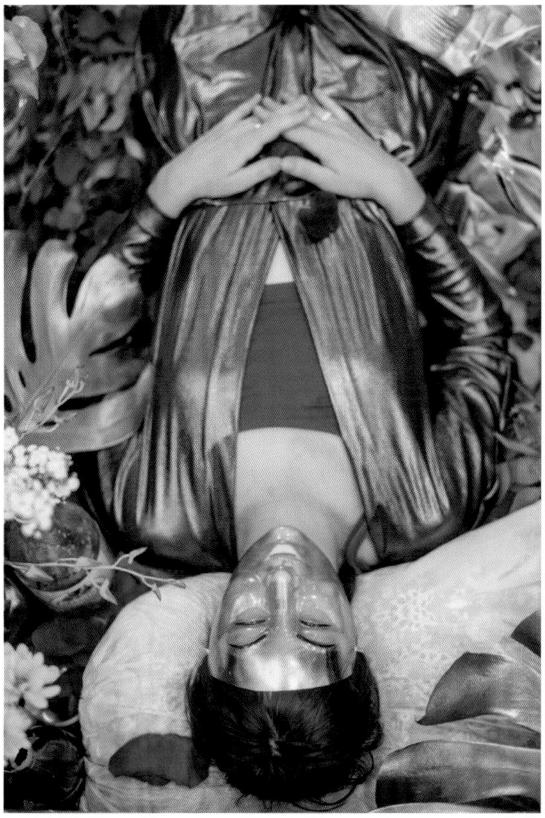

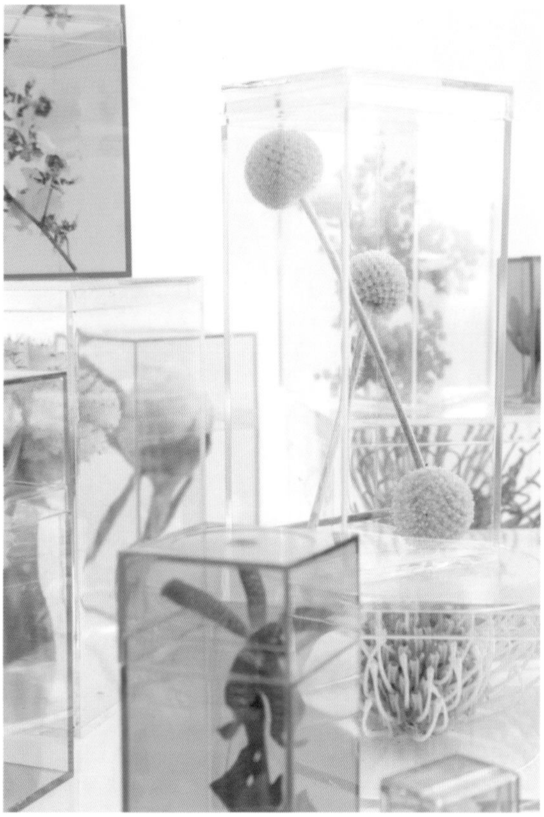

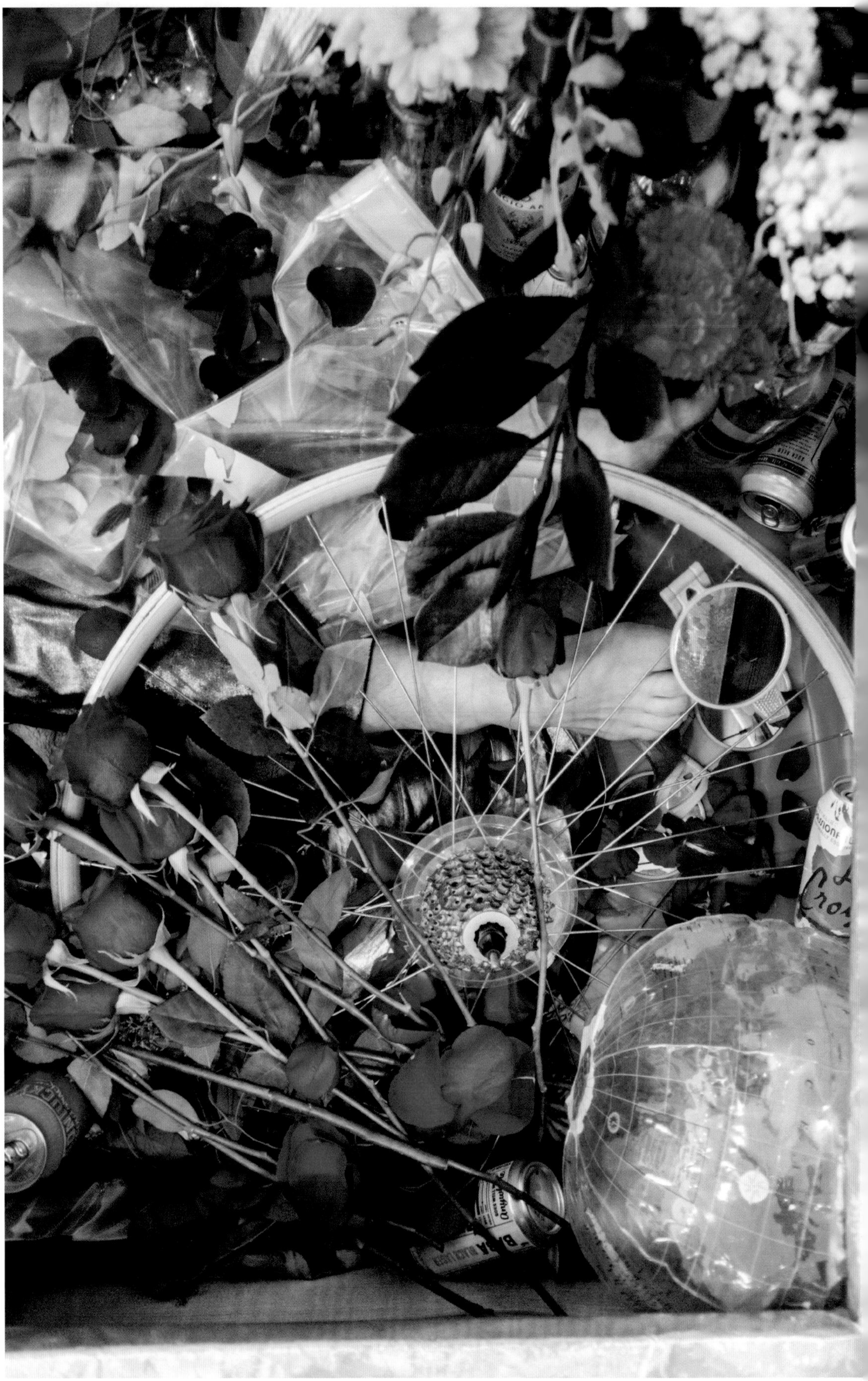

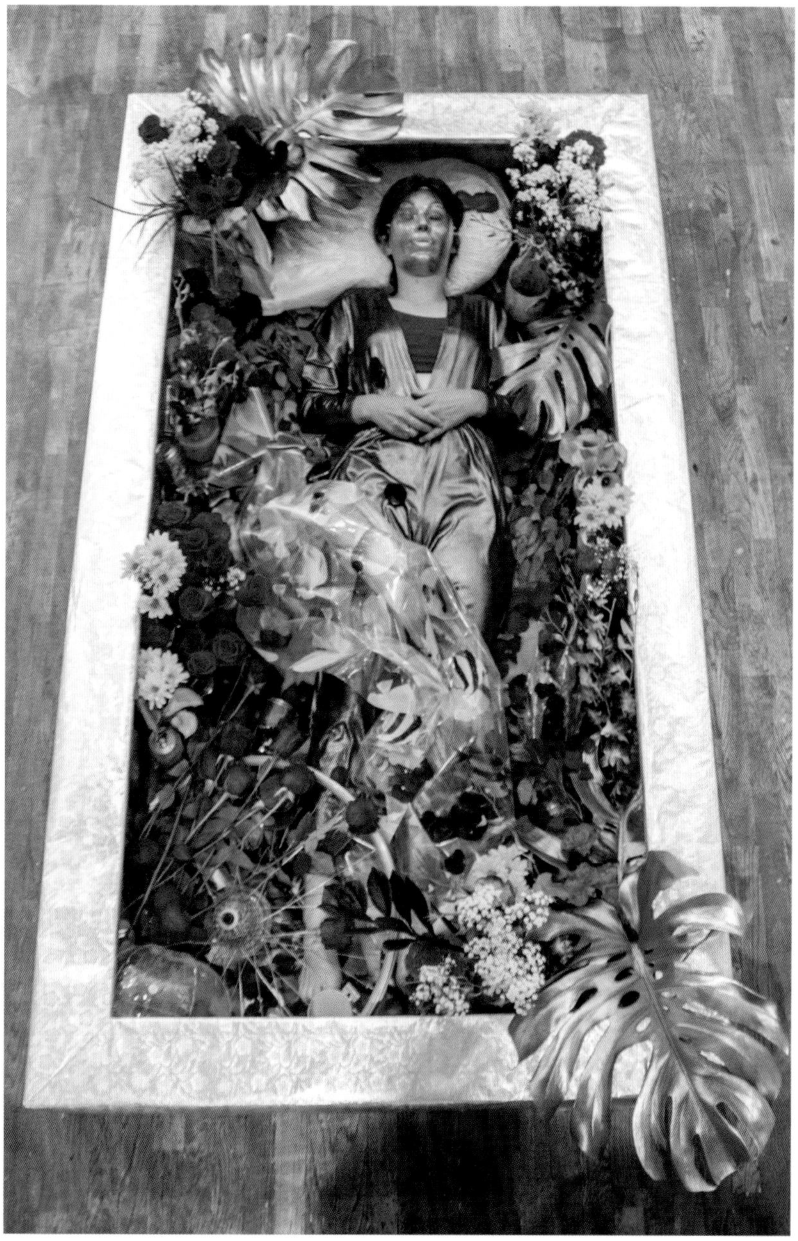

DESIGN BY ARTHUR WILLIAMS | PHOTOGRAPHY BY AMANDA BAKER PHOTOGRAPHY
Leon Gallery, Denver, Colorado | September 2019

TRASH-CAN GODDESS

"Collectively mankind has unleashed countless disasters which continually unfold all around us, reducing culture, natural resources, and ultimately our humanity to meaningless trash."

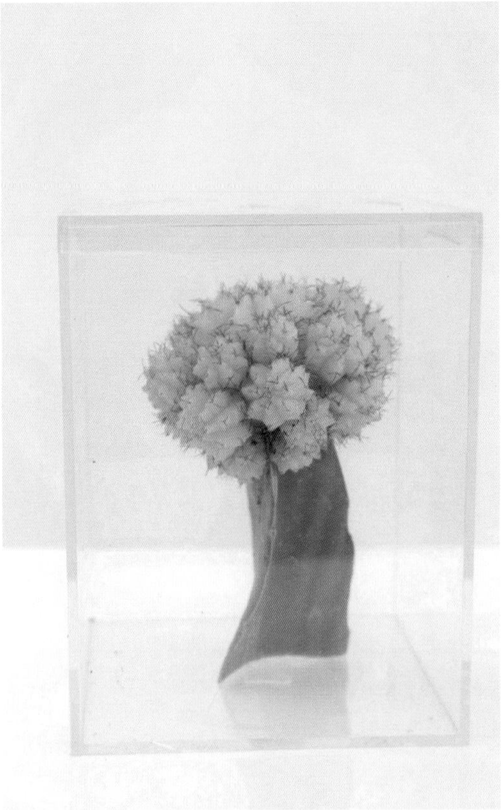

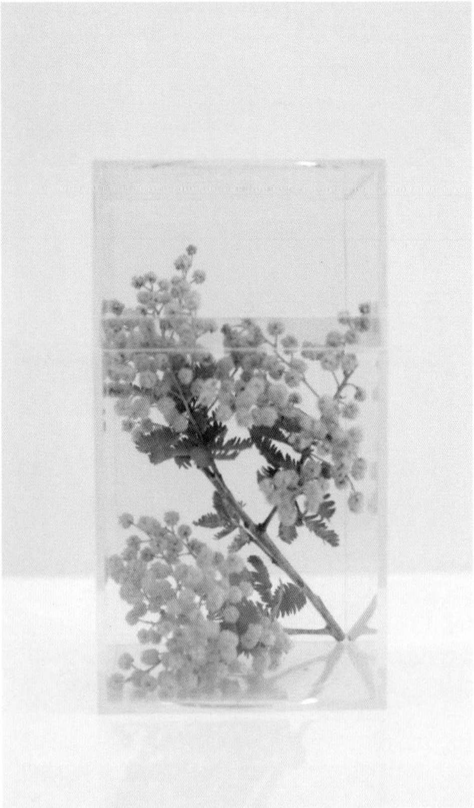

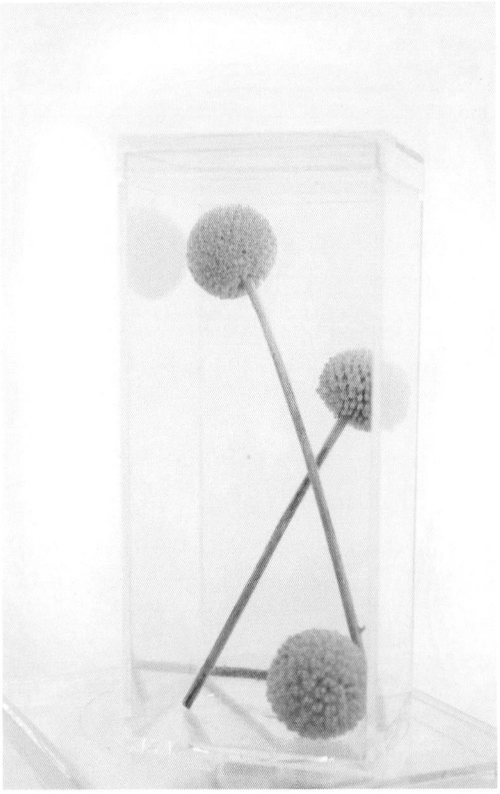

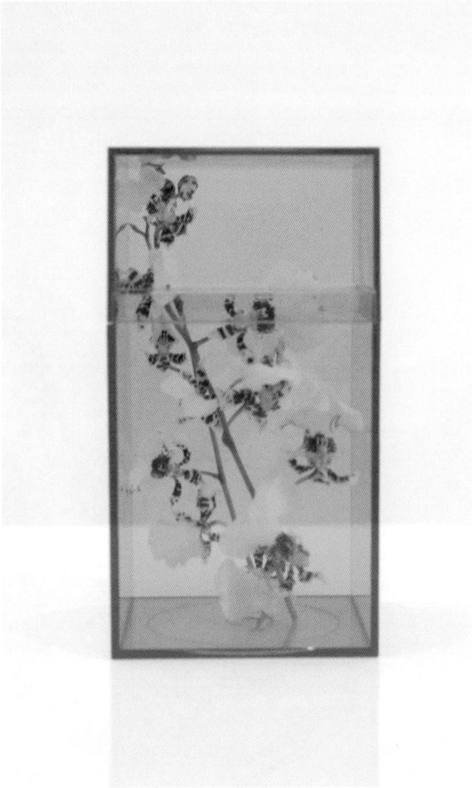

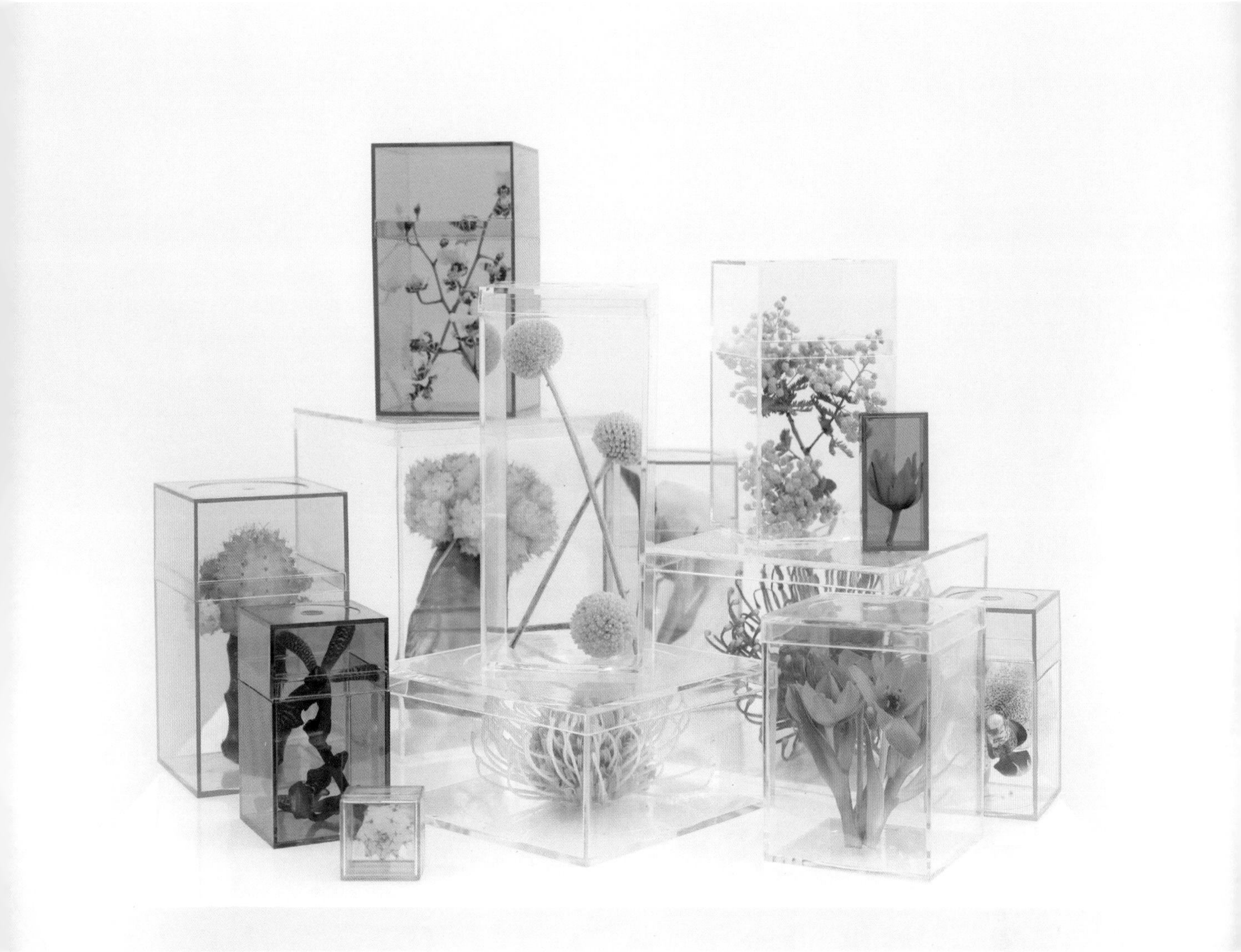

DESIGN BY STACEY BAL | PHOTOGRAPHY BY STACEY BAL
Denver, Colorado | January 2020

TRANSPARENCY

"Inspired by Pandora's unchecked curiosity and disobedience of the unknown, the labyrinth of ironically transparent boxes showcase a playful sense of joy."

PORTAL

To design using the concept
of a gateway, or iconic
circular openings.

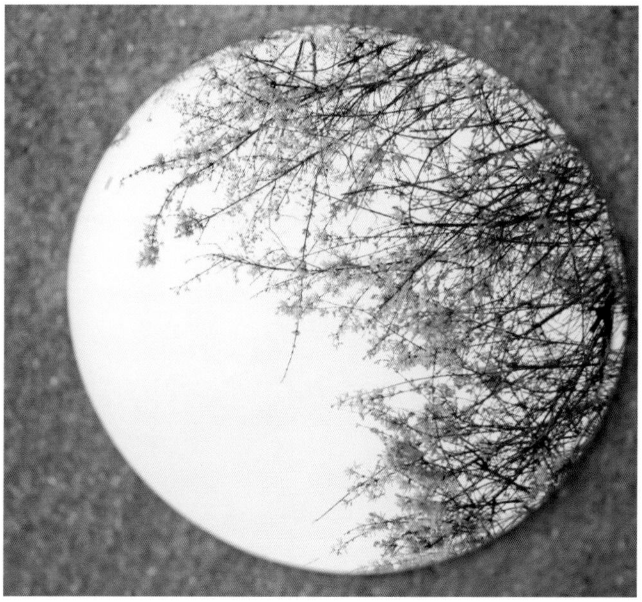

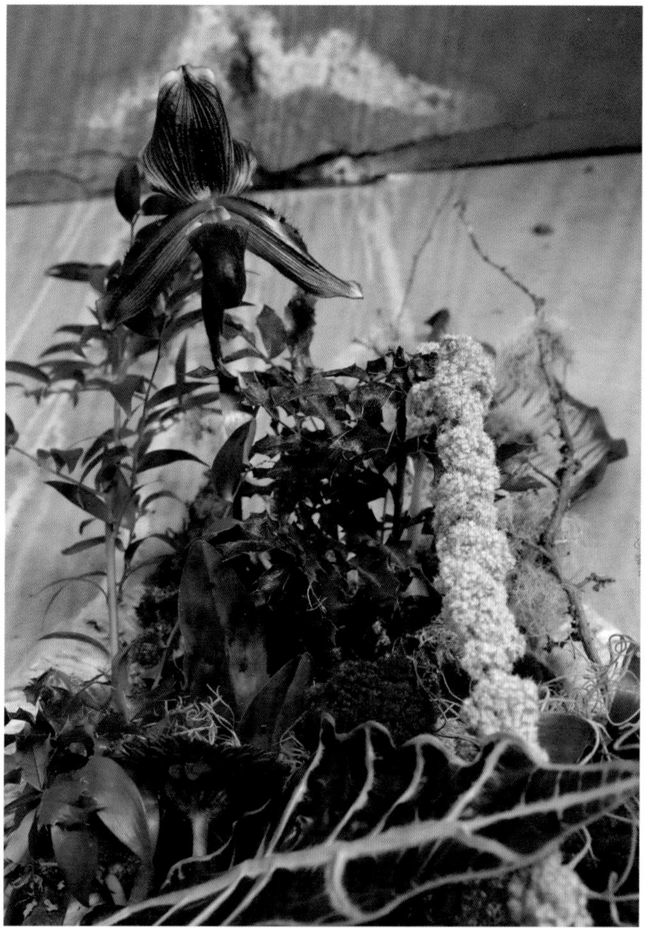

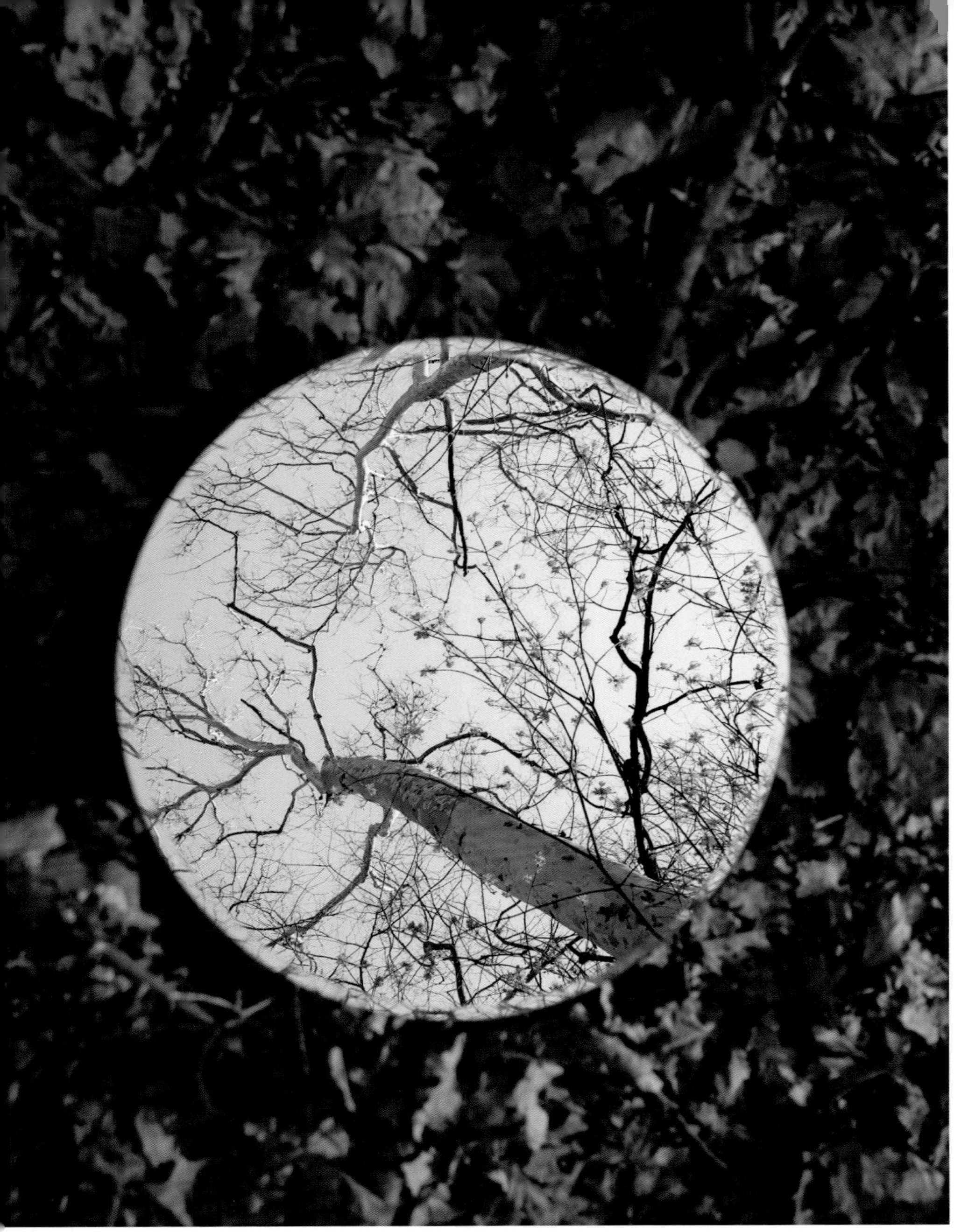

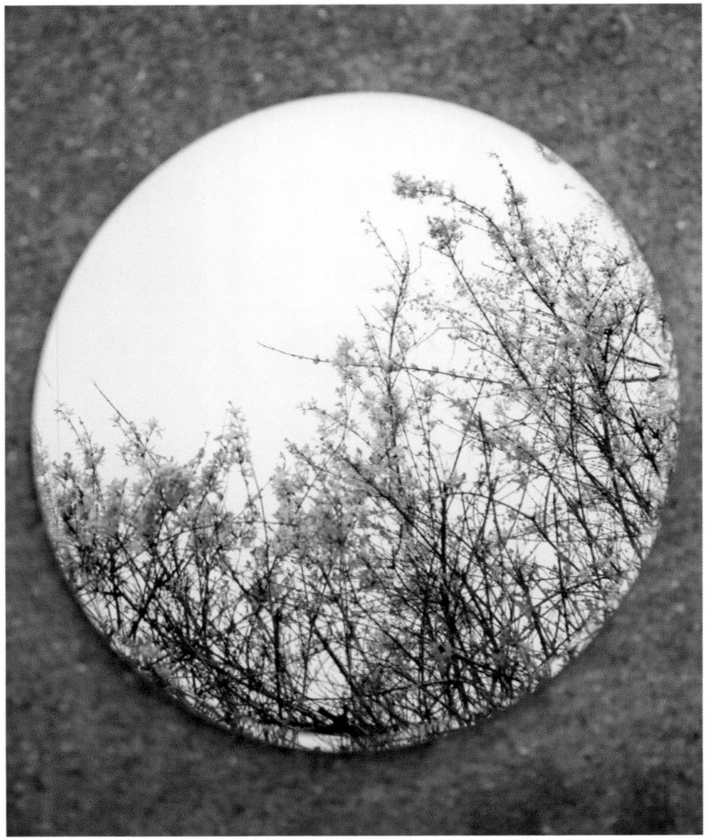

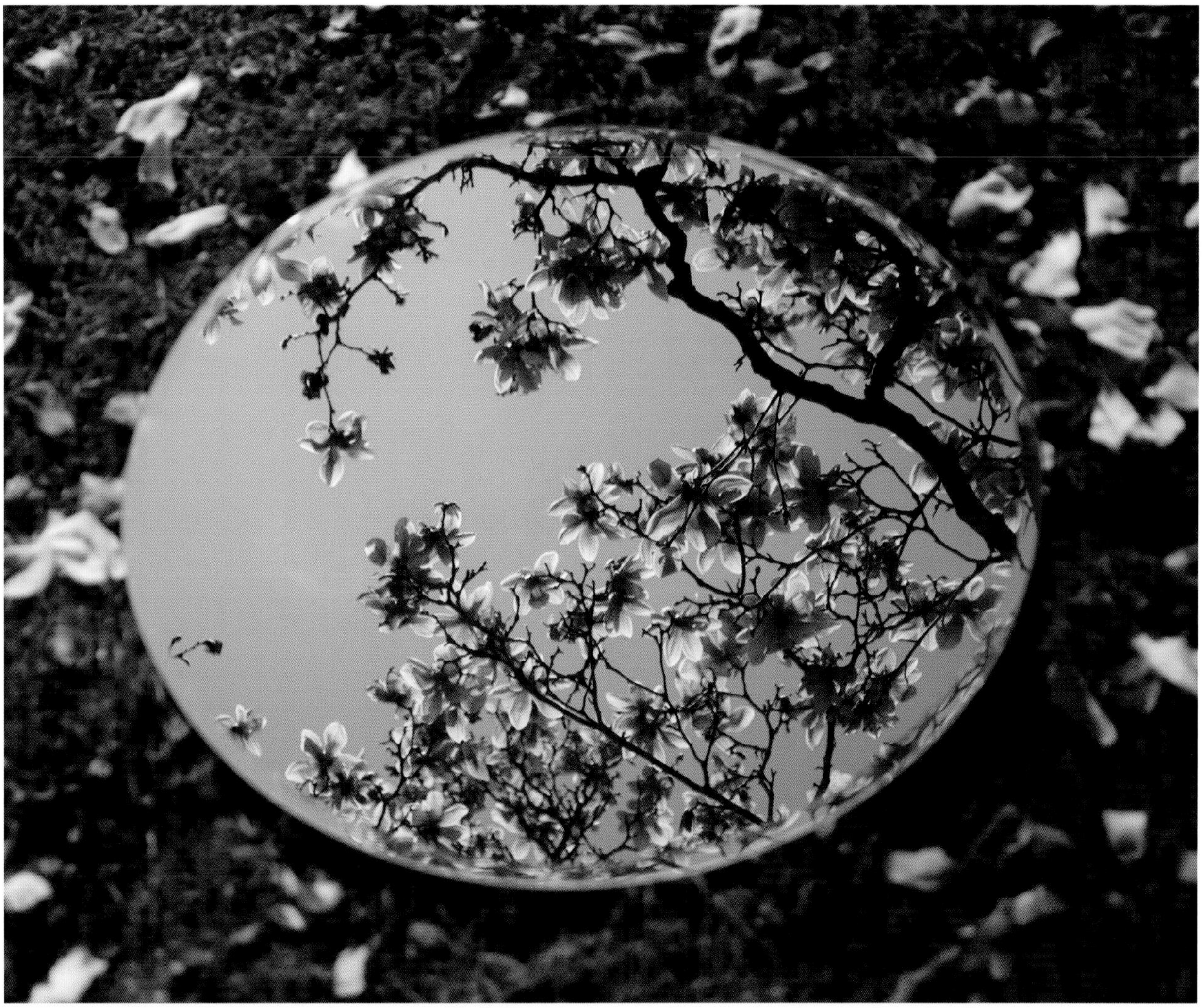

DESIGN BY STACEY BAL | PHOTOGRAPHY BY STACEY BAL

Chicago, Illinois | April 2020

THROUGH THE LOOKING GLASS

"With my thoughts I go; willingly down the rabbit hole."

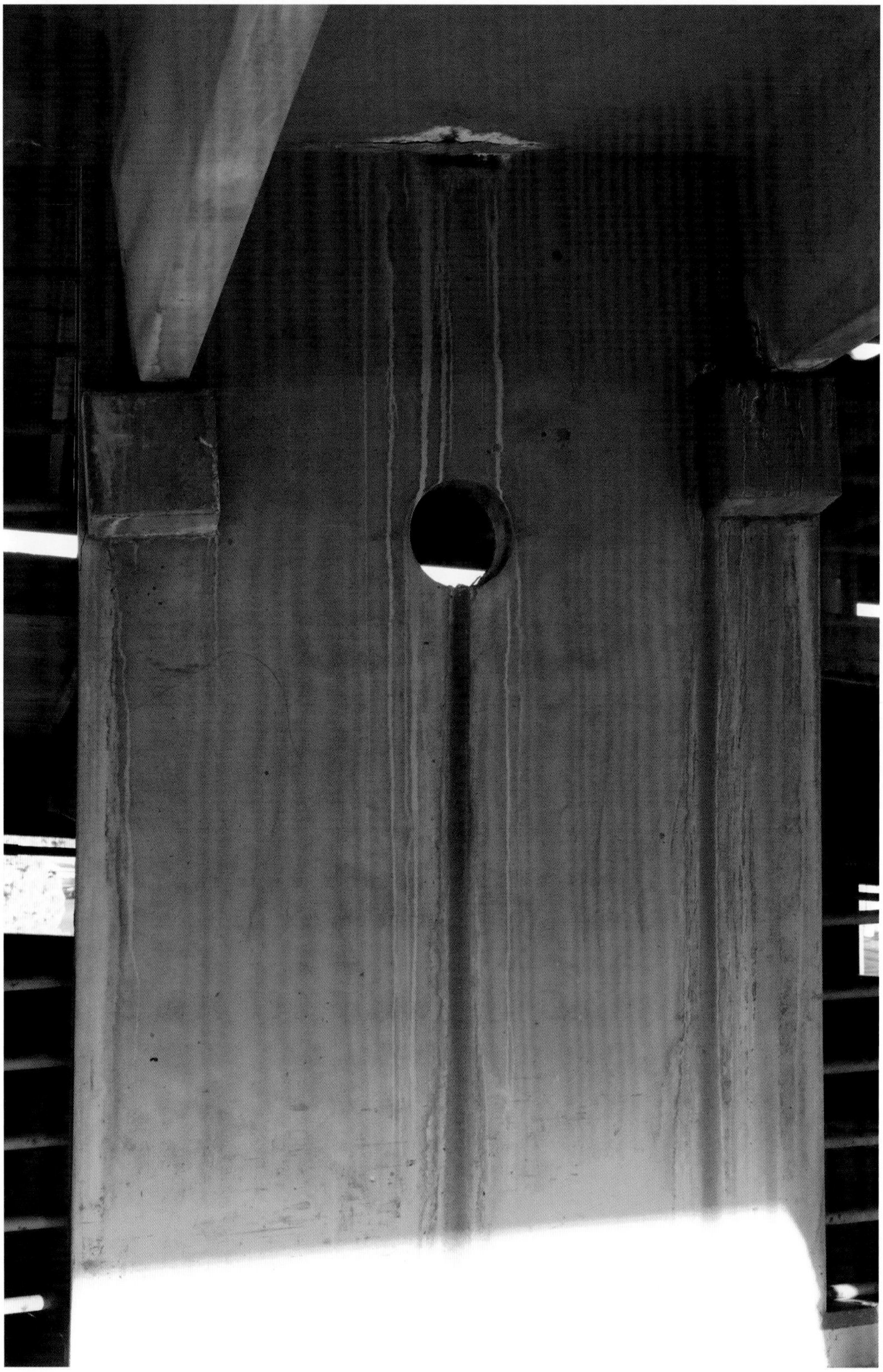

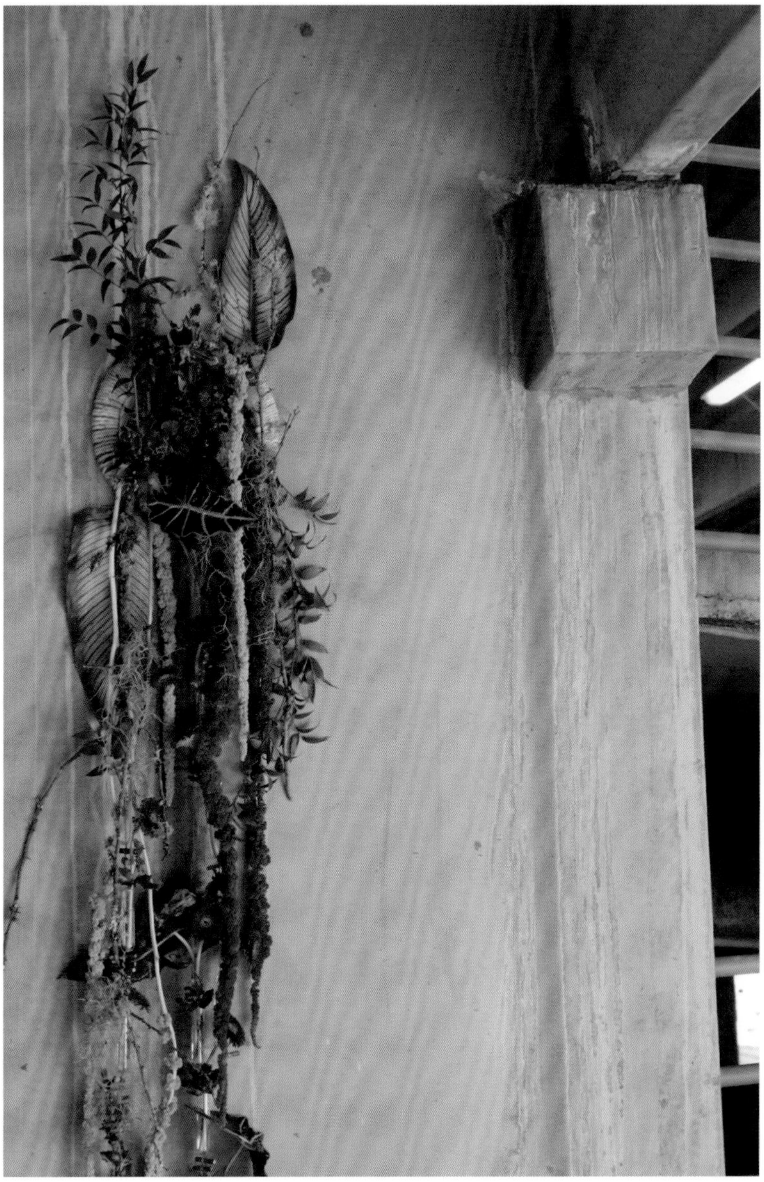

DESIGN BY ARTHUR WILLIAMS | PHOTOGRAPHY BY STACEY BAL
Denver, Colorado | January 2020

ADDER STONE

"They say that if you look through a holed stone bored by water, you can see into the realm of the faery-folk."

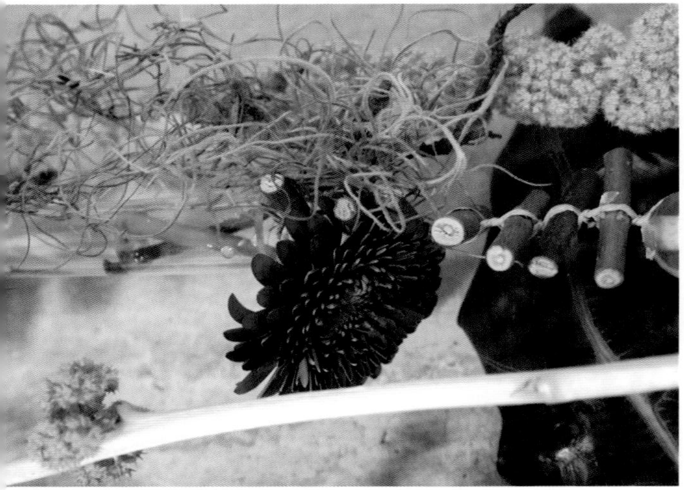

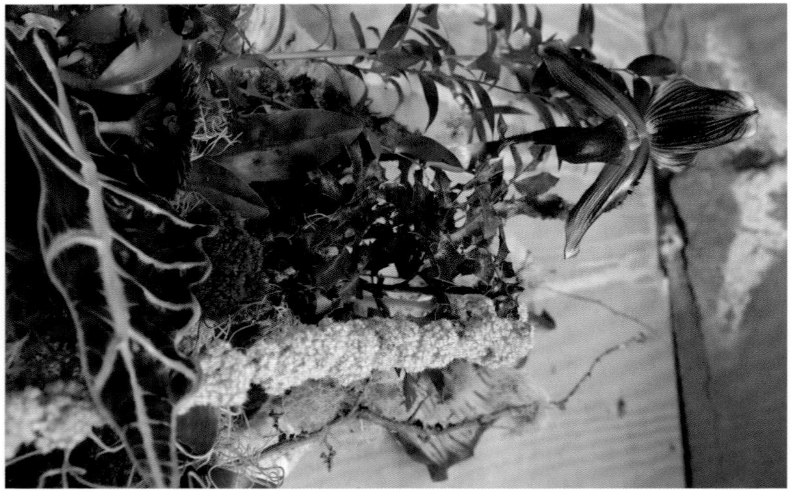

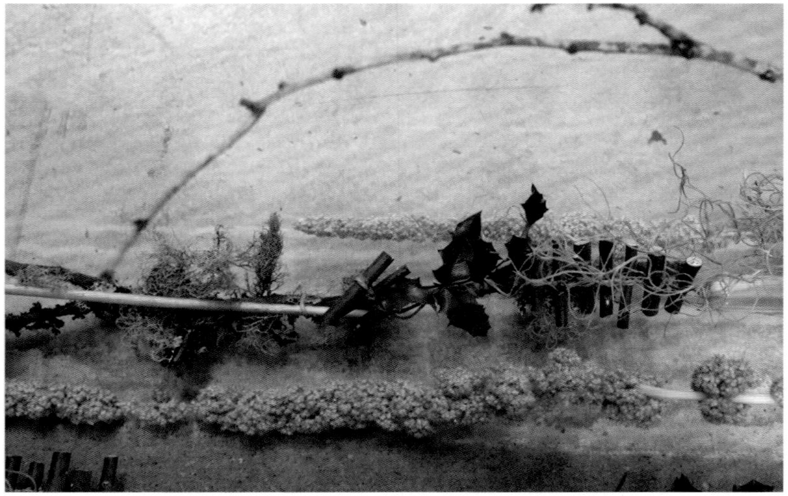

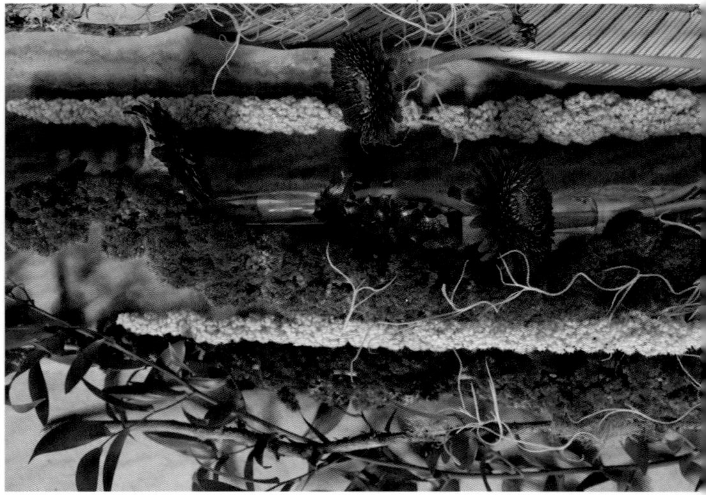

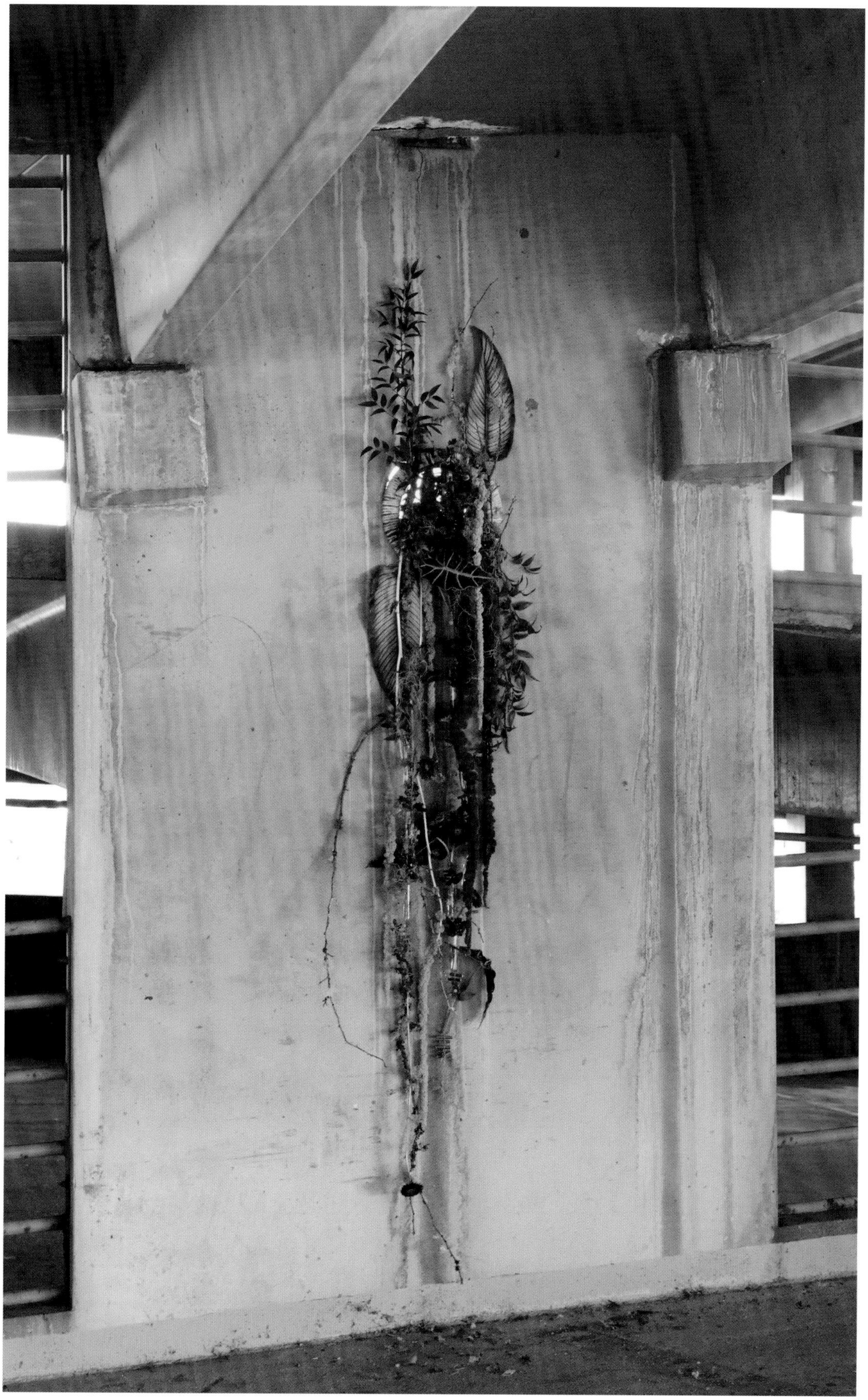

UTOPIA

An imagined place or state
of things in which everything
is perfect - especially laws,
government and social
conditions.

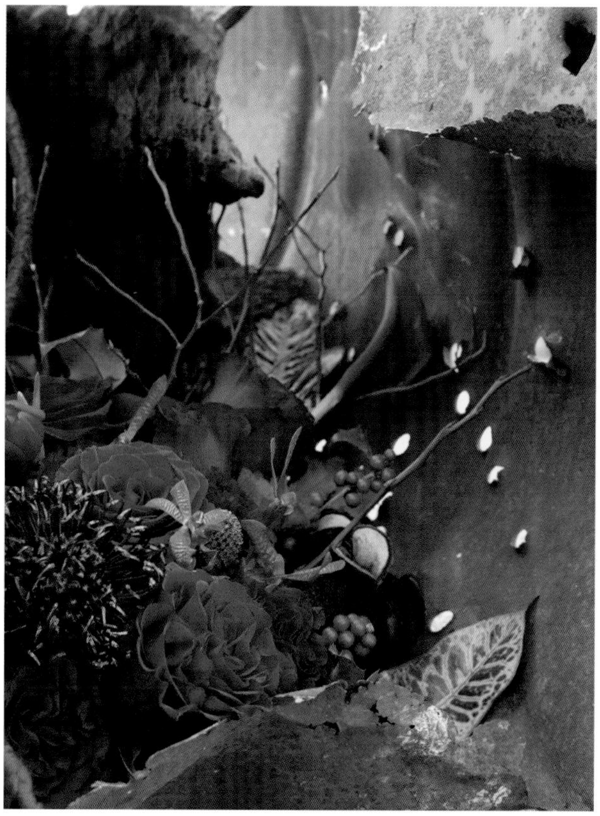

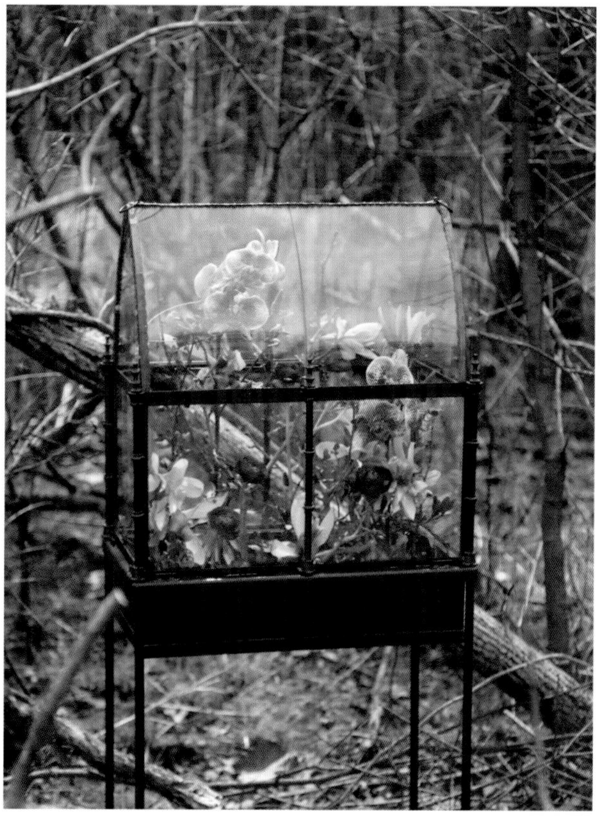

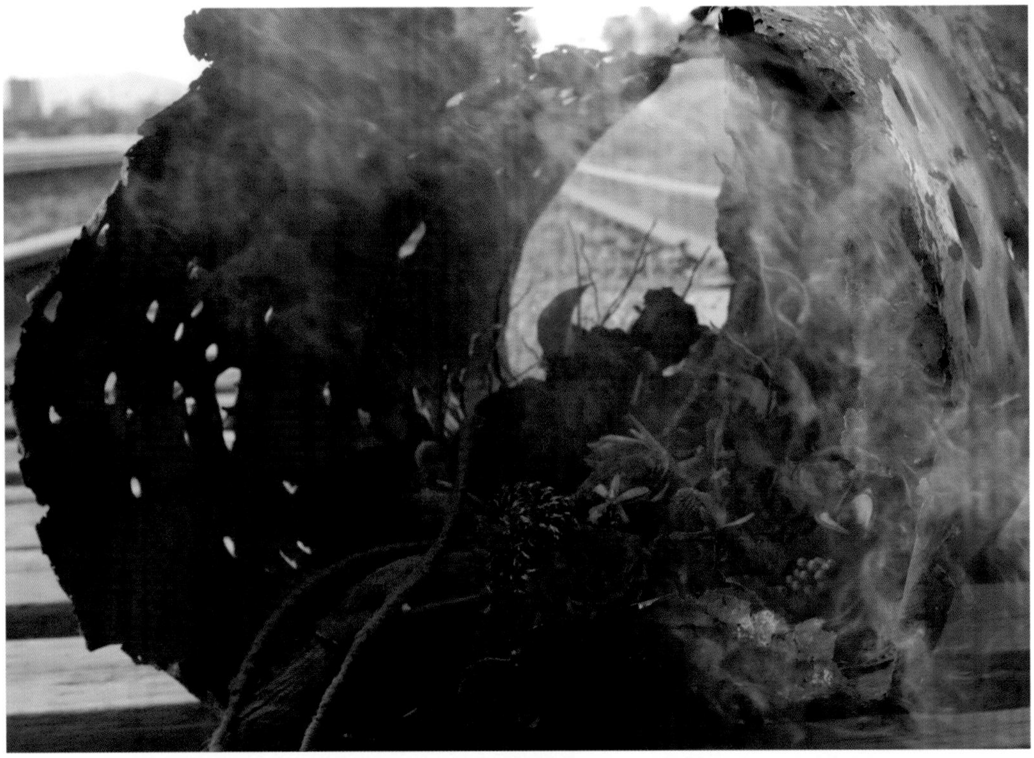

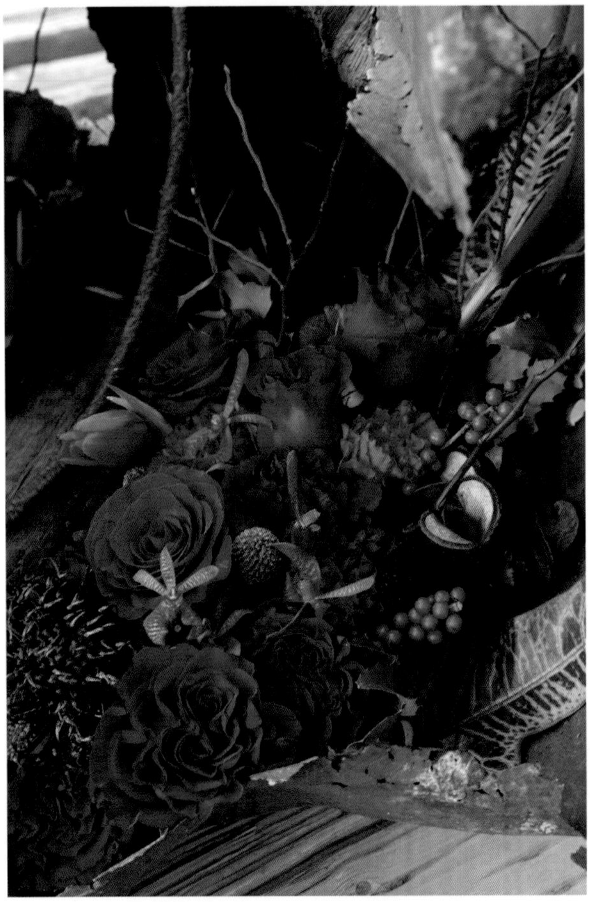

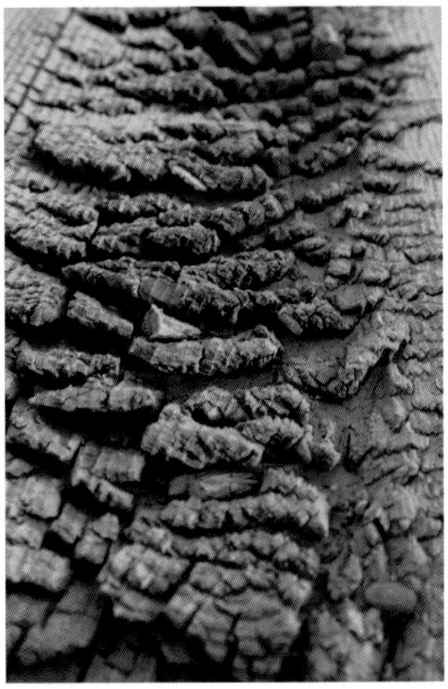

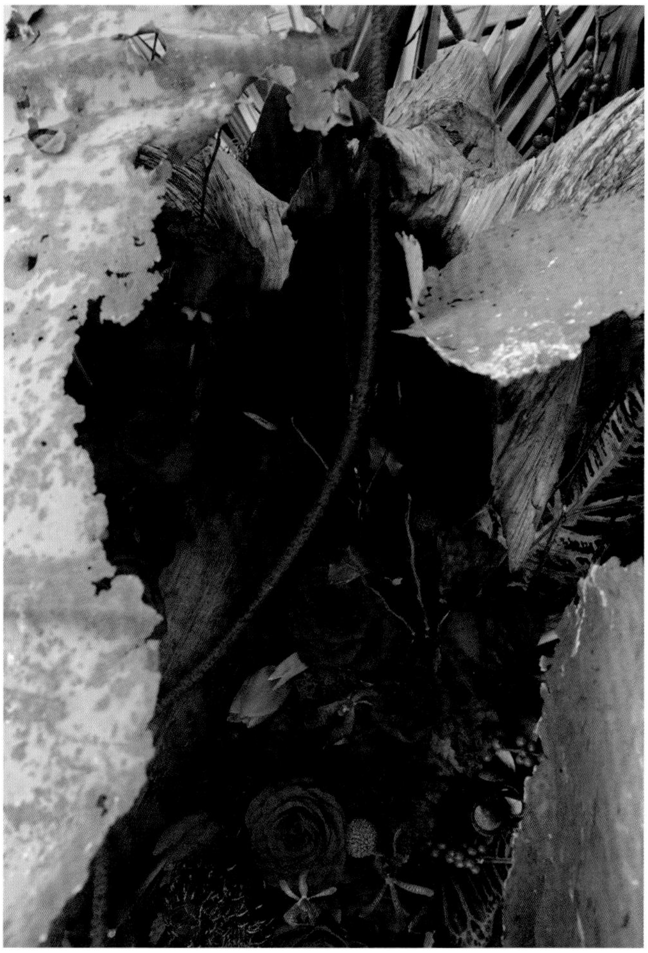

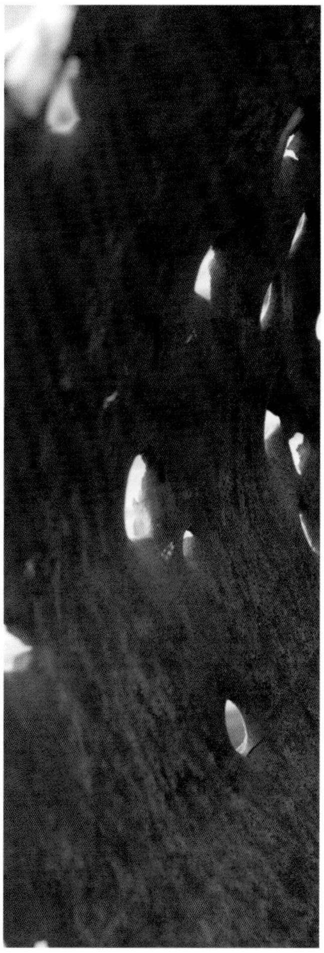

DESIGN BY ARTHUR WILLIAMS | PHOTOGRAPHY BY STACEY BAL
Denver, Colorado | January 2020

BURNOUT

"Chasing the dreams for an unattainable perfect future unavoidably destroys the present, a Sisyphean task to dull the senses of the masses."

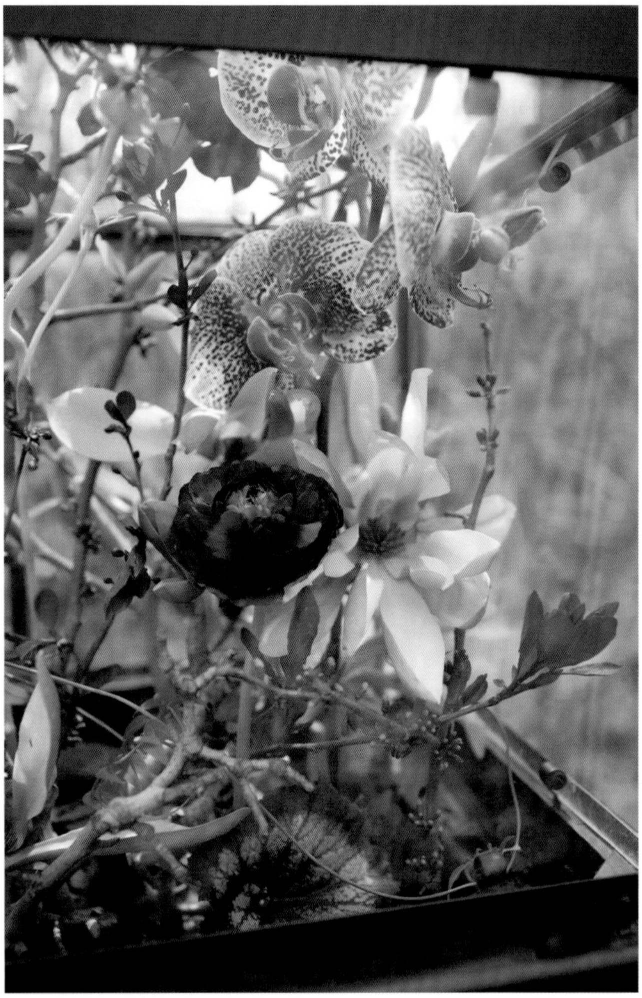

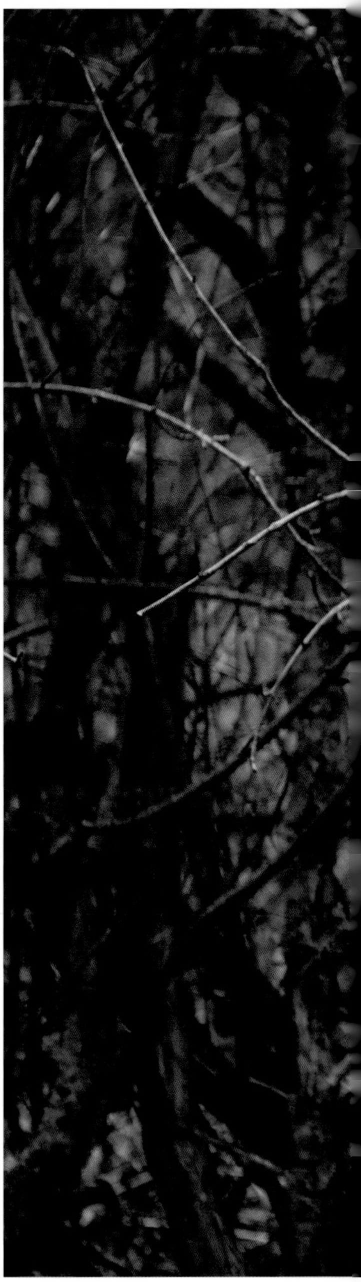

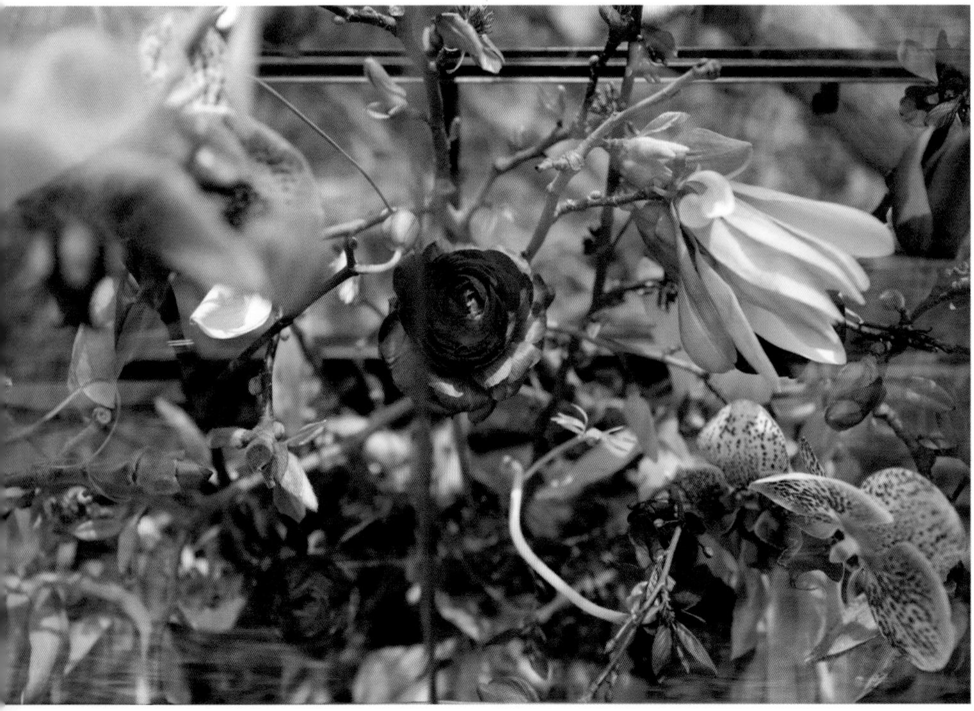

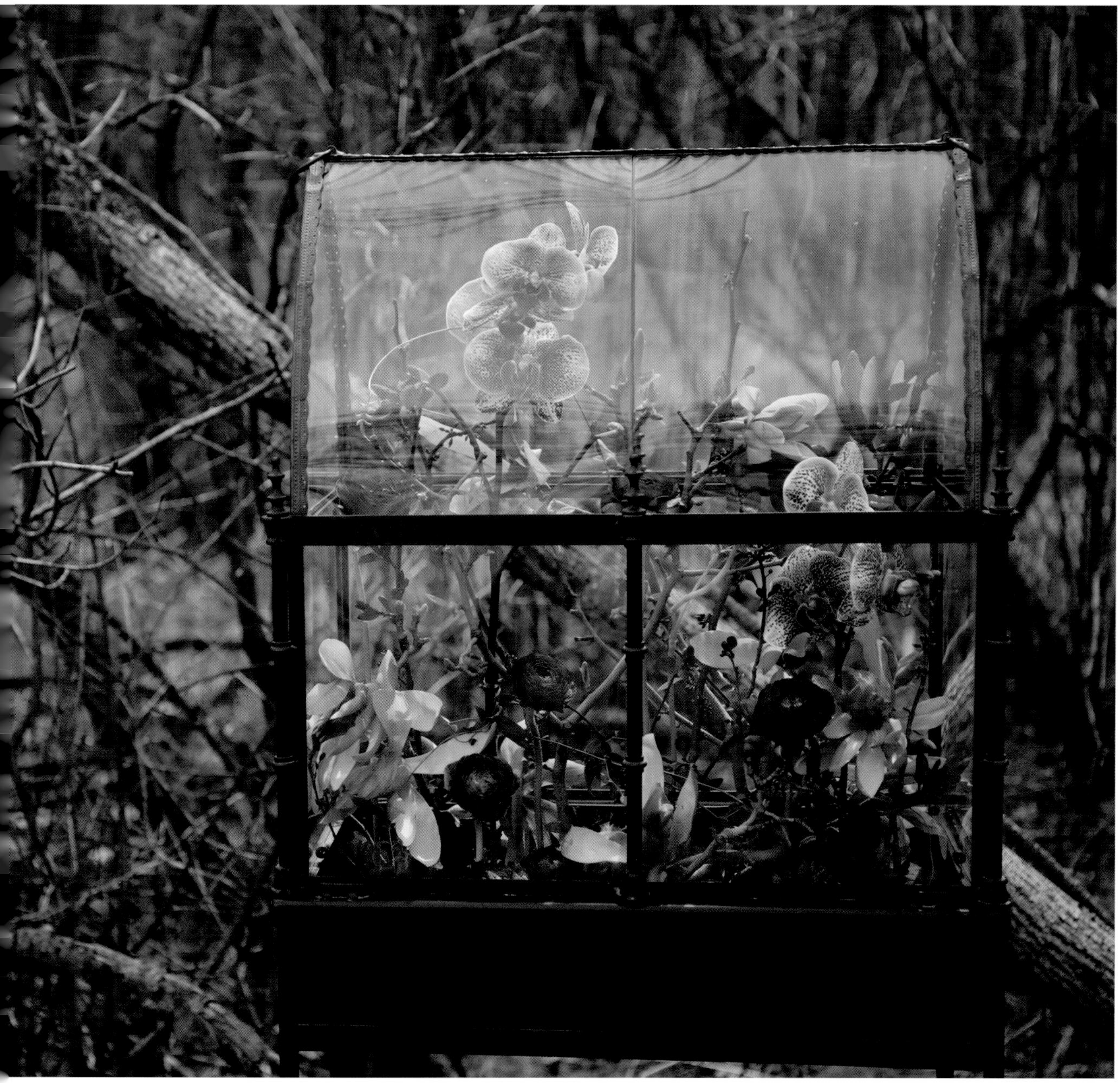

DESIGN BY STACEY BAL | PHOTOGRAPHY BY STACEY BAL

Riverside, Illinois | April 2020

WARDIAN CASE

"A perfect miniature ecosystem existing among chaos, adversity, and the unknown."

AURA

The distinctive atmosphere or quality that seems to surround and be generated by a person, thing, or place. Or, the visual disturbances preceding a migraine emphasized by a distortion of color and the blurring of foreground and background.

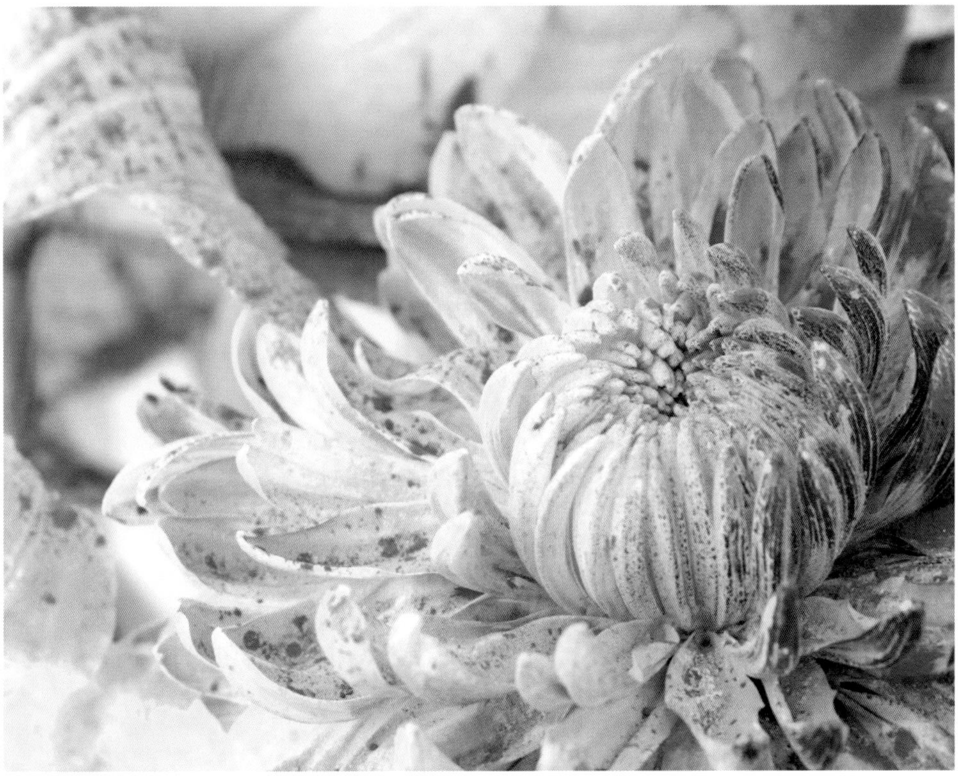

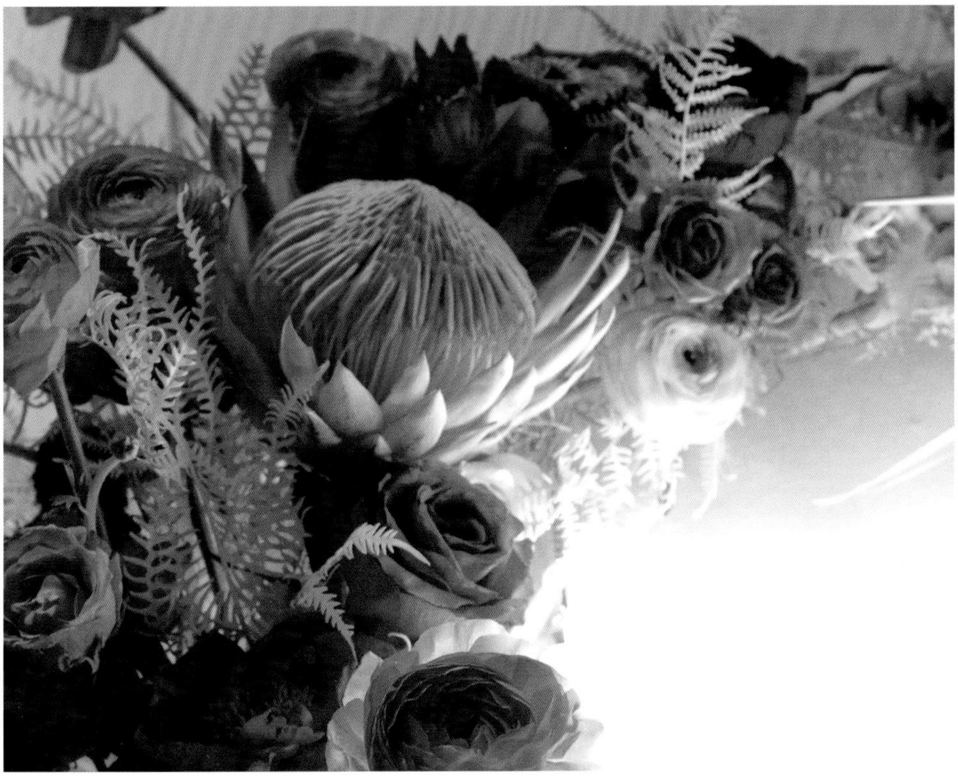

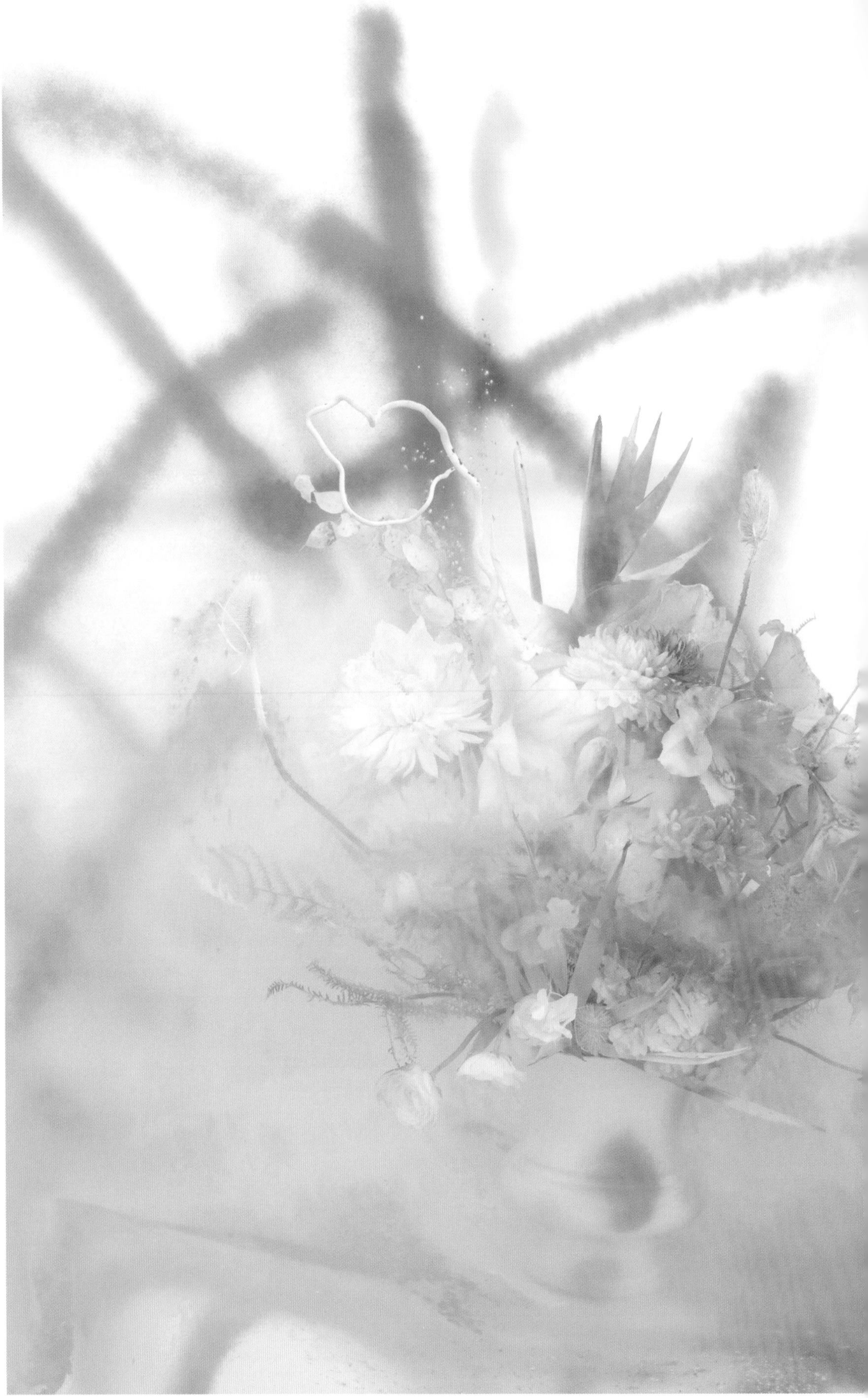

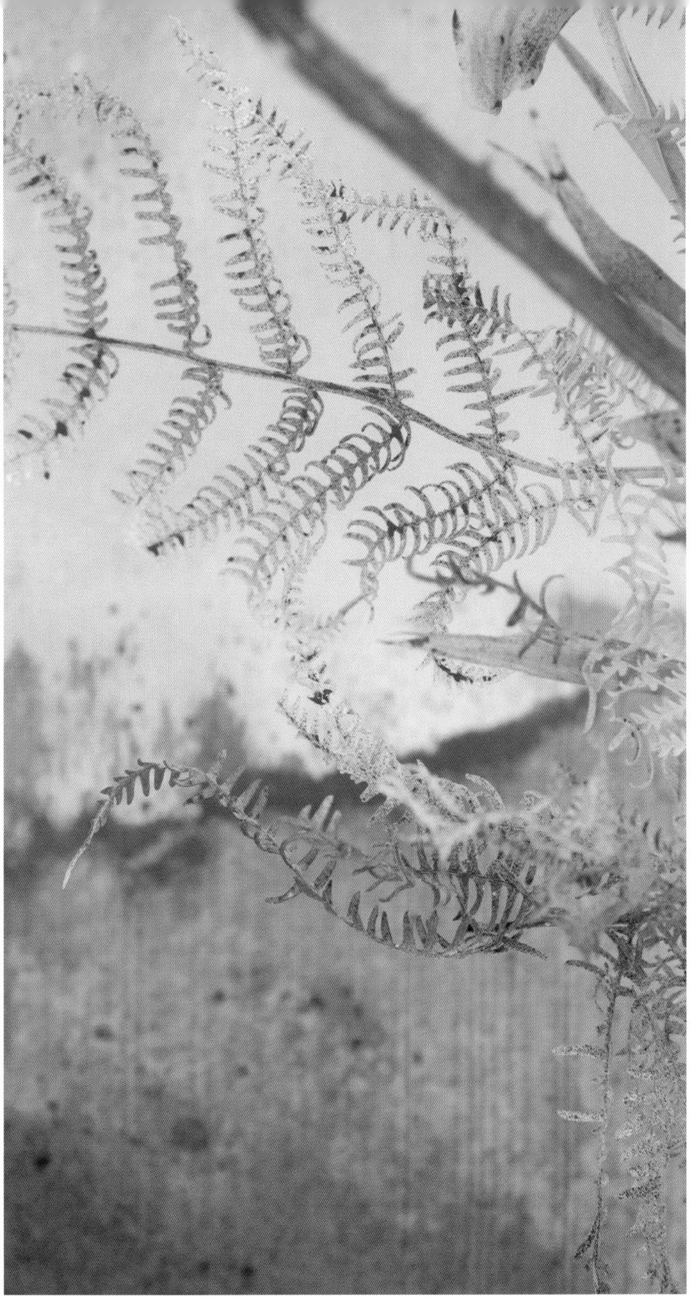

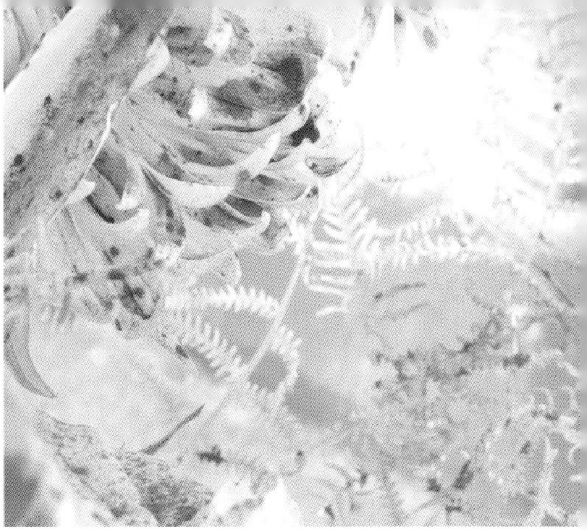

DESIGN BY ARTHUR WILLIAMS | PHOTOGRAPHY BY STACEY BAL

Denver, Colorado | January 2020

OCULAR IGNITION

"Blinding light, lost foreground, reality melting. Trapped in color, a prisoner to one's own senses."

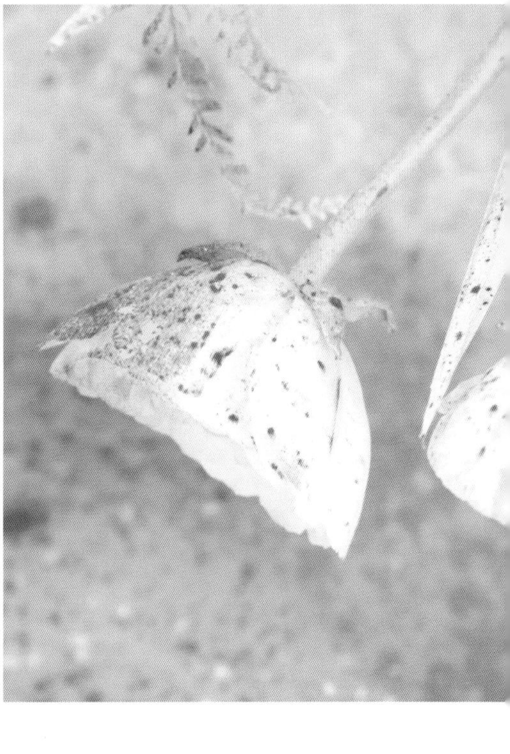

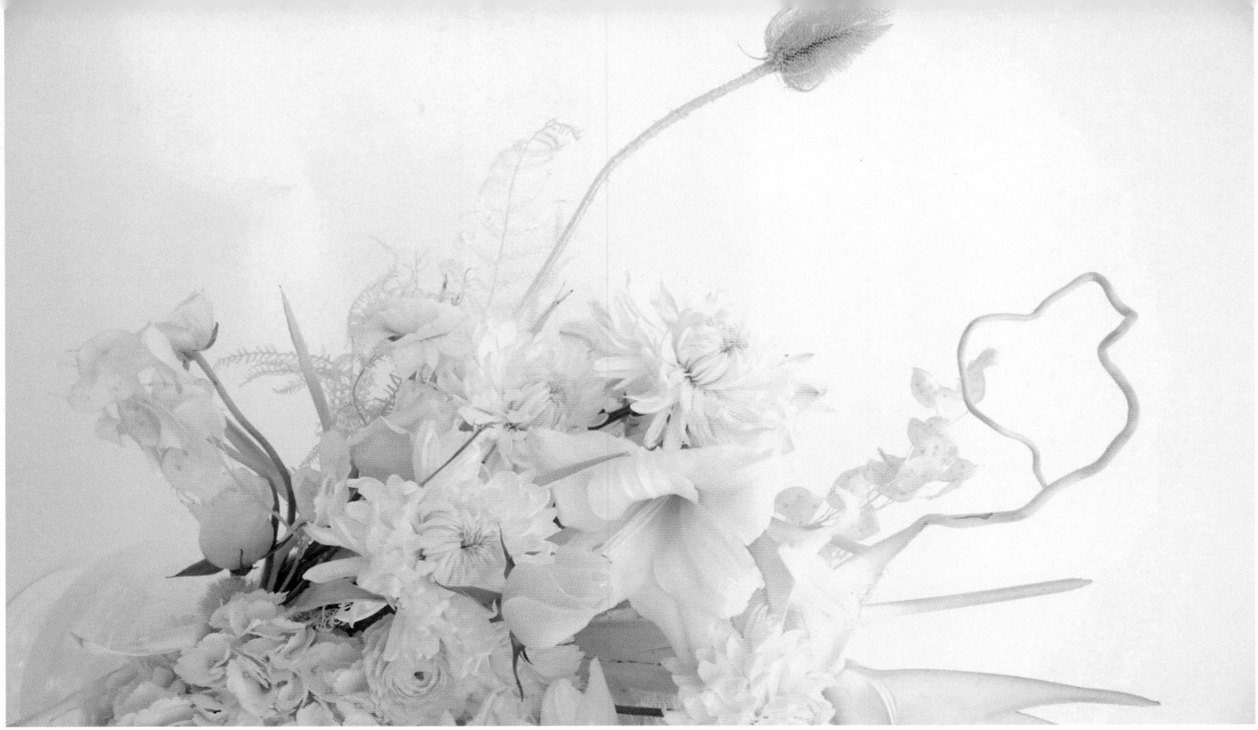

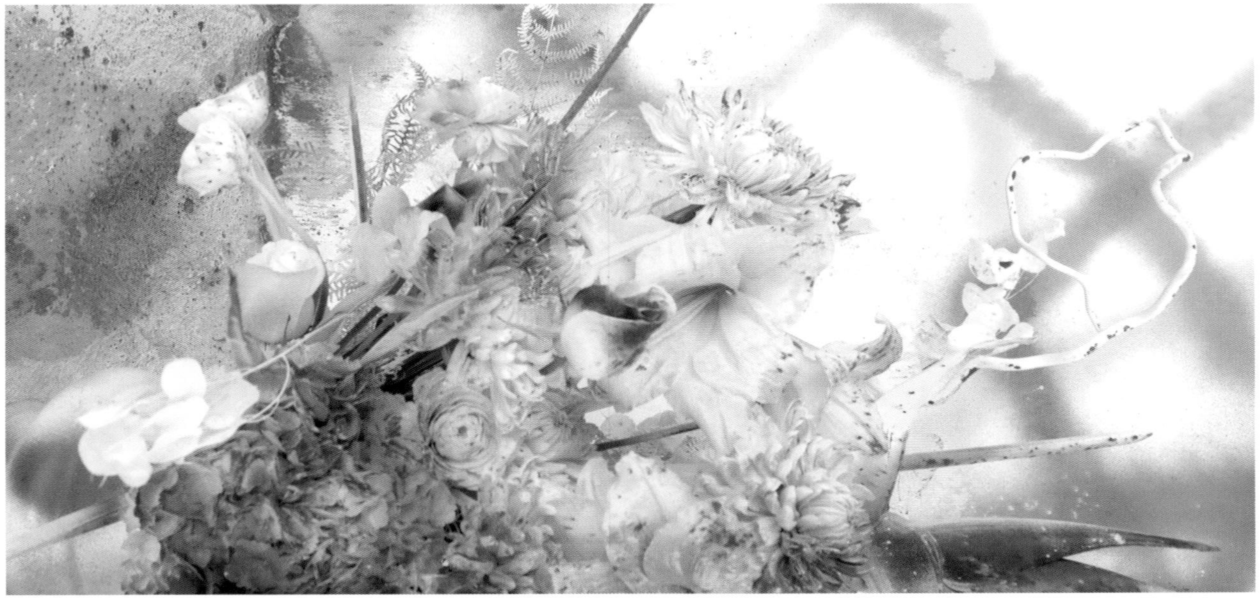

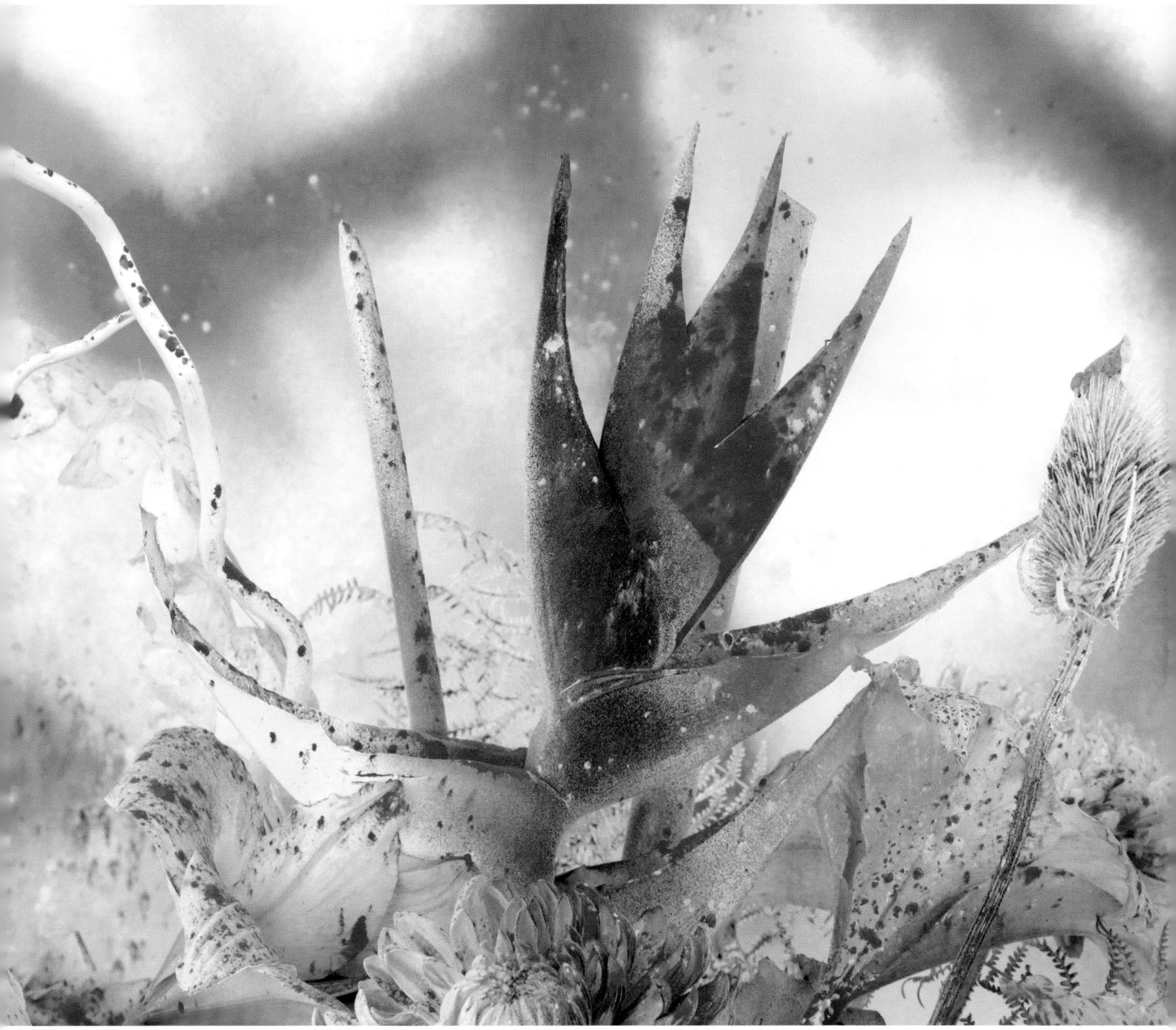

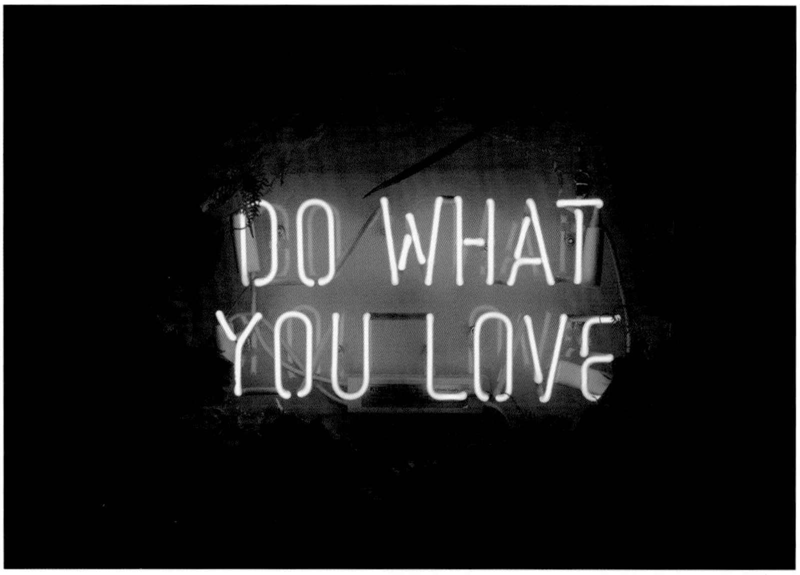
DO WHAT
YOU LOVE

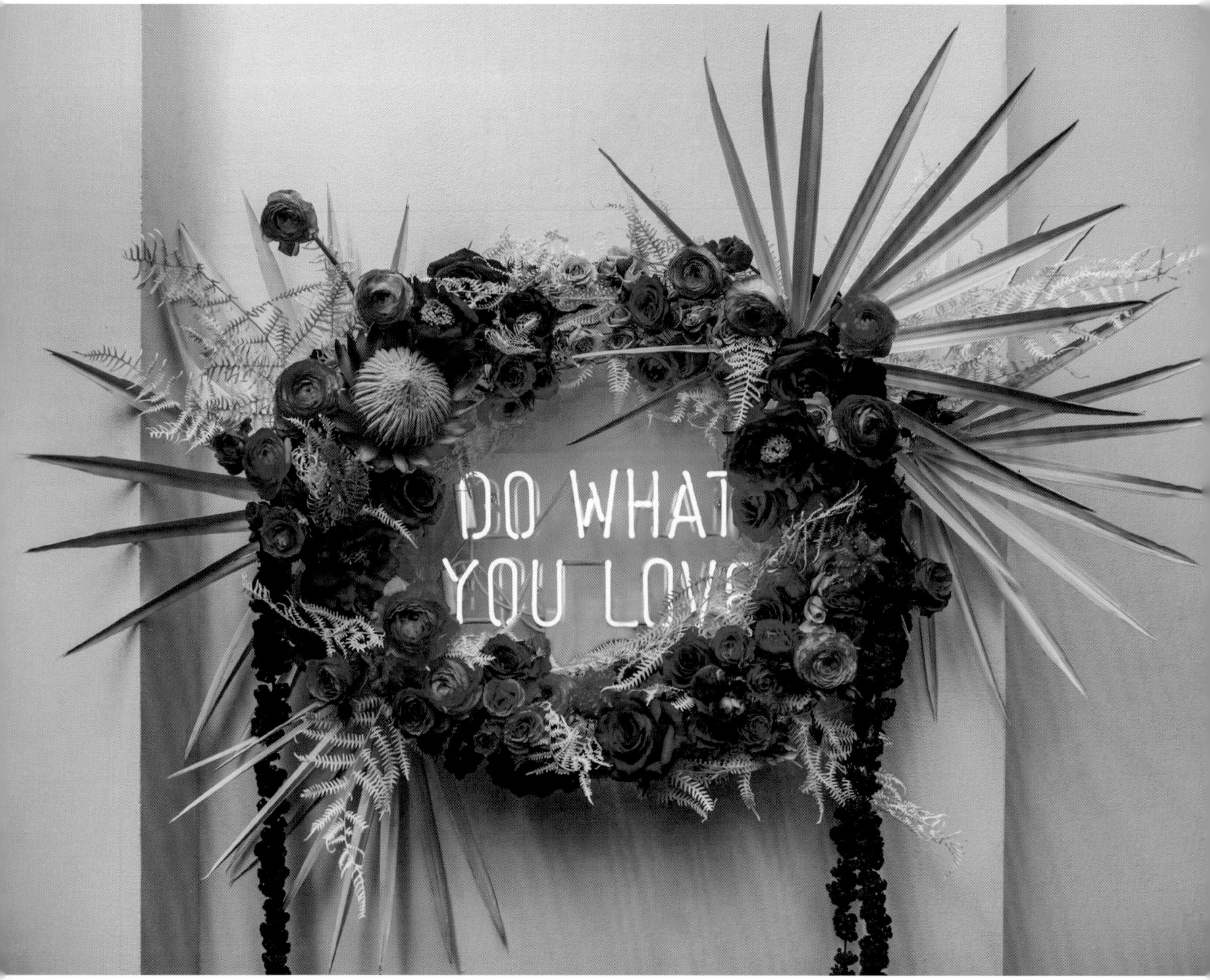
DO WHAT
YOU LOVE

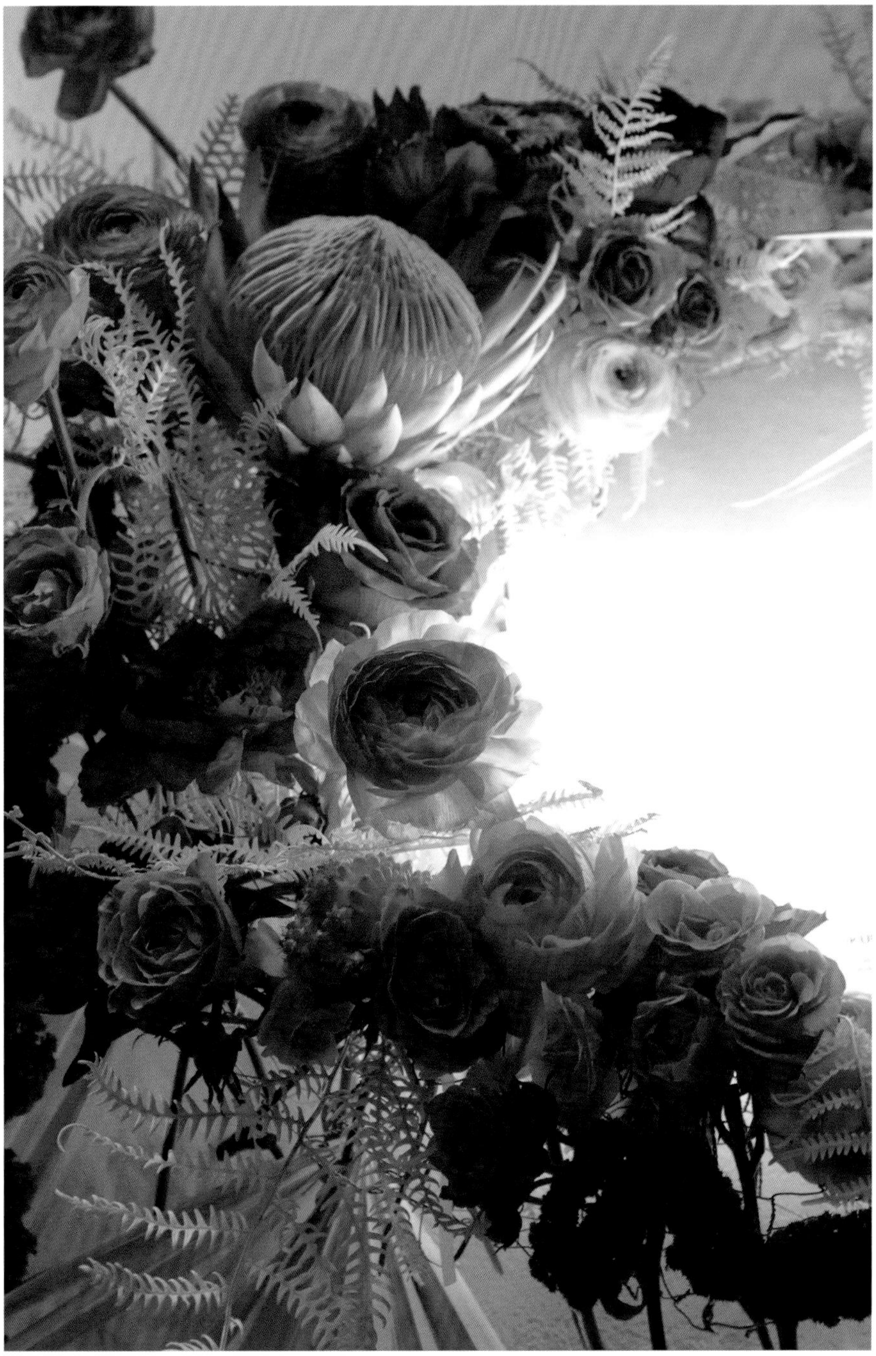

DESIGN BY STACEY BAL | PHOTOGRAPHY BY DAN DE LOS MONTEROS + STACEY BAL

Chicago, Illinois | January 2020

GLOW

"Passion and purpose
lead to luminous living."

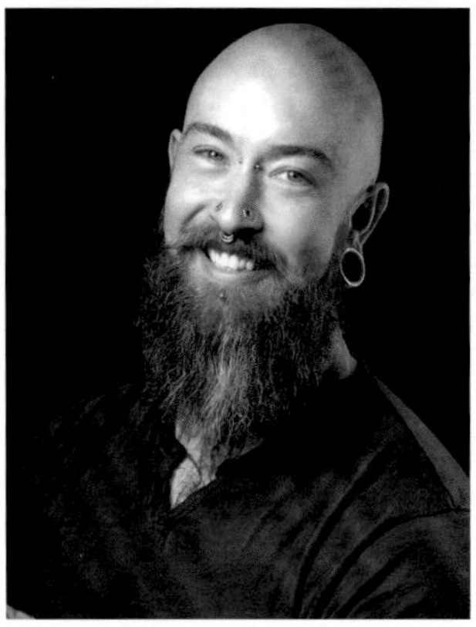

ARTHUR WILLIAMS

Arthur Williams AIFD, CFD, EMC, CPF is known for his floral headdresses and the use of natural tension in his work. With a background in gardening, sculpture, and photography, he entered the floral industry in 1996 and opened Babylon Floral Design, in Denver, Colorado, in 2004. One of the first seven people in Colorado to become a Certified Professional Florist (CPF), he is also a Certified Floral Designer at the national level. Arthur was inducted into the American Institute of Floral Designers (AIFD) in 2015 and completed the European Master Certification (EMC) program in 2016.

Arthur has been featured in the 2012-13, 2014-15, 2016-17, and 2018-19 editions of *International Floral Art*. His floral design work made the spring 2013 cover of the French floral art magazine *Nacre* and was also featured in the winter 2016 edition. Arthur's designs also have been showcased in many Colorado publications, he has contributed to *Florists' Review* magazine, and was profiled in the book *50 Mile Bouquet* by Debra Prinzing. In 2018, Arthur received a bronze medal in the "International Flower Contest" at the annual "World Flower Garden Show" in Japan. He is a past "Creative in Residence" at the Denver Art Museum and is currently on the selection committee for the program.

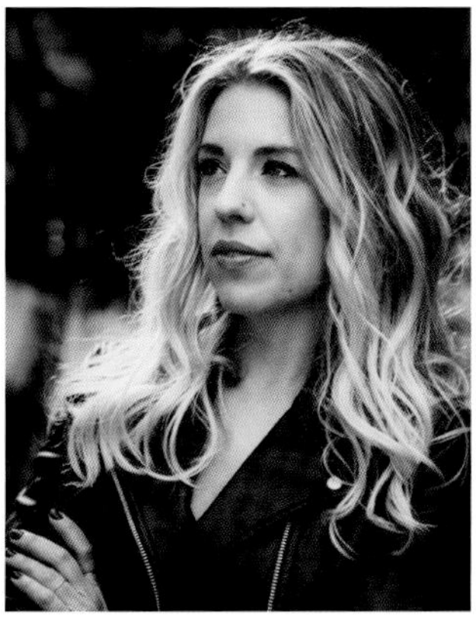

STACEY BAL

Artist Stacey Bal AIFD, CFD, EMC celebrates the value in the vast diversity of the floral industry by wearing many hats including educator, consultant, event designer, magazine contributor, and product developer. As the owner of The Flora Culturist in the Chicagoland area, she energetically expresses her ever-evolving point of view with unexpected materials and unique combinations of botanicals. A lover of adventure, she travels as a freelance artist and speaker. Stacey's continued lifelong educational journey through various arts and horticulture are met with her experience as a second-generation floral designer.

She is recognized for bringing a fresh perspective and strong voice to the visual-arts community, most recently as a feature artist at Art Basel Miami 2019. Stacey was inducted into the American Institute of Floral Designers (AIFD) in 2010. A graduate of the European Master Certification (EMC) program in Bruges, Belgium, in 2018, she is now a member of EMC's Teaching Team.